Kashi

By the Same Author

The Vow of Parvati (2022)
Hindu Love Stories: Dharmically Ever After (2022)
The Curse of Gandhari (2019)
Invading the Sacred: An Analysis of Hinduism Studies in America (2007) with Antonio de Nicolas and Krishnan Ramaswamy

Advance Praise

'[*Kashi*] is a much-needed book about the ancient history and sacred geography of Varanasi, the city at the heart of Sanatan Dharma. Aditi painstakingly delves into the many legends that explain why the city is so sacred to all Hindus.'

Sanjeev Sanyal, economist and bestselling author

'*Kashi: The Valiant History of a Sacred Geography* by Aditi Banerjee, while centred on Kashi and the reclamation of the holiest of Hindu kshetras, serves as a fantastic illustration of the larger Indic movement that seeks to reclaim the agency of Bharatiya civilization in as peaceful a manner as possible. That the reclamation of Bharat's identity and soul is not based on European-style territorial nationalism but on sacred dharmic civilizationalism is made abundantly clear from the title of the book itself, which is a welcome move away from certain attempts to secularize the movement by painting it as mere cultural nationalism. The mountain of material captured by Aditi must inspire irony at the fact of Hindus having to prove the obvious to reclaim their holiest of holies, apart from exposing the glaring hypocrisy of Western decolonial scholarship and academia, which continue to carry the baggage of Orientalism when examining Bharat. One hopes that Aditi's painstaking efforts in charting the journey of invasion, occupation, and reclamation of Kashi lead to conscientious introspection on the part of those who claim to be independent decolonial truth seekers but whose truth seeking decolonial gaze has somehow studiously avoided Bharat (not "South Asia").'

J. Sai Deepak, advocate, Supreme Court of India

'*Kashi* is not just a book but also a journey that begins with time itself and does not end except that it pauses to reflect on the end. This right here is a masterpiece, and it must be read by anyone who has an interest in seeking an answer to the question why civilizations last, but empires do not—a must-read.'

Anand Ranganathan, author and scientist

'Kashi is Shiva's city, and there has been renewed interest in Kashi not merely because of Gyaanavapi. Visitors to Kashi have often asked me about a good book to read on Kashi. I have hesitated. Kashi Khanda of *Skanda Purana*? How do I persuade visitors to look beyond Vishveshvara and the ghats? There is no one more suited than Aditi Banerjee to write such a book on Kashi, and she has filled a much-needed vacuum. Sacred geography, stories (from Sthala Purana too), yoginis and Aditya temples, pilgrimage paths, more recent history of the city—there are all these and more. A wonderful and remarkable book about a wonderful and remarkable city.'

Bibek Debroy, economist and author

'Kashi is not any holy city; Kashi is a microcosm of the ever-prevailing consciousness of Sanatana Dharma in this sacred Bharat bhumi. Aditi beautifully unpacks the civilizational centrality and sacredness of Kashi in the book by taking the readers on a journey from the Puranic past to medieval struggles and the present-day fight for the reclamation of our sacred geography. Delightful, poignant, and informative, all in one!'

Ami Ganatra, author

'A patient poignancy. A picturesque expression. A dip in devotion. And a book that explores tradition and history, assaults and losses, politics and humiliations, and, above all, tells the story of a billion bhaktas yearning for justice. You read Aditi Banerjee's book with a lump in your throat, a heaviness in your heart, and a prayer for restorative balance in the very cells of your being. Her book is a conversation with the wide, deep, and puissant ideas of knowledge traditions of Sanatana Dharma. Respectful to inner traditions of a people who refused to give up their lived reality embedded in the multiple truths of the world's most liberal religion, sensitive to the capture of minds by fake narratives that fan the fires of Hindumisia, *Kashi* reminds us of what we have lost—and must reclaim. This is a well-researched saga of a spiritual geography seen through diverse windows and captured by stories written in blood, faith, and grit. It is an integral handbook of Kashi, the physical, emotional, intellectual, and spiritual hub of the world's oldest civilization that in the 21st century still dares to live.'

Gautam Chikermane, author and vice-president, Observer Research Foundation

'*Kashi* is well-conceived and has been written very nicely. The author has done a commendable job in writing such a book, which is simple and straightforward in presenting all the important facts about Kashi based on the Puranas such as the Kashi Khanda in their translations. She has argued well on the important concept of sacred geography and how the holy city Kashi as a sacred space fulfils the religious and spiritual aspirations of the people of the Bharata country since time immemorial. Putting in place various historical events connected with Kashi, including the recent court litigations, is a special feature of this book. It has come at a crucial period in the history of this sacred place. I fully endorse this book and recommend it for publication.'

Dr T. Ganesan, director, Centre for Shaiva Studies

'It is a daunting task to encapsulate the unique religious markers of a city as ancient as Kashi. It can be a challenge to explain, in layman terms, the concept of a kshetra—sacred space—and its bearing on Kashi. Summarizing, while preserving sufficient detail, the relevant portions from a text as gargantuan as the *Skanda Purana* requires incredible patience and skill. To then sieve through millennia of history, contextualize the current socio-political flavours that colour most modern-day narratives, and stitch together a book as rich in its information and meticulous in its references as *Kashi*, without adding hyperbole, and yet make it as readable as any work of non-fiction could be, is as close to an impossible task as one can imagine. Aditi has achieved all that, and then some more. *Kashi* is an eminently rewarding and engaging book that does justice to the timeless city of an ageless civilization—it will, and must, be the definitive go-to work on Kashi, the eternal city.'

Abhinav, author

Kashi

The Valiant History of a Sacred Geography

Aditi Banerjee

Copyright © 2024 Aditi Banerjee

Aditi Banerjee has asserted her rights under the Indian Copyright Act to be identified as the author of this work.

All rights reserved under the copyright conventions. No part of this publication may be reproduced or transmitted in any form or by any means, electronic or mechanical, including photocopying, recording or any information storage or retrieval system, without the prior permission in writing from the publisher.

This book is solely the responsibility of the author(s) and the publisher has had no role in the creation of the content and does not have responsibility for anything defamatory or libellous or objectionable.

BluOne Ink Pvt. Ltd does not have any control over, or responsibility for, any third-party websites referred to in this book. All internet addresses given in this book were correct at the time of going to press. The author and publisher regret any inconvenience caused if addresses have changed or sites have ceased to exist, but can accept no responsibility for any such changes.

ISBN: 978-93-92209-69-7

First published in India 2024
This edition published 2024

BluOne Ink Pvt. Ltd
A-76, 2nd Floor, Sector 136, Noida
Uttar Pradesh 201301
www.bluone.ink
publisher@bluone.ink

Printed and bound in India at Nutech Print Services

Kali, Occam and BluPrint are all trademarks of BluOne Ink Pvt. Ltd.

To all the rishis and pilgrims
whose footsteps have hallowed the sacred kshetra of Kashi

Contents

Acknowledgements   xiii
Introduction   1

I Overview
Chapter 1: An Introduction to Kashi   21
Chapter 2: Origin Stories of Kashi   31

II Sthala Purana: The Sacred Geography of Kashi from Lore and Legends
Chapter 3: Agastya Muni's Sacrifice   47
Chapter 4: Enlightenment of Shivasharman and the Seven Sacred Cities   57
Chapter 5: The Manifestation of Kaala Bhairava and Dandapani   84
Chapter 6: The Story of Gyaanavapi   90
Chapter 7: Separation of Shiva from Kashi   102
Chapter 8: Origin Stories of Various Sacred Sites and Deities in Kashi   108
Chapter 9: Enlightenment of King Divodasa   125
Chapter 10: The Story of Bindu Madhava   134
Chapter 11: Kashi Pravesha: The Arrival of Shiva in Kashi   142
Chapter 12: The Manifestation of Various Lingas   150
Chapter 13: Origin Stories of the Other Special Lingas   167
Chapter 14: The Greatness of Vishveshvara   193
Chapter 15: The Pilgrimage Paths of Kashi   197
Chapter 16: The Sacred Geography of Kashi   201

III Resistance and Resilience in the Hindu Holy City

Chapter 17: Timeline and Overview — 231
Chapter 18: The Classical Age of Kashi — 237
Chapter 19: Destruction and Devastation: Mughal Invasion and Desecration — 266
Chapter 20: The Warrior Sadhus — 283
Chapter 21: Revival and Renaissance: The Contributions of All Bharatiyas — 303

IV The Gyanvapi Dispute

Chapter 22: The History of Past and Current Litigation in the Courts of India — 313
Chapter 23: Reframing the Dispute: The Sacred Geography of Gyaanavapi — 318

Conclusion — 329
References — 331
About the Author — 336

Acknowledgements

The creation of this book would not have been possible without the guidance, help, and support of many people—too many to name here.

When I first had the glimmerings of an idea to write a book about Kashi, a task that seemed too daunting to undertake, three people were instrumental in giving me the encouragement and inspiration to take on the project. First, Suhail Mathur, literary agent extraordinaire and wizard of the book publishing industry in India, convinced me to write the book and helped me conceptualize it. Second, Prashant from Padhega India. There is no one in the world who is more passionate advocate of authors and books than Prashant, and I am deeply grateful for his unstinting support and for connecting me with the publishing team at BluOne Ink. Third, Otis Haschemeyer, who painstakingly guided me through the writing of the first pages and chapters of the book. There are writing coaches and mentors, but to me, Otis will always be my writing guru.

I am deeply grateful to the BluOne Ink team for bringing this book to life. Anirudh Chakravartty has been nothing less than the godfather of this book. Praveen Tiwari and Thanglenhao Haokip have devoted meticulous attention to the production of the book and all the edits and changes that have made it a much-improved product. I cannot think of a better home for this book, which has been so important to me.

I remain eternally indebted to Hari Kiran Vadlamani for his constant support and encouragement. He motivates me to keep writing and pursuing new projects. He is an inspiration to me and so many others. Were it not for his gentle nudge, I would not have published my first book or found the mentorship, guidance, and support through Indic Academy's various programmes that have kept me going on my writing journey.

Several people in Kashi offered invaluable help and information while I stayed there to research for this book. I am particularly grateful to the various purohitas and panditas who graced me with their knowledge and to Sourav Bhattacharya for arranging and facilitating several such meetings. Ravi Tripathi connected me with various sources. Prof. P.B. Singh has been gracious and generous in sharing his knowledge and scholarship.

Without the love and blessings of my family, I would be nothing. My father, Bhaskar Nath Banerjee, is ever present in my heart and mind even if he is not with us today, and without his blessings, I would not be able to write a word. My mother, Shubhra Banerjee, and my brother, Amit Banerjee, have always encouraged me and supported me to follow my dreams. My sister-in-law, Shilpa Banerjee, is a kindred spirit. My nephews, Avi and Aneesh Banerjee, are the delight of my life.

My husband, Biswajit Malakar, is my beta reader, my muse, my partner, and my better half. One of the first gifts he gave me was a small Ganesha in a rocking chair reading a book. I look at that Ganesha every day for inspiration and to remind myself that I write for Him first and foremost. I could not have a fiercer supporter than my husband. He has sacrificed hours of weekend and vacation time so I can work on my writing; he has insisted on picking up the burden of errands and chores and working around the home to free me up to write; he has pushed me to write every time I did not feel up to it. I am beyond blessed to have him as my husband; he is nothing less than a gift from Bhagavan for me.

If there is any truth to the words I have written and any meaning to be gleaned from these pages, the credit for that goes to my guru, Nagendra S. Rao. All that I have learned about dharma and the metaphysical and philosophical truths that undergird life have come through him. He set me on the path that led me to reading the Puranas, to making teertha yatras to Kashi and other sacred kshetras, and to devoting my life to the pursuit of sadhana and Sanatana Dharma.

All of my other books have been laid at the feet of Sri Krishna, my Ishta Devata; this one, though, belongs to Shiva. That is the beauty of Sanatana Dharma, enabling us to cultivate different relationships with different deities. Many times, throughout the process of writing this book, when I felt discouraged or at an impasse, it was the compassion of Shiva, the feeling that He wanted me to write this, that kept my pen moving (or, rather, my fingers typing). Many times, my eyes teared while reading the *Skanda Purana* and immersing myself in the leela of Shiva. He is Mahadeva. Shiva is my Baba, and this book is nothing but the outpouring of a young child wishing for her Baba to come back home.

Introduction

Seven years ago, I visited Kashi. It was a halt on the way to the Himalayas, where I travel most frequently. Pilgrimage is my favoured form of leisure, and it is, of course, the duty of every Hindu to visit Kashi, the holiest of holy cities. Most destinations are for the living, but Kashi is where Hindus go to die—to spend their last days or perform the last rites for and cremate their loved ones. *Kashayam maranam mukti*, it is said—'To die in Kashi is to attain liberation.'

I did not have high expectations from my trip. I prefer the mountains and the oceanside to the city, and I merely booked a two-day stay. Yet, the experience left an indelible mark on me.

I remember being whisked away in an auto-rickshaw from my luxury resort on the outskirts of the city to a rowdy traffic intersection. There, my guide and I had to descend on foot to make the rest of the way to the Kashi Vishwanath Temple.

Kashi Vishwanath is the holiest temple in the city. The *vigraha* at Kashi Vishwanath is one of the twelve *jyotirlingas*. Jyotirlinga literally translates to a pillar of light, and these twelve pillar-shaped vigrahas of Shiva are said to be *swayambhu*, or self-manifested. Shiva is one among the cosmic trinity of Hinduism, consisting of Brahma (the creator), Vishnu (the preserver), and Shiva (often referred to as the destroyer, but more precisely, the one who prevails over the dissolution of the universe, ushering in a new cycle of creation).

We wound our way through labyrinthine narrow alleyways, jumping aside from darting mopeds that threatened to run us over. The smell of ghee-fried fritters and jalebis, pretzel-shaped sweets soaked in sugar syrup, mingled with the fragrance of sandalwood incense. Soon, our bodies were swept along by a tide of devotees on the path to the temple. We began moving in a frenzied mass, as if none of us could wait a moment longer for the *darshana* of Shiva.

In Hinduism, one does not 'see' a deity. One has darshana, which is to be graced by the vision of divinity. Darshana is bestowed upon us; it is not something that we can take for granted. One is beckoned to a temple or pilgrimage site. Even a place like Kashi, which is easily reachable by a one-hour flight or an hours-long train ride from Delhi, is said to be visited only when one has been called upon by the Devas.

I remember prostrating before Dhundhi Maharaja, the deity of Ganesha, the son of Shiva. One must visit Dhundhi Maharaja in order to complete the Kashi yatra. In this form, Ganesha bears witness to the pilgrimage and records it. I remember circumambulating afterwards the white marble shrine of Annapurna Devi, the consort of Shiva in the form of the Mother Goddess feeding people. I also recall visiting the next morning the shrine of Kaala Bhairava regarded as the protector of Kashi and said to be so powerful that even time turns away from him in fear. My body was covered in chills as I beheld his beautiful and fierce form.

But what I remember the most—that which has seared itself into my consciousness—is not the darshana of any of those deities or even Kashi Vishwanath himself. It is a quiet moment during the prior evening, after my darshana of Kashi Vishwanath, after witnessing the grand Saptarishi *aarti* during which the *purohitas*, officiating priests, energetically bathe and decorate the Shivalinga, chanting Vedic hymns so sonorously and passionately that they go into a trance, leaving a powerful impact on the devotees. Enraptured by that experience, I was dazed as my guide led me to the outskirts of the temple compound.

A mosque towered over the temple compound, its shadow imposing in the evening light. And there, standing alone, facing the mosque, waited an expectant Nandi, his gaze obstructed by the wall of the mosque.

Nandi, the bull, is the constant companion and *vahana*[1] of Shiva. In every Shiva temple, there will be the Shivalinga in the sanctum sanctorum, the main altar, of the temple and facing him will be the loyal Nandi, Shiva's vahana, carved out of stone or metal.

Nandi is no ordinary bull. His four legs symbolize Satya (truth), Dharma (righteousness), Shanti (peace), and Prema (love). Shiva represents the divine and Nandi the devout mortal. Nandi's steadfast gaze upon Shiva represents the steadiness of devotion and focus required on the path to spirituality.

When a Hindu goes to a temple, he or she will not stand between Nandi and Shiva. Instead, the practice is to gently touch Nandi's ears and tail, prostrate to him, and whisper into his ear one's prayer, so that he can convey it to his beloved Shiva. Crouching next to Nandi, we gaze upon Shiva through his eyes.

And so, when the guide led me to the fringes of the compound, I patted Nandi on the back, touched his ears, and crouched next to him, gazing at the mosque. Yet, I could not utter a prayer. I could not muster a word or thought. A visceral pain constricted my lungs and belly, seeing Nandi's gaze unreciprocated. It was like seeing a temple broken in two.

For years, I relived that memory. I took it out and examined it, tried to analyse it. I tried to define and explain it. I tried to find something to do with all the thoughts and feelings churning within me: the long, sacred history of that holiest of holy sites, the heavy

---

1 Vahana literally translates as 'vehicle', but the concept of vahana in Hinduism is much richer than that. A vahana is not only a companion, not only a vehicle for the deity but also spiritually linked with the Deva or Devi and embodying qualities specific and significant to that particular form of the divine.

weight of the violence and bloodshed that led to that split between Nandi and Shiva. It was a feeling of having something robbed from me and my people, and even deeper than my own anguish, surged the vicarious pain of imagining Nandi's long, lonely wait.

I could not articulate it, nor did I know what to do with it.

This is not just a personal story. Centuries of history and current litigation have focused on this very site. Three times, a temple on the site of Gyanvapi was destroyed and then rebuilt. The temple was first attacked by Aibak in 1194 CE and then by Queen Razia, who appropriated the site and built a mosque there during her reign in 1236–1240 CE (Jain 2019, 93). In 1669, Aurangzeb, the Mughal emperor, ordered the demolition of Kashi Vishwanath and other important Hindu temples across India. As renowned historian Meenakshi Jain notes, a portion of the old temple was retained as the rear wall of the mosque (Jain 2019, 96).

A history of litigation, dating back to the early 1990s, is centred on Kashi Vishwanath and the neighbouring Gyanvapi Mosque site. In 1991, a petition was filed by Hindu priests to access the mosque and pray there, based on the claim that the mosque was built atop the original temple. The petition also requested the transfer of the site to Hindu ownership. That case was dismissed in 1998. It should be noted that through all the centuries of destruction and temple-razing, Hindus never relinquished their devotion or claims to the site and numerous attempts were made to rebuild and regain the site, as we will see in more detail in the later sections of this book.

In December 2019, another petition filed in a civil court in Varanasi—the official name for the city of Kashi—sought an archaeological assessment of the origins of the Gyanvapi Mosque. Those proceedings were stayed by a higher court but then the matter was reopened in April 2021 and an archaeological survey was ordered. The management committee of the Gyanvapi Mosque objected and brought this back to the high court, which once again stayed the proceedings in September 2021.

In August 2021, five Hindu female devotees filed a petition in court seeking the right to pray daily before certain Hindu images located on the outer walls of the Gyanvapi Mosque compound. As part of the case proceedings, a videography survey of the compound was ordered. The survey uncovered an object near the *wazookhana*, a well or tank used for washing hands and feet prior to entering the inner premises of a mosque. The video recording was leaked and appears to show an object that resembles a Shivalinga, which some claim represents the original Shivalinga that was worshiped in Kashi Vishwanath. The representatives of the management committee of the Gyanvapi Mosque maintain that the object is a fountain.

In May 2022, the Varanasi civil court ordered that the area where the Shivalinga was found within the mosque compound be sealed and *namaaz* be restricted within the mosque. Later that month, the Supreme Court of India ordered that the object be protected and Muslims be allowed to offer namaaz within the mosque. The Supreme Court then transferred the case from the Varanasi civil court to the relevant district court, stating that such a sensitive case warranted a more senior judge.

The Supreme Court requested the district court to adjudicate first on the plea raised by the mosque committee that the petition was not tenable on grounds of the Places of Worship Act of 1991. This act seeks to freeze the religious classification of a place of worship as it existed on 15 August 1947. An important exception was made for the Ram Janmabhoomi site, the site of the temple consecrating Sri Rama's birthplace, in Ayodhya.

On 12 September 2022, the district court judge dismissed the challenge brought by the mosque committee, which alleged that the plea for year-long worship had no legal standing. The court dismissed the challenge on the basis that the petitioners were not seeking ownership of the site but rather just the right of worship there.

During the autumn of 2022, the court deliberated over the request for carbon dating of the alleged Shivalinga found during the survey, as per the request of four of the five Hindu petitioners; the fifth objected on the grounds that any such testing may harm the Shivalinga. The mosque committee objected to the plea for scientific investigation on the grounds that the original plea pertained to worship at a shrine within the mosque and had nothing to do with the underlying structure. It reiterated its claim that the object is a fountain.

On 11 October 2022, the court denied the request for carbon dating on the basis that the historical status of the object is irrelevant to the plea for worship rights.

This controversy will most likely wind its way through the court system for months, perhaps years, to come. A similar case in Ayodhya roiled through seventy years of litigation before being finally resolved in 2019 with the temple being rebuilt and inaugurated on 22 January, 2024. Suits are pending in Mathura, too. The Ayodhya story caught worldwide attention in December 1992, when a large crowd of Hindu activists tore down Babri Masjid, the mosque erected over the site over a temple consecrating what is believed to be Sri Rama's birthplace. Riots ensued.

In the 1980s, during the popular Rama temple movement leading up to that fateful day in December 1992, a slogan gained currency, becoming the battle cry for the movement that defined Hindu activism and politics for over a generation: '*Ayodhya to bas jhanki hai, Mathura-Kashi baaki hai*' (Ayodhya is only a glimpse; Mathura and Kashi are still left). The other famous slogan from that time is '*Mandir wahin banayenge*' (The temple will be built there and only there).

These three sites are among the most important in all of Hinduism. Ayodhya is the birthplace of Sri Rama, one of the two principal avatars of Sri Narayana. Mathura is the birthplace of Sri Krishna, the other principal avatar of Sri Narayana. And Kashi, the subject of this book, is the abode of Shiva, the city that is his adopted home after Kailasha, his mountainous abode.

While a Westerner can instinctively understand the sanctity of Jerusalem and Mecca to their respective adherents and are sensitized to the religious significance and civilizational relevance of contested sacred sites in Jerusalem, there is no such instinctive understanding in the West of the significance of Ayodhya, Kashi, and Mathura to Hindus from time immemorial. This precludes the nuanced understanding required to address the contemporary issues around cultural ownership and access to these sites.

For a religion that encompasses so many deities and sites of pilgrimage—for which even a tree, a lake, or a pond can become a sacred place; under which, every village, every clan, every household can claim its own specific deity; under which, every home contains a temple within—for such a religion, one could argue that because every place is potentially sacred, no place is particularly sacred. In other words, and this is a common narrative often heard, if every home can have a temple for Sri Rama, if he can reside in our hearts, why is there a need to build a temple for him in Ayodhya?

The Gyanvapi Mosque is lauded under this narrative as a beautiful example of secular harmony—a mosque co-existing with a temple. Under this line of thought, attempts like that of the court petitioners will only cause ancient wounds to fester and threaten to corrode communal relations and risk mob violence. Moreover, as the argument goes, can a nation like Bharat, dealing with widespread poverty and other socioeconomic and geopolitical challenges, afford to be distracted with such Gordian knots of history and religion when attention and resources would be better off invested in improving the quality of life for over a billion people?

In short, can we not do what the law pointed to by the Gyanvapi Mosque committee, the Places of Worship Act of 1991, ordered the state to do and simply freeze history as it existed as of 15 August 1947 and ignore the past? (Even this claim is not so simple, as Hindus have never relinquished their claims to these contested sites, continuously performing worship in the premises or as close to the premises as they were allowed to. In that sense, the religious character of these sites has always been Hindu). Can we not simply proclaim that what was a mosque in 1947 and what was a temple in 1947 remain that way forever?

No, we cannot—and this book attempts to explain why.

Imagine a man, bared to the buttocks, but for a flutter of saffron cloth covering his loin. His body, bronzed by the baking sun and weathered by the wind, through decades spent wandering in jungles and remote mountainsides, is smeared white-grey with the ash of the *dhuni*, the holy fire that is his sole companion. Serpentine twists of matted hair sinuously wind down his back. A *kamandalu*, a gourd-carved round pot for collecting water and rice, lays at his feet. His hand brandishes a curved sword.

Arrayed in front of this naga sadhu,[2] the naked ascetic, stands the sultan's army with cannons. We do not know for certain the identity of this sultan, but in all probability, it was Aurangzeb. This Mughal emperor, still remembered today for the terror and destruction wrought during his reign, destroyed many temples. Oddly enough, his reign inspires admiration and respect from some elite pockets of India and the West even today. A prestigious street in New Delhi was named after him and only in recent years was the street name changed.

The naga sadhu did not stand alone that day in 1664. He stood with sixty thousand other naga sadhus who had come to defend the site of Gyaanavapi, where stood the grand Kashi Vishvanatha Mandir, the holiest of holy sites in Kashi, which had already been rebuilt after having been destroyed twice before.

The naga sadhus have no name, no past, no caste affiliation, no family, and no individual identity. All of this they have renounced,

---

2 'Naga sadhu' in Sanskrit literally translates to 'naked ascetic' in English. It is also the informal term for the religious order organized under this name, as further described in detail in subsequent chapters.

leading a life of incredible asceticism. They prefer a life of solitude, shying away from society. Yet, on that day, they had joined forces to defend this temple of Shiva in this city of Shiva against an invader who would subsequently order the destruction of the most important of temples in Kashi and so many other places.

That day, astonishingly enough, the naga sadhus won and defeated the army of the sultan. The temple was saved and the army retreated.

Scant historical records remain of this incident, while it is strongly supported in oral tradition and secondary sources, which will be described in subsequent chapters. According to Lochtefeld, this incident is described in a handwritten book found in the Mahanirvani Akhada's archives, and this has been further supported by Sir Jadunath Sarkar and other sources (Lochtefeld 2002, 268). The sultan is not identified, but historians speculate that it was indeed Aurangzeb. After all, five years later, in 1669, Aurangzeb had the Kashi Vishvanatha Temple razed to the ground, perhaps, at least in part, seeking revenge upon those mendicants who had dared to challenge him a few years earlier.

This incident fits a well-documented pattern in history of Hindu warrior ascetics who took up arms in defence of Hindu sacred sites as well as to rebel against the rule of the Mughals and later the British. This book will examine the historical significance of these warrior ascetics and their relevance to the story of Kashi.

This battle was fought not only by the naga sadhus but also by innumerable priests and citizens who hid deities in their homes, shielding them from destruction. The citizens of Kashi and devotees from all around Bharat, including kings and queens and generals of various Hindu kingdoms, came together to painstakingly rebuild temples again and again after every round of destruction, which came in waves for over five hundred years. This story of the ongoing resilience and resistance of Hindus who made Kashi their home and protected their deities and temples the best that they could against the tides of history and colonization is the focus of this book.

The battle fought that day in 1664 did not end then; nor did it end in 1669 with the destruction of the Kashi Vishvanatha Mandir. It is a battle that has continued raging for centuries, and even today, access and claims of ownership over the same site within the Kashi Vishwanath Temple compound are being fiercely contested in Indian courts. We have to face difficult truths and come to a more honest reckoning of history. To pave the way for a constructive resolution regarding this and other contested sacred sites in India, it is crucial to rekindle our innate understanding of the concepts of sacred geography that form the basis of cultural assertions to these sites. This forward-looking approach should acknowledge the past without being bound by it.

There is an ancient Hindu literary tradition of recording and transmitting Sthala Purana, texts that, in their simplest form, tell the story of a place. Sthala means 'place', and Purana means 'old or ancient', so the term 'Sthala Purana' can be loosely translated as the old history of a place. Yet, the Hindu understanding of history is markedly different from history as we understand it through a Western lens.

The *Itihaasa Purana* is proclaimed to be the fifth Veda. As per the *Chandogya Upanishad*, '*itihasapuranam panchamam vedanam*' (7.1.2). This genre of Hindu shastra, or sacred texts, distils the corpus of Vedic knowledge into the form of stories and parables accessible to all. *Itihaasa*, literally translated as 'so it happened', exclusively refers to the Ramayana and the Mahabharata, while the Purana has a broader definition. The *pancha lakshana*, or five qualities, that a Purana must possess are as follows: it must explain *sarga* (manifestation and evolution of the cosmos) and *pratisarga* (recreation of the cosmos after its periodic dissolution in *Pralaya*);

it must also include descriptions of *vamsha*, the genealogies of the Devas (the Gods and Goddesses of the Hindu pantheon) and the rishis (sages); it must describe the *manvantara* (the cosmic cycles of time, each of which is presided over by a different Manu or progenitor); and it must contain *vamshanucarita*—accounts of royal dynasties, particularly the solar dynasty (from which Sri Rama hails) and the lunar dynasty (from which Sri Krishna hails).

The Puranas have a loftier goal than merely recounting history. If we think of history as the narration of a sequence of events, fixed in time and space, that are situated in the physical reality of the material world, the Puranas go beyond this to seek and tell us about ourselves in a more essential way. Where did we come from; who were our ancestors; what is the nature of time; and where do we belong in the vast cosmic order? In short, who are we in the most fundamental sense of the word?

Within that genre, a subclass of texts, the Sthala Purana, is focused on the traditions, lore, and history of a particular sacred site. These sites could be a *tirtha* (sacred water body), a *kshetra* (a particular place or territory), or a temple or other site related to a Deva or Devi. For example, hundreds of Sthala Puranas have been written about various Shiva temples and shrines across Tamil Nadu, some in Sanskrit and others in the vernacular.

Maha Periyava, the late Shankaracharya of Kanchi, Sri Chandrasekharendra Saraswathi Mahaswami, said of the Sthala Puranas:

> In my opinion, the Sthala Puranas not only enables us to have an insight into history but also enrich our knowledge of local culture and local customs. It seems to me that if they are read together in a connected manner they will throe [sic] more light on our history than even the 18 major Puranas and Upapuranas. In fact, they fill the gaps in the major Puranas.

Local legends do help in a proper understanding of history. For instance, educated people today do not believe that Sankara Bhagavatpada visited any of the temples or that he brought the puja performed there under a certain system. [...] But let us examine the stories that tell us that he gave new life to certain temples, temples that are thousand [sic] miles or more apart. Their connection with the Acharya is confirmed from such stories and local legends.

[...]In teaching us lessons in dharma also the Sthala Puranas are in no way inferior to the major Puranas. It is in fact these local Puranas which are a few hundred in number that throw light on the finer points of dharma. (Importance of Sthala Puranas from the Chapter 'Puranas' n.d.)

Thus, oral history and the traditional lore associated with a sacred site are a core component of the Sthala Purana. This also connects Sthala Purana to the larger global tradition of cultural transmission and initiation that is often nowadays derisively referred to as 'mythology'. 'Mythology' has come to mean falsehood. A mythological story is assumed to be fictional; myth-busters exist to show us the truth. Popular myths are mistaken notions that we are duty-bound to correct.

Yet, in the original sense of the word, in ancient Greek and then Latin, the word 'mythos' is something more complex:

The word 'myth' originates from the Greek word mythos, meaning 'word' or 'tale' or 'true narrative', referring not only to the means by which it was transmitted but also to its being rooted in truth. Mythos was also closely related to the word myo, meaning 'to teach', or 'to initiate into the mysteries'. This is how the word was interpreted by Homer—who is generally identified to have lived in the 7th or 8th century BCE—when composing his great works, including *The Iliad*, in which he meant to convey a truth. (Black 2012)

A paper by Brezinski delves into the various interpretations given to the word 'myth' by scholars, sociologists, and historians over time. He notes the following:

B. Malinowski expressed his views in the same vein as Eliade. He observes that the most important characteristics [sic] of myth is the fact that it testifies to the past truth, however, always present and vital for reality. For a native, myth is neither a fictional story nor an account of the past; it proves the existence of important reality which is partly alive nowadays.

...

Myths, as Eliade notes, narrate not only the origin of the World, of animals, of plants, and of man, but also all the primordial events in consequence of which man became what he is today – mortal (in some myths immortal), sexed, organized in a society, obliged to work in order to live, and working in accordance with certain rules. If the World exists, if man exists, it is because Supernatural Beings exercised creative powers in the 'beginning'. But after the cosmogony and the creation of man other events occurred, and man as he is today is the direct result of those mythical events, he is constituted by those events. He is mortal because something happened in illo tempore. If this 'something' had not happened, man would be immortal.

Modern history of religion and ethnology borrowed from historians and ancient philosophers this division into 'mythical' and 'true' statements, i.e., 'verifiable'. However, let us repeat it once again that for our historical and theological reflection at this point it is of no importance whether all characters and situations presented in mythological accounts are the creation of human spirit and mind and in this sense are objectively false. It should be underlined that for a religious man in a given community mythology is understood and lived through in the perspective of the real world and not the world of fantasy. Mythology explains and 'validates' the existence of the world, man and society. This last statement is the main reason why a religious man considers his mythology as a true story which gives meaning to his action. In somewhat simplified terms, it might be stated that the 'true' nature of myth is not based on its historiography but historiosophy.

...

Myths act in favour of cultural stability, stimulate to action and provide with patterns of behaviour. Thus, it is said that a sociological function of myths implies certain ethical norms of a

> given individual and community. Finally, myths fulfil pedagogical function providing man with knowledge about himself and others. They demonstrate how to live with integrity in all circumstances. Man referring to his ancestors and preserving 'mythical memory' derives from their lives wisdom which applies to his life in perspective of his own destiny.
>
> ...
>
> No myth might be understood differently than as a vital cultural power. Thus no researcher can collect and analyse myths out of context. They must notice the influence of myth on social life, morality, law and also religious life with its entire rituals. (Brezinski 2015, 21-24)

Thus, we see that myths are not just flights of fanciful imagination or stories to be taken lightly or mocked. Rather, the mythos a society believed in and propagated was the organizing principle for its cultural and ethical norms and the bedrock of its metaphysical, religious, and civilizational identity. It was the story by which a people could understand and express themselves at the deepest and most fundamental levels. This is how cultures were preserved and evolved for much of human history. Less focus is on factual history than on the essential nature of life, human nature, the cosmos, and the workings of the world. For example, a myth will be more concerned about the essential nature of war itself than the factual sequence of any particular war; it will use storytelling devices to accentuate those important civilizational, spiritual, psychological, and philosophical lessons embedded in history to act as a memetic device to pass on insights and cultural norms down the generations. It will focus on archetypes rather than any particular individual—on the metaphor and allegory of an event than the reportage of facts and dates and times.

Some of the most ancient Sthala Puranas delve into the sacred geography of Kashi, one of the oldest inhabited cities in the world. Kashi, according to Hinduism, transcends the cosmic cycle of time. It is said, when *Pralaya*, the moment of cosmic dissolution, comes, Kashi alone will survive.

This book uses the term 'sacred geography' for this intertwined concept of mythos, tradition, and history that has, in Hinduism, been captured within the tradition of Sthala Purana and its associated literature. In a broader context, the ancient world and indigenous traditions globally have since the dawn of history ascribed to certain sites an elevated status based on their inherent sanctity. That sanctity could come from the energies and geographical features of the site itself or from the lore and mythos of the site, its connection to the gods, and the enhanced prestige by being hallowed by the footsteps of sages and other holy ones.

This sacred geography was not just metaphysical. Great civilizations were built around holy sanctuaries like Delphi and Delos; these sites were not just temples for pilgrimage but centres that became the beating heart of the civilizations to which they belonged, important for purposes of trade, politics, and education. It is only after the destruction of the classical world with the onset of the Abrahamic faiths that many of us, at least in the West, lost this understanding of the role of sacred geography in traditional societies. Instead, we have fallen under the spell of historicity, such as the use of archaeology, maps, dating technologies, and property deeds, to try to establish ownership and claims to sites. But this is not workable for a system based on sacred geography.

In this context, the courts of India find themselves on a quixotic quest to prove or disprove, via narrow notions of historicity and archaeology, whether Hindus have a valid claim of access to or ownership of disputed sacred sites. By attempting via legislation to freeze history as of the arbitrary date of India's independence as a nation-state, the Indian state is essentially asking the Hindu people to forget the sacred geography that is integral to their faith and that has shaped the geographical and cultural conception of Bharat itself from time immemorial.

Diana L. Eck's book, *India: A Sacred Geography*, makes this point compellingly: India, that is Bharat, came together as a nation not in 1947 but since millennia through the conceptualization of Bharat within the prism of sacred geography. Asking a people to erase their own history and the way that they have understood themselves and their nation for thousands of years is not tenable. The conversation around Gyanvapi and similar disputed sites cannot take place without fully acknowledging the relevance and role of sacred geography. Sacred geography speaks to a people's communal claim over a particular site, one that cannot be summarily dismissed.

That does not mean that sacred geography can or should always be determinative. A native community will always have the weight of hundreds or thousands of years of history against a new arrival seeking to establish a new site of worship. In that regard, sacred geography cannot be used to ossify a society or nation. There must be space and accommodation for others. In looking at the issue, however, in trying to analyse it, we must allow for the relevance of sacred geography to inform us how a community has revered and understood a particular site through its traditions, texts, and lore. If nothing else, it will enrich the analysis and bring much needed sensitivity and compassion to debates that can too often be polarizing.

What it boils down to is this: a Eurocentric approach to disputed sites like Gyanvapi ask who was here first and who built the first religious structure, and try to uncover ownership through legal records like property deeds and historiography based on archaeology. Sacred geography takes a step back and looks at the mythos and lore of a place—not seeking to prove the historicity of such lore, but merely taking it at face value—to understand the specific relevance of a site for a community and its meaning and importance to that community. It is then that the relative weight of meaning and spiritual and civilizational importance for one community must be weighed against other considerations, including access to sites of worship for minority communities. In the current discourse, though, there is no space given to even acknowledge this notion of sacred geography. No meaningful or constructive discussion or resolution can proceed without such acknowledgement.

This book is written in honour of, reverence for, and in the spirit of the tradition of Sthala Purana. This book seeks to integrate the sacred geography and traditions of Kashi, stretching back to time immemorial, with modern-day documented history of the people of Kashi who have strived to preserve and protect the traditions and sanctity of this kshetra. Both aspects are needed to understand the history and significance of Kashi, and more importantly, to experience its powers for ourselves.

Visiting Kashi is different from having *darshana* of Kashi. The purpose of all Sthala Puranas is not just to inform but also to inspire, to motivate one to undertake pilgrimages, which in earlier times were arduous, months-long, and often dangerous journeys. Today, it is easy to visit Kashi. However, it has perhaps become more difficult to have darshana of Kashi, to experience the true essence of Kashi.

When we steep ourselves in what the Sthala Purana of Kashi holds, our vision expands and becomes purified for that true darshana.

It is the humble hope of this book to make the sacred literature relating to Kashi from the Puranas more accessible. This book also aims to pay homage to all those devotees, sadhus, and kings and queens who dedicated their lives to preserving the sacred sites of Kashi, whether by physically building and rebuilding temples or meticulously documenting and sharing the sacred lore of each and every one of the thousands and thousands of holy places in Kashi.

Many of us know about the Vatican, Jerusalem, and Mecca as holy cities. Very few people outside India, however, know much about Kashi, other than snippets of documentaries they may have seen of an exoticized image of a naked sadhu with matted hair smoking a *chillum*. In 2017, CNN featured a documentary on Kashi titled *City of the Dead*, referring to the city as 'one large crematorium', and focused ghoulishly on a cannibalistic sect of naked sadhus (Safi 2017). One of the primary objectives of this book is to cleanse the reader's perception of Kashi from this kind of colonialist, racist, distorted taint.

The desire is to present the story of Kashi authentically from the perspective of the devout, to give voice to those whose narratives have been forgotten or been silenced over the past few centuries, and to raise awareness of the complex entangled history of sacred sites that are now disputed and being hotly contested in the courts of India. In that sense, this is not just the story of Kashi but also the story of Mathura and Ayodhya and many other sacred Hindu sites that have been usurped from Hindu custodianship through successive waves of invasion and colonization. This is a story of a city and a civilization.

I
Overview

CHAPTER 1

An Introduction to Kashi

Om.
gaṅgātaraṅgaramaṇīyajaṭākalāpaṃ
gaurīnirantaravibhūṣitavāmabhāgam/
nārāyaṇapriyamanaṅgamadāpahāraṃ
vārāṇasīpurapatiṃ bhaja viśvanātham[3]

(Salutations to Sri Vishvanatha), Whose bundle of matted hair is beautifully decorated by the waves of the Ganga
Who always keeps His consort, Gauri, in the left half of His body
Who is dear to Narayana (the Preserver of the Cosmos) and Who has destroyed the pride of Kamadeva (the God of Desire)
Hail that Vishvanatha, the Lord of the city of Kashi/Varanasi

A Misunderstood City

If you are from outside India, you may never have heard of Kashi—also known as Varanasi, also known as Benares—a city with a continuous recorded history of at least 2,500 years, a city whose civilizational and historical significance rivals that of Jerusalem, Babylon, and Peking that is now Beijing. If you are from India, you have heard of Kashi but may have never seen it, dismissing it

---

[3] This is the first verse of the śrīviśvanāthāṣṭakam, an eight-verse stotra, or hymn, on Shiva in the form of Vishvanatha. It was composed by Adi Shankaracharya.

as a city where old people go to die or the religious go to cremate and perform the last rites of their loved ones. If you have visited Kashi, you may have experienced a whirlwind of crowds swarming narrow labyrinthine paths winding towards innumerable shrines and temples, the series of eighty-four ghats, rows of steps, leading from the lofty heights of the city down to the sacred Ganga river, oil lamps nestled on betel leaves floating on the serene grey waves, the drone of Vedic prayers being recited by pilgrims standing waist-deep in the water and purohits presiding over funerary and other rites. You may have glimpsed during a scenic boat ride balls of orange fire billowing out from the Manikarnika Ghat, where cremations are performed incessantly day and night, the special site where Shiva himself comes to liberate the dead.

To see Kashi is not necessarily to understand Kashi, however.

In 2017, CNN aired a short-lived documentary series entitled *Believer*, hosted by Reza Aslan, intended to showcase different world religions. As *The New Yorker* put it, 'The show is a kind of spiritual "Parts Unknown," in which religions are ingested like sea-urchin roe—but without Anthony Bourdain's lovable loutishness' (Muhanna 2017).

The first episode centred on Kashi drew widespread outrage. Kashi was referred to as 'the city of the dead'. A promo for the episode by CNN was titled, 'Face to face with a cannibalistic sect' and had the following description: 'Reza Aslan learns why some fear the Aghora Hindu sect when he sits down with a bizarre guru covered in cremated ashes' (CNN 2017). The promos for the episode depicted Kashi as a giant crematorium and referred to dumping ashes in the Ganga.

In the course of the documentary, an Aghori smears the ashes of cremated humans on his face and invites Aslan, the host, to drink alcohol from a human skull then eat what was claimed to be a piece of human brain. At one point, the Aghori threatens to cut Aslan's head off if he continued to ask questions and began flinging his faecal waste at him and the camera crew.

When the episode aired, there were pockets of appalled outrage across the Indian and Hindu community worldwide. The episode was aired after a spate of killings that targeted Hindus and Sikhs across the US, and there was concern that this kind of sensationalized reporting would make an already vulnerable religious minority the target of more bigotry and attacks.

It is not that Aghoris do not exist in Hinduism. The Sanskrit term '*aghori*' literally means one without fear. The path of *aghora* is for the rare few who can transcend societal conventions and walk the path of extremes. It is not mainstream and was never meant to be. In India, Aghoris are respected, while, at the same time, most people give them wide berth. Indians recognize the path of aghora as valid but one that should not be treated or tampered with lightly. To depict Aghoris without this important context within the broader framework of Hinduism and Indian society was a disservice to CNN's audience, generating buzzy ratings at the expense of genuine understanding. This thwarted the purported purpose of the show to develop a multicultural understanding of global religions.

That episode is but one incident in a long chain of exoticized caricature that has persisted since colonial times in Western portrayals of Hindus and Hinduism. In popular culture, Hinduism and India are often reduced to stereotypes surrounding caste, cows, and widow-burning. The litany of side characters like Apu on *The Simpsons* and Raj on *The Big Bang Theory*, who are laughed at more than taken seriously, makes many Hindu-Americans ashamed of their background.

The perfect example of this phenomenon is the 1984 movie *Indiana Jones and the Temple of Doom*, the second in the blockbuster Indiana Jones franchise. Directed by Steven Spielberg, the movie was intended to be shot in India, but the Indian government refused and later banned the movie, finding the content to be racist and offensive (the-take.com n.d.). The story depicted Kali, a revered Hindu Goddess (and consort of Shiva), as a bloodthirsty demoness whose devotees maniacally chanted to kill for Kali while performing violent sacrifices. The Tantric priest who played the villain pulled beating hearts out of his victims. He had been stealing Shiva deities to harvest their power and take over the occult world. At dinner, Indiana Jones and his companions were served spiders and snakes, eyeballs, and monkey brain soup. On a tangential note, the Indian actor who played the villainous priest—and received flak for it in India—received numerous invites for Hollywood movies after *Temple of Doom*, but he rejected them because all the roles were to play a Red Indian chief, continuing the confusion and conflation between Indians and Native Americans from the time of Columbus (the-take.com n.d.).

This kind of depiction has coloured Western thinking about India and Hinduism, clouding the gaze with which Kashi is viewed today. And because of the hold that Western thought increasingly has on young people worldwide, including in India where English is perhaps still the main lingua franca among the educated and affluent classes, it has obscured the understanding of Indians and Hindus about their own traditions and holy places, including Kashi.

It is time to lift that veil and try to see Kashi for what it is, within the context of the 'modern' world.

A Brief Overview of the Geography and History of Kashi

The city of Kashi is situated on a high bank overlooking the Ganga in the central part of India. The quintessential image of Kashi is that of the wide curve of the river Ganga, and on its bank, terraced steps that lead up to edifices of temples and ashrams, behind which stretches a maze of narrow alleyways and footpaths now leading to a dense urban centre.

Mark Twain described it poetically:

> The Ganges front is the supreme showplace of Benares. Its tall bluffs are solidly caked from water to summit, along a stretch of

three miles, with a splendid jumble of massive and picturesque masonry, a bewildering and beautiful confusion of stone platforms, temples, stair-flights, rich and stately palaces—nowhere a break, nowhere a glimpse of the bluff itself, all the long face of it is compactly walled from sight by this crammed perspective of platforms, soaring stairways, sculptured temples, majestic palaces, softening away into the distances; and there is movement, motion, human life everywhere, and brilliantly costumed—streaming in rainbows up and down the lofty stairways, and massed in metaphorical gardens on the miles of great platforms at the river's edge. (Twain 1898, 496)

At Kashi, the Ganga, the most sacred of the rivers within Hinduism, flows as Uttarvahini, meaning while it mostly flows north-to-south from the Himalayas to the Bay of Bengal, it reverses course and flows south-to-north near Kashi. It is said that the reason for this is Ganga, who is borne on Shiva's head, wishes to pay homage to Shiva who resides here in the form of Kashi Vishwanath.

Within Kashi proper, which stretches out into the countryside, there is the area known as Varanasi situated between the Varana and Asi rivers. Over time, that name has morphed into Banaras or Benares in common parlance.

Varana and Asi: these are no ordinary rivers in Hindu cosmology.

The *Vamana Purana* describes the origin of the two rivers from the body of Purusha, the cosmic man, with Varana flowing from his right foot and Asi flowing from his left foot and the tract of land in between praised as a site of pilgrimage without peer. The first two sections of the *Jabala Upanishad* identify the eternal soul (atma) with that which is sought out and served in *Avimukta*. When pressed about the location of Avimukta, the teacher reveals that it is between the Varana and the Asi in the place where the nose and eyebrows meet, where Dyu, the celestial realm, touches earth. This mystical interpretation of Avimukta is quoted and discussed by the author of the *Kashimoksha Nirnaya* and is referred to by Shankaracharya in his commentary on the *Brahma Sutras* (Eck 1993, 19).

Kashi is an ancient city. As Mark Twain famously observed—you will be hard-pressed to find a tour guide in Kashi who does not quote this line: 'Benares is older than history, older than tradition, older even than legend, and looks twice as old as all of them put together' (Twain 1898, 480).

On a more serious note, a Christian missionary from the mid-1800s noted:

> Twenty-five centuries ago, at the least, it [Kashi] was famous. When Babylon was struggling with Nineveh for supremacy, when Tyre was planting her colonies, when Athens was growing in strength, before Rome had become known, or Greece had contended with Persia, or Cyrus had added lustre to the Persian monarchy, or Nebuchadnezzar had captured Jerusalem, and the inhabitants of Judaea had been carried into captivity, she had already risen to greatness, if not to glory. (Sherring 1868, 7)

Unlike other ancient cities of yore, Kashi has maintained civilizational continuity without break for over 2,500 years. As observed by Professor Diana Eck:

> There is another important difference between [Kashi] and its contemporaries: its present life reaches back to the sixth century BC in a continuous tradition. If we could imagine the silent Acropolis and the Agora of Athens still alive with the intellectual, cultural, and ritual traditions of classical Greece, we might glimpse the remarkable tenacity of the life of Kashi. Today Peking, Athens, and Jerusalem are moved by a very different ethos from that which moved them in ancient times, but [Kashi] is not. (Eck 1982, 19)

Right next to Kashi is Sarnath, one of the most sacred areas for Buddhists. Gautama Buddha—known as the Buddha in the West, although, really, he is one of many Buddhas to have come in the past and still to come in the future—first turned the wheel of

Dharma in Sarnath and delivered the first of his sermons here after his great awakening. For the next 1,500 years, Sarnath continued to be a prominent and important Buddhist centre, attracting pilgrims from Nepal and other areas outside of India. When Hiuen-Tsiang visited Kashi in the seventh century CE, he observed that there were thirty Buddhist monasteries and three thousand Buddhist monks in the vicinity (Eck 1982, 91).

While the ascent of Shankaracharya led to a Hindu renaissance that overtook Buddhism in prominence across India, Kashi continued to have significant Buddhist monastic presence until the twelfth century when Qutb-ud-din Aibak's forces destroyed Sarnath and the temples of Kashi. Hindu society eventually recovered, but the Buddhist community, dependent upon the institutional infrastructure of the monastic system, was virtually eradicated (Eck 1982, 91).

Kashi has also been historically significant to Jainism and the evolution of classical Hinduism. The city went through a dark period during the Mughal invasions and British rule but still maintained its resilience and religious and civilizational continuity. This history will be explored in-depth in subsequent chapters.

Today, Kashi—or Varanasi, as it is officially called in India today—is a bustling urban centre. The current prime minister of India, Narendra Modi, carefully selected Varanasi as the constituency from where he contested for election. In 2022, a revitalized Kashi-Vishwanath corridor was unveiled by the prime minister with great pomp and fervour. The reconstruction of the area of the city in which the Kashi Vishwanath Mandir stands was meant to beautify the city, make it more accessible to tourists and pilgrims, and consequently attract more tourism. The campaign was not without controversy, as many small shrines were destroyed or constructed over in the process and sacred deities were allegedly also destroyed and/or uprooted. In fact, in Kashi, many vigrahas were taken from temples and hidden in homes over the course of attacks and invasions during the past few centuries, when temples were purposely targeted, looted, and destroyed. At risk to their lives, many ordinary Hindus hid the deities within their own homes and built underground temples to continue their worship.

In fact, it is difficult to move a stone in Kashi without disturbing a deity.

A City of Many Names

As we have already seen, the city of Kashi goes by many names. In Sanskrit etymology, Kashi is derived from the root 'kash', which means 'to shine'. According to the *Skanda Purana*, the city became famous by the name of Kashi because it illumines the path to *moksha*, or liberation from the apparent cycle of birth and death, and because the radiant light of Shiva shines forth there. It is also referred to as Avimukta, the city that Shiva never forsakes; Anandavana (the forest of bliss); and Rudravasa (the city in which Rudra/Shiva resides).

Civilizational and Religious Significance

The significance of Kashi can perhaps best be understood through the story of the Kashi yatra *prayoga*, a traditional component of the Hindu marriage ceremony across various regions of India. As part of this custom, before the wedding commences, the prospective groom will make preparations to leave for Kashi. This is what, after all, Kashi represents for the devout: the pathway to enlightenment and the *summum bonum* of a spiritual life—one that is devoted to the study of the shastras (the Hindu scriptures), religious penance, and asceticism. Ultimately, it is the place where one goes to abandon their mortal coil. The groom must remove all costly adornments from his body, leave behind all of his material possessions and family, and set out on the road to Kashi.

At that time, his prospective father-in-law will approach him. He will tell the young man that Kashi is indeed the ultimate destination of human life, but along the way, the prospective bride, his daughter, can be a partner and helpmate. Through the path of *grhasthashrama*, the life of the married householder, they together can pursue the four principal aims of human life: Dharma (the path of righteousness), Artha (the pursuit of wealth through dharmic means), Kama (the pursuit of desire through dharmic means), and Moksha. The groom accepts (or not!) the father's proposal, and the wedding rites proceed.

Nowadays this custom is often treated as an occasion of merriment, perhaps as something superstitious. But the roots of this custom come from a deep place. It is meant to set the tone for a harmonious married life, one devoted to mutual spiritual support and evolution, symbolized by Kashi. Kashi becomes the metaphorical North star for the couple and the ritualistic enactment is a reminder that wherever life may lead them, Kashi and all that it represents is their ultimate destination.

And for millennia this is what Kashi has come to mean for Hindus. From the time of the Vedas, Kashi has been referred to as an affluent kingdom and a centre for learning, as cited in the 'Shatapatha Brahmana' of the *Shukla Yajurveda, Kaushitaki Upanishad*, and *Brhadaranyaka Upanishad*, for example (Medhasananda 2002, 10). Kashi is also one of the *Saptapuri*, the seven cities capable of bestowing moksha, according to the Puranas. The others are Ayodhya (the birthplace of Rama), Mathura (the birthplace of Krishna), Haridwara (at the foothills of the Himalayas), Kanchi, Ujjain, and Dwaraka.

The City Where People Come to Die

Most great cities in the world are places where people long to come to live. Kashi is perhaps one of the only places where millions of people come expressly to die. The unique aspect of Kashi, as we will explore further in Chapter 2, is that Shiva himself is believed to come at the time of death for anyone who dies in Kashi and whisper into their ear the *Taraka mantra*, the final instruction that leads them to moksha or liberation.

As a result, from time immemorial, people have been coming to Kashi at the end of their lives to die in this holiest of places. And family members will often come to Kashi to cremate the remains of their loved ones or to bring the ashes for immersion into the Ganga to allow the departed one to dissolve into and become one with the sanctified environs of Kashi.

CHAPTER 2

Origin Stories of Kashi

Where and how did Kashi come to be? It is a deceptively simple question. We could look to recorded history. When were the first human settlements formed? What was the topography and climate of this place? When was it conquered by this or that king, and what kind of lives did the people lead? This is our modern conception of history, one that is evidence-based, documented, and ideally speaking, provable. This is one type of history, and it is an important one.

Sacred Geography

But there is another type of history, one that is less concerned about what happened when and more concerned with who we are as a group of people and how did we come to be. Who are the archetypal figures, divine and human, that define our ideals and heritage? How did they create and navigate the mortal world and what can we learn from them? How was the world around us created and what are its secrets? These are some of the questions that the other type of 'historical' analysis tries to answer.

In the case of Kashi, this can best be understood through the perspective of sacred geography, distilled through the Puranas, specifically the Sthala Purana associated with the city.

In order to understand sacred geography, we should first understand the concept of humanistic geography. As Seamon and Sowers ask, 'Is [place] merely a synonym for location, or a unique ensemble of nature and culture, or could it be something more?' (Seamon and Sowers 2008, 44). They note the movement in the early 1970s to develop a study of 'humanistic geography', devoted to a more philosophical and experiential exploration of place and space. Edward Relph was a major figure in that movement and his work is referred to frequently even today.

Relph's work distinguished between place and space. Place has the 'power to order and to focus human intentions, experiences, and actions spatially' (Seamon and Sowers 2008, 44). People then experience that space through different lived realities, which gives rise to spatial modes like sacred space and gendered space. On the other hand, space is about the physical dimensions of a site. In the words of Lawrence-Zuniga (n.d.), 'Space is often defined by an abstract scientific, mathematical, or measurable conception while place refers to the elaborated cultural meanings people invest in or attach to a specific site or locale.'

Relph believed that a phenomenological approach—one grounded in the lived experience of place and space—is essential to understand why a particular site is important and how to repair or restore it or create a new site in its place. As Seamon and Sowers pithily observe, 'In short, before we can properly prescribe, we must first learn how to accurately describe—a central aim of phenomenological research' (Seamon and Sowers 2008, 44).

Relph's research examines the three aspects of place: the place's physical setting; its activities, situations, and events; and the individual and group meanings created through people's experiences and intentions with respect to the place.

A crucial insight from Relph is the concept of 'insideness', which is 'the degree of attachment, involvement, and concern that a person or group has for a particular place' (Seamon and Sowers 2008, 45). Existential insideness is the most intense sense of insideness, referring to a deep unconscious immersion in place and experience, when people feel at home.

Kari Forbes-Boyte links the notion of existential insideness with the idea of sacred geography. She explains how the Lakotas believe that their religion cannot be practiced without access to their sacred places, causing severe psychological alienation and cultural disintegration upon separation:

> Many Native American peoples' sense of identity comes from walking on land also walked on by their ancestors, or by being able to identify places that are not only significant to them as individuals but also significant to their ancestors. To lose this identity, through loss of sacred lands, would have devastating consequences for generations to come. (Forbes-Boyte 2011)

Sacred geography comes in various forms and manifestations, according to different cultures and civilizations. Often, sacred sites are places of creation that are 'revealed through the society's mythology (sacred truth), thereby becoming the physical manifestations of the mythological system' (Forbes-Boyte 2011).

For example, the Aborigines of Australia believe that when the world was first formed, at the time known as 'dreamtime', animals and humans emerged from the core of the earth and walked across the land. Along the way, as they cried, laughed, danced, and played, the landscape was moulded into mountains and lakes and other topographical formations. These beings are regarded as ancestors by the Aborigines, and therefore these sites are sacred to them. The paths walked by these beings are 'songlines' or dreaming tracks that connect the sacred sites. These have served as pilgrimage treks for the Aborigines for over forty thousand years (World Pilgrimage Guide n.d.).

Similarly, Hindu and Buddhist conceptions of mandalas, sacred geometric patterns, and shapes, have been projected over wide expanses of land and territory. For example, Buddhist monks would often travel from mountain to mountain to honour the Bodhisattvas and Buddhas who manifested there. Specific routes are prescribed to allow for a gradual progression through the landscape that mimics the different states of experience a person goes through psychically and spiritually during the journey.

Ancient Chinese culture focused on interpreting the natural landscape through the conception of feng shui that seeks to optimize the flow of chi, to bring in and let flow positive energy with the most effectiveness. Temples and monasteries would be established based on locations with the most harmonious flow of chi. Sometimes, the landscape would be altered—hills shaped and the course of rivers reversed—to make it more conducive for the proper flow of chi.

Forbes-Boyte explains how the Great Plains Indians centre their religious practices and rites around the locations of sacred sites:

> The locale where a ritual takes place is as significant as the ritual itself. [...] [T]he religious perceptions that Plains Indians have of their physical environment lead to a psychological stability evident in a condition referred to as 'existential insideness'. Existential insideness is knowing that a particular place is where one belongs, completing the self-identity of an individual. Existential insideness is supported through the spiritual system of the culture when there is an acknowledgment of sacred places. (Forbes-Boyte 2011)

Consecration is an ongoing process that maintains and enhances the sanctity of a sacred site. This is part of the synergistic relationship between deities and ancestral beings, on the one hand, and humans, on the other. In veneration and gratitude, humans make pilgrimage to such sites and perform the prescribed rites and observances to reinforce and preserve the sacred space for future generations.

Sacred geography permeated the ancient civilizations of Europe, too. Jean Richer observes:

> The evidence of the monuments shows in an undeniable way, but not yet clearly perceived, that during more than two thousand years, the Phoenicians, the Hittites, the ancient Greeks, and then the Etruscans, the Carthaginians, and the Romans, had patiently woven a fabric of correspondences between the sky, especially the apparent course of the sun through the zodiac, the inhabited earth, and the cities built by humanity. (Richer 1994, xxv)

The oracle temples at Delphi and Dodona, the sacred site of the Parthenon in Athens, the island of Delos—none of these locations were randomly selected. A mandala or zodiac circle was laid over wide expanses of territory and marked by numerous significant pilgrimage centres, including these particular sites. Similar care was given in marking the sacred sites of Egypt with meticulous measurements and understanding of astronomy and astrology. While the locations of many such sites are still known today, the history and mythos of these sites—the ways they were used and understood in the context of sacred geography—have to a large extent, sadly, been lost or at the very least largely ignored.

India is one of the few places in the world where the history and continuity of this sacred geography still thrives. And Kashi is one of the most important and prime examples of this living sacred geography. Therefore, to understand Kashi and its origins, we need to go back to its sacred geography.

The Origin Story of Kashi from the *Skanda Purana*

Come on. Come on. Give unto me the contact with your body, O noble sage of holy vows.

Even the contact with the wind blowing from Kashi is desired (and welcomed) by me who stays here. But you yourself have come from there.

The dust particles from the feet of those who stay at Kashi even for three nights with the senses under control, can purify invariably when touched.

But you have stayed there for a very long period; you have performed many meritorious rites there and your hairs have become tawny-coloured through (continuous) ablutions in the current flowing northwards.

Skanda, the son of Shiva, to Agastya Muni, the rishi[4]

---

4   Adapted from Tagare 1950, Chapter 25.

There are many texts that comprise the Sthala Purana for Kashi. A key core text is the Kashi Khanda of the *Skanda Purana*. There are eighteen Mahapuranas—Great Puranas. Each is devoted to a particular Deva or Devi. The *Skanda Purana* is eponymously dedicated to Skanda, the son of Shiva, while major sections of it are devoted to Vishnu and Shiva, for example. In the *Skanda Purana*, we find an entire section entitled the Kashi Khanda, explaining the formation and glories of Kashi.

A significant aspect of the stories from the Puranas is that the content is delivered in the form of dialogues, often dialogues within dialogue. This hearkens back to the tradition of *smriti*, that which is remembered and transmitted, often from the Devas to the rishis and then to the mortals. When we hear a story, we honour not only the content of the story but also the unbroken transmission of it, from the hoary ancient past to the present, from guru to *shishya*, teacher to disciple.

In this case, when the renowned rishi, Agastya Muni, is forced to leave his beloved Kashi, he visits Skanda, the son of Shiva, and asks him a number of questions about Kashi and its origins. Skanda proceeds to narrate the story of Kashi as he heard it from his mother, Parvati Devi, the mother of the universe and the consort of Shiva.

It was the time of Pralaya, the phase of cosmic dissolution, when all life in the universe had been extinguished; the sun and stars had winked out, leaving the universe in total darkness. There was no moon, no day, no night, no fire, no wind, no earth to hold up the skies, no firmament to behold. There were no rishis, no smell, no sight, no sound.

Brahman alone existed, formless, or rather, beyond form, without differentiation, without a second, beginningless and endless. Simply *sat-chit-ananda*—truth, consciousness, bliss—was all that there was. From Brahman emanated Shiva, the form of the formless Brahman, endowed with all the qualities, glories, and opulence befitting Ishvara. The closest equivalent to Ishvara in English would be God, or rather, Godhead, the essence of Godness, or Saguna Brahman, Brahman with form or multiple forms.

From the left side of his own body, Shiva manifested Devi, 'a being that does not swerve away from [his] person' (Tagare 1950, Chapter 26). Simultaneously, Shiva created Anandavana, the forest of bliss, described as extending to five or *pancha krosha* in distance, equivalent to roughly fifteen kilometres. Because Shiva and Devi never leave this site, even at the time of Pralaya, it is known as Avimukta, the place that is never forsaken. Avimukta was created before the earth or the waters had appeared.

Wanting to enjoy the bliss of Anandavana with Devi, Shiva manifested Vishnu in the role of the Preserver and commanded him to establish the world. He instructed Vishnu that the Vedas would arise out of Vishnu's exhalation and that he would understand everything through the Vedas. His role as Preserver would be to maintain the world in accordance with the Vedas. Shiva and Devi then retreated into the forest for meditation and enjoyment.

Vishnu dug a beautiful lotus pond with the *Sudarshana chakra*, the golden serrated discus that always hovers above his right hand. As Vishnu dug the pond with his hands, it filled with the sweat dripping from his limbs. The pond came to be known as Chakrapushkarini, the pond dug by his discus. He sat on the banks of the water there and motionlessly observed penance for fifty thousand years.

When he finally roused from meditation, Shiva and Devi stood before him. Shiva was so pleased with Vishnu's penance that he shook his head and a pearl earring, encrusted with gems, fell from his ear. Shiva said that the site had already become well-known as Chakrapushkarini from Vishnu's penance, and now it would also be known as Manikarnika, literally, an earring, a gem adorning the ear.

Vishnu requested and obtained a number of boons, including anointing the site of Anandavana with the name of Kashi. He also sought that from Brahma (the Creator Deva) to a blade of grass, every living organism within Kashi should attain moksha.

He was fervent in his plea: 'Let those who die at Kashi be initiated into [salvation]; let even rabbits, mosquitoes, worms, locusts, horses or serpents dying within the five kroshas of the Kashi perimeter attain salvation' (Tagare 1950, Chapter 26).

Shiva assured Vishnu that Kashi was to be one of his sacred abodes, where his command alone would prevail. Not even Yama, the Deva of Death and Righteousness, could carry away anyone from Kashi without Shiva's explicit permission. Shiva would be the sole chastiser and enforcer of the laws of karma and dharma in Kashi.

Shiva then proceeded to explain the process to Vishnu. The fierce and ferocious *ganas*, the attendants of Shiva, would guard the city of Kashi with their nooses and tridents in order to keep out all sins. So, if a person entered Kashi, all their sins would remain outside the city, since nothing could penetrate Kashi without Shiva's permission. Thus, a person would become sinless when they entered Kashi.

By bathing ritualistically in the waters of Manikarnika, a person attains merit equivalent to that of ritualistically bathing in all the sacred waters or tirthas and all the merits obtained through the bestowal of elaborate gifts and offerings. Even if one bathes at Manikarnika without faith, Shiva explained, they will still ascend to *Swarga*, the heavenly realm where one can find enjoyment until his or her store of good karma is exhausted.

Further, Shiva explained, by worshiping Vishveshvara a single time, one obtains the benefits of having performed Shiva worship for an entire lifetime. Vishveshvara is the manifestation of Shiva within the city of Kashi, proclaimed Shiva. Vishveshvara assumed the form of a *linga*, specifically a Jyotirlinga, the Linga of Light. It is said by Shiva in the *Skanda Purana* that just as the sun, though stationed in one place, is perceived everywhere by everyone, so also is Vishveshvara perceived by everyone everywhere in Kashi. It should be noted that in this context Vishveshvara is the same as Vishvanatha, the Shivalinga found in Kashi Vishwanath Mandir; this is just the preferred term of reference in the *Skanda Purana* and some of the older texts.

Shiva promised, 'There is no question of fall[ing] into hell in the case of those creatures that die in Kashi by chance, though they might have been perpetrators of sins, because I am their chastiser and controller' (Tagare 1950, Chapter 26).

Shiva and the Taraka Mantra

Purvamimamsa is one of the six *darshanas*, or epistemological schools, of Hinduism. It uses an incredibly sophisticated methodology for interpreting Vedic texts, one that is relied upon even by the other schools of Hinduism of differing philosophies. Within that epistemology, the concept of *arthavada* explains the meaning of statements according to four different categories: (i) *ninda* (censure) meant to prevent or disincentivize certain acts; (ii) *stuti* (eulogy or praise) meant to encourage the undertaking of certain acts; (iii) *parakrti* (performances by another great person) meant to praise certain acts committed by others and induce us to repeat them; and (iv) *purakalpa* (description of occurrences from the olden days) to demonstrate the value of an act.

The purpose of arthavada is to explain and contextualize what may appear to be embellishments in a scriptural text. For example, if it is said that by bathing in the Ganga, all the sins from our past lives are expiated, applying the heuristic of arthavada would reveal that this may not be a literal statement but rather a statement of stuti meant to encourage us to revere the Ganga and make the effort to bathe in the waters of the Ganga.

It is, therefore, easy to dismiss the idea that every being who dies in Kashi attains liberation directly through Shiva as a type of arthavada, i.e., it is an exaggeration not to be taken literally.

But there is a careful and precise theology that treats Shiva's promise as a literal fact. In Kashi, Shiva takes over the responsibilities and duties of Yama Deva, who otherwise presides over matters relating to death and justice. Shiva personally attends to the death of every creature in Kashi and whispers the Taraka mantra into their ear. This immediately liberates them.

This causes an ontological conundrum if not understood properly. According to Advaita Vedanta, only wisdom can bring about moksha or liberation. There is no action or shortcut that can replace the dawning of wisdom, including an apparent divine intervention.

Hindu pandits have painstakingly reconciled this Vedantic view with the theology of Kashi. They have reiterated that it is indeed wisdom that bestows liberation. Death by itself, even in a sanctified place like Kashi, cannot be a sufficient condition to attain moksha. Neither the personal presence of Shiva nor the mantra that he whispers in and of themselves bring liberation. No, it is specifically the wisdom that dawns after hearing the mantra from Shiva's lips that bestows liberation. In other words, Shiva becomes the guru in that moment—the one who removes darkness and brings the light of enlightenment. It is the wisdom that Shiva brings to the dying person that liberates them, not Shiva himself.

The renowned scholar Narayana Bhatta, whose life and importance to Kashi we will explore in more detail in later chapters, explains, 'There is no liberation in the absence of wisdom—that is clear from statements in both the revealed and remembered tradition, such as "[f]rom wisdom alone comes liberation". Therefore, knowledge of the atman arises here from the Taraka, which is taught by the guru, Vishveshvara' (Eck 1982, 484–85).

Bhatta goes on to quote the Kashi Khanda: 'Creatures are released by knowledge of Brahman and never in any other way. I am that knowledge of Brahman for those who die in Kashi. I teach the Taraka at the time of death, and they are released at that moment' (Eck 1982, 484–85).

Sureshvaracharya clarifies that death in Kashi does not 'cause' liberation but rather is the occasion of liberation. It is the time when the veil of ignorance is lifted and the light of day shines:

> Receiving knowledge from the Great Lord Shiva at the time of death, all creatures, bound by beginningless ignorance, are liberated. Liberation for them means absolute unity, like the unity

of the air that is inside a pot with that that is outside the pot. There remains no cause at all for the creation of another body. God, the Supreme Lord, destroys ignorance [...] merely by rising, just as the sun destroys darkness, merely by rising! (*Kashi Mriti Moksha Vichara*, verses 3–4, 20, in Eck 1982, 485–86)

The moment before enlightenment, one experiences *Bhairavi yatana*, the punishment of Bhairava. This punishment is brief, lasting but a moment, and very intense. Sureshvaracharya compares the experience of this punishment with the experience of dreaming. Just as in a dream one might experience a whole lifetime of activity in a very brief moment, so also in Bhairavi yatana, one might take on many bodies, one after another, and live through many lives, in a single moment (Eck 1982, 492).

The mantra that Shiva whispers into the ear of the dying one is referred to as the Taraka mantra. The word 'taraka' means to ferry across; in this context, it means transporting one across the turbulent waters of *samsara* to liberation. This mantra is a secret, whispered by the guru into the ear of the shishya.

In the *Skanda Purana*, it is explained, 'Into the ear of the living being about to die, [Shiva] whispers that syllable on hearing which even the dead one becomes immortal' (Tagare 1950, Chapter 39).

A great spiritual master and the guru of Swami Vivekananda, Sri Ramakrishna, once travelled to Kashi in the late nineteenth century. When he passed by Manikarnika on boat, Sri Ramakrishna went into a deep trance. He later described that he had witnessed Devi in the form of Annapurna, holding in her lap the body of a dead man, while Shiva knelt to whisper the Taraka mantra into his ear. He saw in practice, through his meditative vision, what Shiva had promised in the *Skanda Purana*.

The experience so moved Sri Ramakrishna that from then onward for the duration of his trip, he left Kashi when he had to go to the bathroom, so keenly did he feel the divinity of the consecrated city.

The Story of Ganga and Kashi

There is no city more hallowed than Kashi for Hindus and no river more sacred than the Ganga. This is the story of how they came together, again from the *Skanda Purana*.

Once upon a time, there was a great king named Bhagiratha. He wished to rescue his ancestors, the sixty thousand sons of Sagara, his great-grandfather. They were stuck in the underworld or *Patala*, where they had been reduced to ash by a sage's curse. The responsibility of performing their funerary rites had passed down the generations to Bhagiratha.

Bhagiratha was determined to rescue the spirits of his ancestors. Only Ganga was capable of descending to Patala and then ferrying their spirits up to Swarga, the heavenly abode. Bhagiratha went to the Himalayas to propitiate Ganga. She told him that if she were to descend to the mortal realm, the force of her fall would be unbearable for earth.

Ganga advised Bhagiratha to go to Shiva and ask for his help. Bhagiratha propitiated Shiva for one thousand years at Kailasha. Shiva granted him the boon that he would allow Ganga to flow through his hair. He then stood and allowed Ganga to descend upon his head.

Ganga flowed along Shiva's matted locks for another thousand years. Once more, Bhagiratha undertook penance to please Shiva. Finally, Shiva shook his hair so that a drop of the mighty Ganga fell upon earth and became the river that flows from the Himalayas to the Bay of Bengal today. The river also descended to Patala so that Bhagiratha was able to finally perform the funerary rites for his ancestors.

The place where Ganga landed on our world, by Bhagiratha's request, was Manikarnika, thereby triply blessing that site. It was already blessed as Chakrapushkarini of Vishnu, Manikarnika of Shiva, and now the site of the descent of Ganga Devi, the most sacred and purest of rivers.

As Kashi became anointed as the city where one could attain liberation, the Devas were moved to protect the city. They fashioned the Asi river, a tributary of the Ganga, to the south, warding off entry by the wicked. They made the Varana, another tributary of the Ganga, to keep out all obstacles and hindrances. Shiva established Ganesha, his other son, to guard the western border of Kashi. Thus, all three guard the city and accord entrance to only those who are allowed by Shiva.

Kashi on Shiva's Trident

We began the origin story of Kashi with Pralaya, the time of the great cosmic dissolution. It is with Pralaya that we will end this story, too.

In the *Skanda Purana*, Shiva explains that at the time of Pralaya, the earth dissolves into water. The water dissolves into the mouth of fire, which dissolves into the wind, which dissolves into the firmament, which dissolves into ego consciousness, which, with its by-products, dissolves into the cosmic intellect, which then dissolves into *Prakriti*. Prakriti is the material nature consisting of the three *gunas* or building blocks of the material universe. Brahma, Vishnu, and Rudra also dissolve into Ishvara who assumes the form of Time.

Only that Ishvara, that Shiva, remains. He lifts Kashi, his very own city, at the tip of his *trishula*, his trident, and holds it aloft. Thus, Kashi alone remains immune from the ravages of Time and Death, from the destruction of the universe itself. It remains alone with Shiva: the abode of Shiva.

II

Sthala Purana

The Sacred Geography of Kashi from Lore and Legends

CHAPTER 3

Agastya Muni's Sacrifice

> Life and different types of wealth are as fickle as the tips of the ears of an elephant. Hence, the only thing to be carried out by a learned man is rendering help to others.
>
> *Skanda Purana*

The *Skanda Purana* provides a large portion of the canonical lore about Kashi. Even today, many of the temples, sacred sites, and pilgrimage routes in and around Kashi have their origins in the stories from this Purana. This section of the book, therefore, summarizes the Kashi Khanda portion of the *Skanda Purana*. Without understanding this lore, one cannot truly understand and appreciate the sanctity of Kashi.

While this is a condensation of the Kashi Khanda, it still carries a lot of the meticulous detail and specificity of this section of the Purana. That is deliberate. The detail is intentional to document, remember, revise, and experience Kashi tirtha by tirtha. The Puranic accounts lead us from the abstract to the experiential. There is a magic, a trance-like feeling of immersion, in ensconcing ourselves within the intricate textual passages of the Purana. After all, traditionally, passages from the Puranas were used as guides on *upasana*, or meditation. To the extent possible, this section of the book attempts to retain that ethos.

The Arrogance of the Vindhya Mountain

Once the great sage Narada, after bathing in the holy waters of the Narmada, encountered the Vindhya Mountain. The *Skanda Purana* poetically describes how the sanctified mountain scattered leaves and flowers all around, as if in an offering of *arghya* to the sage, welcoming him through the cries of peacocks. The mountain was eager to talk to the sage, who shone with the radiance of hundreds of suns.

Narada's brilliance was such that the mountain's ignorance as well as the darkness of caves was immediately illuminated. Vindhya was so awed by the magnificence of Narada that, forsaking his hard mountain nature, he became soft and helpless in front of the sage's spiritual might. The lofty mountain bent his head to the ground in obeisance to the sage.

Narada was gratified by this humble reception and lifted him up with the tips of his fingers, bestowing his blessings upon him. Narada sat before him with a sigh.

Vindhya asked what had perturbed the sage. But before he could answer, the mountain went on to describe his own perceived plight. He complained that he alone sustained the earth, though Meru and other mountains were credited for it. Himavan was honoured because of his daughter, Parvati, he claimed. Why should Meru be singled out for honour simply because the mountain was full of gold, the ridges heavy with precious stones, and its terrain the abode of the Devas? Other mountains could also support the weight of the earth, but their fame was confined only to their localities, lamented Vindhya.

Narada was displeased by this show of vanity. The sage spoke cryptically. 'In pointing out the capabilities of the various mountains, you have spoken the truth. Meru does actually disparage you among the mountains. This is indeed why I sighed. Or why else should we mahatmas, the great ones, worry about such trivialities?'

With that, the sage left. We often find Narada as the instigator in many of the stories in the Puranas. Part of his function is to catalyse the causes and conditions for the *leela* of Ishvara to unfold. While Narada is famed for his devotion to Narayana, he is also devoted to Shiva.

Vindhya Mountain realized his mistake and remonstrated with himself. But rather than correcting his own behaviour, the mountain decided that he had to take on his perceived enemies and defeat them. Thus, Vindhya began to increase his own height, with the desire to pierce the firmament, so that the sun would no longer be able to circumambulate and pay obeisance to Mount Meru. He was determined to make himself so powerful that nobody would ever look down upon him again.

It is important to note that this was all going on within Vindhya's head. There is no indication that anyone had actually mocked or laughed at him in the past. But Vindhya himself was full of these insecurities, as so often we are plagued with our own self-created fears and doubts.

Having achieved his objective, Vindhya calmly awaited the dawn. He had become so tall that the sun's path across the skies was now obstructed. It could not rise and set as before. The performance of rites, dependent on the sun's cycle, was interrupted. The disruption of the *Rtam* of sacrifice and offerings was of grave concern to the Devas. One of the functions of the Devas is to maintain the order and harmony of *Rtam*; when this natural balance is disturbed, it interrupts the function of the Devas and becomes an obstacle to the performance of their fundamental role in the carrying out of the work of the cosmos.

One of the lessons of this episode is that as mortals we must be especially careful in the presence of holy ones. We are unable to maintain our presence of mind when overwhelmed by the power of their presence. While we may initially be in a state of reverence and awe, this quickly devolves to a preoccupation with our own petty desires and fears. Instead of asking after their well-being in a mode of service or seeking their words of wisdom, we pour out the pollution of our thoughts and fears in the hope that the great ones can assuage them.

The Parting of Agastya Muni from Kashi

As is tradition, the Devas took refuge at the feet of Brahma, seeking an answer to their plight. Brahma directed them to seek Agastya Muni, who was presently residing in Avimukta, immersed in devotion to Shiva's Vishveshvara form. Brahma instructed them to ask the sage to stop Vindhya Mountain from competing with Mount Meru and disrupting the natural order of things.

The Devas were delighted. Not only would they find a solution to their problem but they would also be able to visit Shiva and Gauri in their abode. They proceeded to Kashi, accompanied by many rishis. The Devas bathed at Manikarnika Ghat. They performed *sandhyavandanam*—offerings to be made at dawn, noon, and dusk—and other rites, offering *tarpana*, or libations, to the *pitrs*—the ancestors and other departed ones—with a mixture of water, sesame seeds, and scented substances. They then bestowed gifts upon the residents of the city, including gold, jewellery, clothes, horses, cows, and ornaments. Dormitories for the students were supplied with food and collections of manuscripts. Scribes and clerks were given livelihoods, and guesthouses were funded. Medicine and water tanks for pilgrims travelling during the summer season as well as iron ovens with fuel for the winter were all provided. Umbrellas and clothing to shield against the rain were gifted. Lamps for reading at night were also given. Ointments for massaging feet were gifted. Temples were given grants to retain expounders of the Puranas and also to provide for temple music and dancers.

Temples were given funds for whitewashing, repairs, and decorations. In addition, lamps with many wicks, *sambhrani* incense, camphor, and other paraphernalia for Deva worship were amply provided. Conches, kettledrums, and other instruments to delight the ears of the temple *Devatas* were provided. Other things were bestowed as well, such as substances for the *panchamrta* made with milk, yogurt, honey, ghee, and sugar used for bathing the temple deities; white cloth for wiping and drying the deities; sweet scents to perfume their breath; materials for fire sacrifice; arrangements for the loud chanting of Shiva's names; and arrangements for offering *pradakshina*—circumambulations performed clockwise, usually thrice—around the temple perimeter.

Why does the *Skanda Purana* go into such detail on the various donations and gifts provided by the Devas? It is a good reminder to us that our wealth should be used to support the humanitarian needs of society as well as provide for the temples and the performance of rites. The Devas did not make these provisions for their own convenience. Rather, the virtuous circle of offering and sacrifice is what sustains the natural order of the universe and provides for *loka sangraha*, the wellbeing of the collective whole. It is through such worship and sacrifice, through the mutual responsibilities undertaken across all segments of society, that dharma is sustained.

The Devas spent five nights performing these rites and bathing in the sacred rivers and ponds of Kashi. They frequently visited the Vishveshvara Linga. After concluding the required formalities, the Devas finally proceeded to meet with Agastya Muni, who was always eager to help others.

Agastya Muni had established a Shivalinga for worship and had dug a pit in front of it. There he sat reciting the *Shatarudriya* hymn, his mind steady. In fact, that temple still exists in a small compound in the lanes of the old city. When I visited this place, standing there, I could still feel the powerful presence of Agastya Muni and the force of his devotion to Shiva.

The Devas marvelled at the sight of him. The force of his *tapasya* was such that in his hermitage the elephant sat comfortably next to the lion. The lion, in turn, slept on the lap of the *ashtapada*, a fabled animal of eight legs. The hog roamed along with the jackals and tigers. The hog dared not dig up the earth, for the entirety of Kashi is so full of lingas that the hog was afraid to disturb any of them. The hyena played with the hog's baby. The fawn of the deer was being suckled by a tigress.

The crane rested his neck on the neck of a goose, and the Devas saw that it was not sleeping but rather meditating upon Vishveshvara. When the male swan approached the female swan for mating, she fluttered her wings and warded him off, appearing to say that it was inappropriate to exhibit sexual desire in such a sanctified place. The other birds remained silent while the female parrot seemed to be saying that Shiva takes one across the sea of samsara, and the cuckoo seemed to say that the age of Kali and Death do not trouble those who live in Kashi.

From this passage, we see that animals too are spiritually charged in Kashi.

The Devas felt that Kashi was better than their own heavenly realms. After all, these birds and animals would be liberated from the cycle of birth and death while the Devas would be subject to rebirth once their storehouse of good karma was exhausted.

The Devas pleaded their case with Agastya Muni, who then felt compelled to leave Kashi in order to find a solution to the Vindhya Mountain issue. This has always been the way of rishis. Left to their own desires, they would stay in isolated retreat within the havens of their hermitages in remote jungles and caves. The only thing that can rouse them from the fathomless depths of meditation is the need to intervene in samsara to uphold dharma and protect sentient beings.

Agastya Muni, accompanied by his wife, the renowned *rishika* Lopamudra, made preparations to depart from Kashi. He grieved to leave this city so beloved to him. He lamented that in the entire universe there was no linga comparable to Vishveshvara. One may wonder why a *muni*, who, by definition, has mastered his emotions, would be subject to such sadness. We must understand that this is not the typical emotion we feel, driven by our baser material and physical urges; rather, this is a *bhava*—a steady state of experiencing a particular flavour of sentiment that comes from absorption in *bhakti* or *dhyana*—associated with the leela (divine play) of the intimate relationship a highly attained devotee has with his or her *Ishta Devata*, the form of a Deva one is most attracted to and chooses for personal worship.[5] This grief was but an expression of the great sage's depth of devotion to Shiva.

Agastya Muni offered prostrations to Kaala Bhairava and requested his permission to leave the city. Even now, Kaala Bhairava is held to be the police chief protecting Kashi. It is said that his attendants, Sambhrama and Udbhrama, are expert chroniclers of the various karmic and biographical details of the people inhabiting Kashi, and they drive out the wicked from the city by creating great confusion in their minds.

Still today, the residents of Kashi follow the tradition of taking permission from Kaala Bhairava before leaving the city. Because Kashi is so sacred, it is considered inauspicious for a resident to go elsewhere, even for a visit. It can only be done with Kaala Bhairava's permission. This is sought by visiting his temple in Kashi.

Agastya Muni then called out to Dhundhiraja Ganesha, proclaiming that all obstacles were under Ganesha's control, and pleading to not be driven away by the obstacles put forth by the Devas. He called out to all the Devis of Kashi—Vishalakshi, Bhavani, Mangala, Jyestha, Ishi, Saubhagya-Vidhana-Sundari, Vishve-Vidhe, Chitraghanta, Vikata, and Durgika—asking them to bear witness to his statement. He proclaimed,

> I am not going away from this place for my own sake. It is because I have been requested by the gods that I am doing this. What all is not done for helping others? Did Dadhichi not give his bones? Did Bali not give the three worlds to Vamana? Did Madhu and Kaitabha not offer their heads to Vishnu? Garuda himself at the request of Vishnu became his vahana.

After circumambulating the premises of Kashi, Agastya Muni took leave of the city with Lopamudra. As he stepped out of the city,

---

5 A muni is described by Sri Krishna in the Bhagavad Gita as one whose mind is not shaken by adversity, who does not hanker after pleasure, and who is free from attachment, fear, and anger (Bhagavad Gita, 2:56) (Sivananda 2000, 2:56).

Agastya Muni was so distraught that he fainted, crying out, 'Alas! Kashi, O Kashi, come again and glance at me.'

Agastya Muni's departure from Kashi sets the frame narrative for the rest of the Kashi Khanda. He leaves Kashi and then meets with Skanda, from whom he hears about the glory and various stories about Kashi, just the way Shiva had once recounted them to Devi. After leaving Skanda's presence, presumably Agastya Muni proceeds toward the Vindhya Mountain, the taming of which is left for another story.

The Description of Tirthas and Saptapuri

Describing Agastya Muni's sacrifice in leaving Kashi for the sake of helping the Devas, Sri Veda Vyasa explains to Suta the importance of helping others. He says,

> If a keen sense of helping others is ever wakeful in the heart of the good, all their adversities perish and riches accrue at every step. What is obtained by extending help [to others] cannot be derived through severe austerities; that purity cannot be had through the holy ablution and the sacred waters; that benefit cannot be had through plentiful gifts. The piety resulting from helping others and the piety born of gifts, etc., were weighed together in one balance by Brahma. The former was weightier. After churning through the network of verbal discussions, this is the conclusion arrived at—there is no piety greater than helping others and no heinous sin greater than injuring others. (Tagare 1950, Chapter 6)

After departing from Kashi, Agastya Muni and Lopamudra bathed in sacred waters and from a distance they could see Sri Shaila, the mountain sanctified by the presence of Shiva. This mountain was eighty-four yojanas in breadth and full of Shivalingas, deserving to be circumambulated with devotion. Delighted, Agastya Muni told his wife that simply by perceiving this sacred site, mortals would be freed from rebirth.

Lopamudra thought about how distressed Agastya Muni was at leaving Kashi and tried to reconcile it with his statement that other places, like Sri Shaila, could also provide liberation. To remove her own doubt and to provide a clarification that would be beneficial to all, Lopamudra asked her husband, if simply by glancing at the peak of Sri Shaila one could escape rebirth, then why was Kashi sought by him and the others.

Agastya Muni was delighted and praised his wife for asking such a question; he encouraged her and all women to ask such questions of their husbands. He then explained the various tirthas and their significance and hierarchy. He acknowledged that many such holy sites can indeed bring about *mukti*. According to the list made by Agastya Muni, such sites include Prayaga, Naimisharanya, Kurukshetra, Gangadvara (present-day Haridwara), Avantika (present-day Ujjain), Ayodhya, Mathura, Dwaraka, Amaravati (the place where the Saraswati and Sindhu rivers join the sea), the meeting place of Ganga and the ocean, Kanchi, Tryambaka linga situated on the Brahmagiri mountain, Saptagodavari (in present-day Andhra Pradesh in the West Godavari district), Kalanjara (the site of a svayambhu linga in present-day Uttar Pradesh), Prabhasa, Badrinath, Mahalaya, Amarakantaka (near the source of the Narmada river), Jagannath Puri (cited as the holiest of all the temples of Vishnu), Gokarna, Bhrgukaccha (in present-day Baroch, Gujarat), Bhrgutunga (in present-day Nepal), Pushkar, Shriparvata (identified with Sri Shailam/Mallikarjuna), and Dharatirtha (on the northern bank of the Narmada river). He specially cited Gaya as the tirtha that bestows salvation upon the pitrs.

He went on to explain that there are also tirthas that reside within. For example, truth, forbearance, control of the organs of sense and action, compassion for all living beings, straightforwardness, religious gifting, self-restraint, contentedness, speaking pleasing words, knowledge, courage, penance, and celibacy are the greatest of all tirthas, while the absolute purity of the mind is the holiest of all holy tirthas. What makes certain sites sacred is the result of 'the mysterious influence of the ground, of the water and of the fire thereof as well as of the backing and acceptance [as holy] by sages' (Tagare 1950, Chapter 6).

Going back to Lopamudra's specific question, Agastya Muni said that indeed the entire area of Sri Shaila bestows mukti. Still, Kedarnath is superior to it, and Prayaga exceeds them both in glory. Avimukta or Kashi excels Prayaga, which is the foremost among sacred sites. The key is that pilgrimage to the other tirthas makes the tirtha to Kashi accessible. If one is unable to attain liberation after reaching Kashi, then they cannot get mukti even by visiting millions of other sacred sites.

Agastya Muni illustrated this through the story of Shivasharman and the wondrous way in which he achieved mukti.

CHAPTER 4

Enlightenment of Shivasharman and the Seven Sacred Cities (Saptapuri)

Once, there was a Brahmana in Mathura named Shivasharman, a great scholar steeped in the study of the Vedas, Puranas, Vedangas,[6] Mimamsa,[7] and Dhanurveda.[8] He was also an expert in dance and political economy, and conversant in the languages of different countries. He earned wealth through dharmic means and thoroughly enjoyed his life. One day, he realized that he was old and greying.

It dawned on Shivasharman that he had not spent time on *adhyatma* or propitiating the Devas. He had not planted trees or fed the poor or donated to public works. He reckoned that mere scriptural study and the acquisition of family and wealth would not be sufficient for moksha. He, therefore, resolved to go on a pilgrimage, or a *tirtha yatra*, acknowledging that as long as the body is capable one must undertake pilgrimages beneficial to one's spiritual development.

Within five days of taking this sacred resolve—a *sankalpa*—Shivasharman set out on his journey. Resting on the road,

---
6 The Vedangas are the six auxiliary limbs of Vedic study: shiksha (phonetics), kalpa (rites), vyakarana (grammar), nirukta (etymology), chandas (metre), and jyotisha (astronomy).
7 The study of how to interpret Vedic literature.
8 The study of warfare.

he wondered where he should go. After all, there were many holy places in the world worth visiting. He decided to visit the Saptapuri, or the seven sacred cities capable of bestowing mukti. He went to Ayodhya and bathed in the Sarayu river. After staying there for five nights, he left for Prayaga. There he bathed in the black waters of the Yamuna and the white waters of the Ganga. It is said that the Sarasvati river is *rajasic* in nature; the Yamuna is *tamasic*; and the Ganga is *sattvic*. All three lead to Brahman, which transcends all three attributes. Accordingly, it is said that Prayaga, as the confluence of the three rivers, leads one towards Brahman.

Revelling in the wonders of the city, Shivasharman remained in Prayaga for an entire month before proceeding to Kashi. At the entrance to the city, he beheld Dehali Vinayaka, the form of Ganesha who protects the threshold of the city. He then proceeded towards the Ganga flowing northward at Manikarnika. Immediately, he immersed himself, fully clothed, into the river. He then performed the rite of *panchatirthika*, bathing in the five holy water bodies at Varana, Asi, Panchanada, Manikarnika, and Dashashvamedha. He circumambulated the city and marvelled at it, recognizing how futile his life had been until then. He spent an entire year in pilgrimage yet could not visit all of the tirthas in Kashi. It is said that there is a sacred site at every place in Kashi; no place the size of a sesame seed is bereft of sacredness in the entire kshetra of Kashi.

A doubt struck Shivasharman's mind. He thought, 'I know that Kashi is the chief of the Saptapuri, since it is the most efficacious in bestowing liberation. But since I have not visited the other four cities, let me complete those tirthas and then return to Kashi.'

Because Shivasharman lacked the necessary reverence for Kashi, he was compelled to leave and wait to return. This is a common problem that plagues the spiritual aspirant. Doubt is the destroyer of all. A lack of *shraddha* in the words of the *shastras* or the wise words of counsel from a guru or acharya will often lead to such destructive speculation or corrosive doubt. This leads to confusion and erroneous actions based on such confusion. This is the play of Maya. In this sense, Maya is the cosmic force that bewilders and cloaks the mind. Maya at once conceals and reveals; through his own delusion, Shivasharman left Kashi, but then that journey was also what ultimately led him back to Kashi, as we will see.

Eventually, Shivasharman reached Ujjain. From there, he proceeded to Kanchi and Dwaraka,[9] finally reaching Haridwara. After fasting and bathing in the Ganga there, Shivasharman was struck by a terrible fever. He was anxious at the prospect of dying without having attained mukti. Thoughts of the holy cities and what had befallen his wife, sons, and his accumulated wealth, riddled him with fear. What solace could that collection of texts that he had mastered give him now? He failed to understand how he had fallen into this state after having visited the Saptapuri. Soon after, he died.

Presently, a *vimana* descended from Vaikuntha, the celestial abode of Vishnu, bearing the flag of Garuda and two attendants of Vishnu. Shivasharman boarded the aerial chariot and began traveling to various worlds. The two attendants, Punyasheela and Susheela, were votaries of Vishnu. First, they took him to the world of the *pishachas*—loosely translatable into what we colloquially call 'ghosts'. This is the world that is inhabited by flesh-eaters, by those who give gifts and then resent it, those who are reluctant to give but then do give, in other words, those of low merit.

Soon, they proceeded to another world, the world of the *guhyakas*. The inhabitants of this world were big-bellied with thick lips and dark, hairy limbs. They attained this world by being hoarders in their past lives. They had earned their wealth legitimately but held on to it in a miserly way. They sought

---

9 Since Shivasharman was from Mathura, one of the Saptapuri, Prayaga has been included as an addition to his pilgrimage to the Saptapuri. The meaning here is that tirtha yatra should include exertion and travel, some amount of effort by which the merits of pilgrimage are earned. Being born and living in Mathura, in that regard, would not count for Shivasharman as a pilgrimage and thus another sacred site was added to his journey.

pleasure and did not understand the finer points of dharma. They were not attuned to the lunar cycle, the religious observances to be maintained on particular days, and other such practices. But they did know enough to gift cows to the Brahmanas and follow their words. And, devoid of anger and jealousy, they shared their food with others. The accumulation of these merits allowed the guhyakas to lead a prosperous existence in this world, living in pleasure and without fear.

Next, Shivasharman and the attendants journeyed to the world of the *gandharvas*, a splendid place beautiful to behold. The gandharvas sang praises of the Devas and were beings of splendid holy observances. In the course of their days, they delighted kings and the wealthy and were sometimes overcome by greed. Yet, their minds always dwelled on the Vedas through their persistent study of dance and music. They thus earned great merits and after death resided in a special world.

Next, they reached the world of the *vidyadharas*. The vidyadharas are expert in various types of lore and arts. They were generous to their pupils, treating them as their own offspring. During their lifetimes, they performed *kanyadana* and worshipped the Devas, albeit with *kamyakarma*—desire for certain fruits. Through their merits, they earned this world.

As the attendants and Shivasharman were conversing, Yama Deva, also known as Dharmaraja, appeared in their midst. He congratulated Shivasharman for studying the Vedas, observing the pious practices set forth in the Dharmashastras, and making pilgrimage to the Saptapuri. Yama Deva commented that mortals only live for a brief span of five moments; what, then, he asked, was the use of indulging in licentiousness? He praised Shivasharman, saying that wise men should exert themselves in noble activities like he did. He offered to render any help that Shivasharman may need.

Yama Deva then entered his own city of Samyamini, leaving Shivasharman behind with the two attendants of Vishnu. Shivasharman marvelled at how gentle and kind Yama Deva was, in contrast to the perception in the mortal world of his terrifying nature.

The attendants explained that Yama Deva is gentle to those who are not afraid of death, since he is the personification of piety. Otherwise, he is terrifying as the tawny-eyed deity, the edges of his eyes red with anger, his tongue lolling like lightning, his voice as fearsome as a thundering cloud, his brows savagely knit.

Then they proceeded to the world of the *apsaras*, numbering sixty thousand. The women who reside in this world exude radiance that never fades and a youth that never diminishes. They can assume any form they like. Some women, who while on earth, observed monthly fasting but from time to time violated the vow of celibacy, are also to be found in this world.

Afterward, they reached the world of the Sun. From a distance, Shivasharman saw Surya Deva holding two lotuses, seated in a chariot with one wheel drawn by seven horses. Aruna, the reddish hue of dawn, drove this chariot, which was adorned by apsaras, rishis, gandharvas, nagas, yakshas, and rakshasas.

Shivasharman was so moved by this sight that he joined his palms together and bowed down. Surya Deva acknowledged the obeisance with a slight movement of his eyebrows and crossed the breadth of the sky in a moment.

Shivasharman eagerly asked the attendants how to attain the world of the Sun. The attendants explained that Surya Deva is to be worshipped thrice a day. The devotee should continue *japa* while facing the rising sun, then the midday sun, and, finally, the setting sun while it is still present in the sky until the stars appear. This is the performance of sandhyavandanam which is not to be transgressed. In addition, the attendants said, Surya Deva wishes for three handfuls of water, offered as *archana* accompanied by the utterance of mantras, at the time of sunrise and sunset. The attendants revealed the special relationship between Surya Deva and the Gayatri mantra: Gayatri is the great expression and the Sun is the object of that expression. Through the offering of gifts and the performance of *japa*, *homa*, and *shraddha*, Surya Deva is invoked and becomes manifest.

In this way, Shivasharman and the two attendants of Vishnu journeyed through multiple worlds. They came to the world of Indra, built by Vishvakarma. The splendour of moonlight shines there, even during the day. Kamadhenu, the wish-fulfilling cow; Uccaishravas, the jewel among horses; Airavata, the four-tusked elephant; and the Parijata tree, all reside here.

Then they proceeded to Archishmati, the city of Agni Deva. Those devoted to the God of Fire and the observers of excellent vows reside in this city, along with people of high sattvic attainment. Here reside those Brahmanas who had in the past practiced *agnihotra* (a particular form of daily Vedic fire sacrifice performed at home), those who had observed celibacy, and those who had observed the *Panchagni vrata* (undergoing penance while being surrounded by four fires to the side and the fire of the sun above). These men shine with fiery splendour.

Vaishvanara: The Story of Agni Deva

Shivasharman then learned from the attendants of Vishnu the origin story of Agni Deva.

Once, there was a great sage named Vishvanara. He was an ardent devotee of Shiva. One day, he offered his wife a boon and she asked to bear a child equal in resemblance and stature to Shiva. Vishvanara immediately understood the folly of such a wish. But, being a sincere husband, the sage set about trying to fulfil the boon requested by his wife.

He departed for Kashi. He bathed in all the holy waters and visited all of the lingas, chief among them, Vishveshvara. He prostrated to all the Vinayakas and *Gauris*. He worshiped Kaala Bhairava and others. He made obeisance to all the deities of Surya Deva, chief among them Lolarka. He performed *sahasra-bhojana*, feeding a thousand individuals simultaneously.

He wondered which of the exalted lingas would be most appropriate to propitiate for the sake of his wife. He reasoned that Siddhikshetra, the site of the Vireshvara Linga, would be the most appropriate. In Kashi, there is not even a piece of land the size of a sesame seed where there is not a Shivalinga, and various lingas have unique properties. The unique property of this linga was that it bestowed *siddhi* (a power or ability that appears to be paranormal or supernatural but is acquired through yoga or sadhana or the blessings of a guru or Deva) quickly.

Vishvanara recalled the story of an apsara who began to dance with great bhava in front of the linga and how her body had soon merged with the linga. Shankachuda, a great serpent, offered the waving of lights through the gems of his own hood at night and attained siddhi within six months. Hamsapadi attained mukti along with her husband, Venupriya, as they sang sweetly in front of the linga. Jayadratha had lost his kingdom, but after propitiating Vireshvara, he could kill his enemies and was able to maintain his kingdom without interference. Thus, Vireshvara became known as the greatest Siddhalinga.

Vishvanara resolved to worship Vireshvara thrice a day to beget a son as desired by his wife. For a month, he only took a single meal a day. Eventually, he gave up food altogether. For another month, he took only milk. Then, only water. The for the next month, he observed the vrata of Chandrayana—modifying the quantity of his food per the waxing and waning cycles of the moon. Eventually, he subsisted only on air.

Thirteen months passed in this way. One day, after taking his bath in the Ganga, early in the morning, the sage saw in the middle of the Vireshvara Linga an eight-year-old boy wearing *bhasma*, the white ash that is the sacred mark of Shiva. Shiva, in the form of the boy, promised to be borne by Vishvanara's wife.

Thus was Vaishvanara born to the great sage and his wife. He brought happiness to all, spreading fragrant aromas in all directions. The rivers and the minds of all living beings became translucent. Darkness attenuated. Dust particles settled, clearing the air. Animals became sattvic.

After some time, Narada came to visit the family. He praised all the wonderful qualities of the boy and warned that he should be guarded carefully for a calamity was likely to befall him around the time he reached twelve years of age.

Vishvanara and his wife tumbled from joy to abject despair as they feared losing their son. Such is samsara: the replacement of joy with the fear of losing that which brings us joy. But the boy consoled his parents. He established a linga that became known as Agnishvara, a linga that increases the brilliance of all who worship it. At the age of twelve, the boy was tested by Shiva in the form of Indra. In the guise of Indra, Shiva offered the boy any boon of his choosing. Vaishvanara refused to accept a boon from anybody other than Shiva, the only form of Ishvara he recognized.

Pleased, Shiva blessed him to take on the post designated for Agni Deva. Thenceforth, he would be the mouth of all the Devas, move among all the living beings, and become one of the *dikpalakas*. Shiva also proclaimed that anyone who propitiates the Agnishvara Linga on the western bank of Ganga, to the east of Vireshvara in Kashi, would stay in the world of Agni Deva along with his parents, kin, and friends.

The Journey of Shivasharman Continues: Varuna Loka and Other Worlds

Shivasharman and the attendants of Vishnu journeyed on to the worlds of Nirrti, Varuna, and others. He learned that those who dig wells, tanks, and lakes are granted residence in Varuna Loka. There was once a great sage, Kardama, who had a son named Shuchishman. One day, Shuchishman was bathing in a lake of pure water when an alligator took him away. The boys who had accompanied him went to his father, Kardama, and reported the incident.

Kardama's mind remained fixated on Shiva, even after he heard the harrowing news about his son. Meditating on Shiva, he saw, in a vision, the fourteen worlds filled with various kinds of living beings, all within the great cosmic egg; he saw the moon, sun, stars, mountains, rivers, seas, forests, and cities. He identified his son's location. Shuchishman had been taken to a lake and handed over to the Lord of the Rivers. The copper-hued Rudra, the fierce form of Shiva, then rebuked the Lord of the Rivers. Kardama saw it all unfold in his vision.

The child was given back to Shiva. And the alligator was bound with a rope and handed over to the child. Kardama opened his eyes. He beheld his son in front of him, holding the alligator at his side. The father and son were happily reunited. After some time, Shuchishman took leave of his father and journeyed to Kashi. There, he observed a terrible penance for five thousand years. He established and worshiped a Shivalinga in Kashi. At the end of his penance, Shiva appeared before him and offered him a boon.

The son of Kardama requested sovereignty over all waters and aquatic beings. Shiva agreed and bestowed upon him the position of Varuna Deva. He said,

> Be the overlord of all jewels issuing from the ocean, of the rivers, of the lakes, of the puddles, of all water-sources, nay, of all those places where water collects and also of the Western quarter. Be the favourite of all Devas. You shall be known hereafter as Pashapani (the one with the noose in his hand).

Shiva granted him another boon that the linga installed by him would come to be known as Varunesha, stationed to the southwest of the Manikarnesha Linga. The special powers of that linga are that it destroys sluggishness and removes fear of water, distress, heat, and thirst. Simply by remembering the Varunesha Linga, food and drinks that otherwise taste bad turn delicious.

North of Varuna's capital was Gandhavati of Vayu, the Lord of the Northwestern quarter. Through worship of Shiva, he had attained the guardianship of the direction. He had performed his penance for ten thousand centuries, installing the Pavaneshvara linga in Kashi. By seeing this linga, a person is purified. Shiva blessed Vayu Deva that he would embody a form of Shiva, that he would be all-pervasive and the knower of all principles. Vayu, in the form of *prana*, would alone be the main feature of the life of all beings. Shiva promised that those who have darshana of this linga that he established would be endowed with pleasure and happiness and be honoured by Shiva himself. This linga is to the west of Jyeshthesha and north of Vayukunda.

The Story of Kubera

To the east of Gandhavati was Alaka of Kubera, who had always been a loyal friend of Shiva. Once, in the city of Kampilya, there was a man by the name of Yajnadatta, an expert in performing *yajna*, born to a family who had performed *soma* yajnas for generations.

Yajnadatta had a son called Gunanidhi, who was an extremely learned person, engaged in maintaining the sacrificial fire. Alas, he became addicted to gambling and abandoned all his virtuous pursuits. He even took money from his mother to pay off his gambling debts.

Yajnadatta was not aware of his son's gambling addiction. Gunanidhi's mother tried to mend her son's ways, but he was impervious to her attempts. Eventually, Yajnadatta found out about Gunanidhi's gambling and thievery. Disgusted, he abandoned both his son and wife, for she had deceived him for so long.

Gunanidhi left the kingdom, shamed by the disastrous end he had brought to his family. He was remorseful that he had been born to a family of pious yajna-performers while he had become a man of vice.

As he was reflecting on his own actions, the sun set. A devotee of Shiva came out of the city, bearing baskets full of sweets and puddings to be offered to Shiva at the temple. Gunanidhi plotted to take the food out of the temple after it was offered and eat it himself. After the evening puja was completed, the music and dances concluded and all the devotees in the temple fell asleep.

Gunanidhi entered the *garba griha*, the sanctum sanctorum, to take the *naivedyam*—the food that had been offered to Shiva. There was no light in the inner shrine, for the oil lamp had dimmed. So, he tore off a piece of his clothing and used it to reignite the light in order to see the food that he meant to steal. Taking the sweets, he quickly exited the temple. In his haste, he kicked one of the sleeping devotees.

All the devotees awakened and realized that Gunanidhi was attempting to steal from the temple. This was amongst the greatest sins that an individual could commit. They raised a cry, and the city guards quickly came to the rescue. They struck Gunanidhi as he was fleeing, and he died instantly. Because of his good karma from lighting the lamp for Shiva in the temple (albeit unintentionally), he died without eating the stolen naivedyam. Otherwise, the magnitude of his sins would have increased enormously.

The soldiers of Yama Deva, bearing nooses and hammers in their hands, came to take Gunanidhi away to the abode of Yama Deva. But before they could carry him away, Shiva's trishula-bearing attendants arrived on the scene. The servants of Yama Deva were frightened. Bowing down, they explained how wicked Gunanidhi's conduct had been during his past lifetime. Shiva's attendants were unmoved.

They explained that Gunanidhi had lit the lamp with the corner of his own clothing, preventing darkness from engulfing the top of the Shivalinga. Moreover, while he was waiting for the devotees to fall asleep, he had heard the holy names of Shiva being recited and witnessed the puja performed there. They announced that therefore Gunanidhi would become the king of Kalinga. With that, they dispatched Yama Deva's attendants.

As foretold, Gunanidhi took birth as the son of the king of Kalinga, Arindama. The reborn Gunanidhi was now known as Dama. Eventually, when the king passed away, Dama became the king of Kalinga. He knew no other practice than lighting lamps in the temples of Shiva. When he was crowned, he summoned all the village leaders within the kingdom. He ordered that in all the temples in all the villages of the kingdom, lamps would always remain lit, and that if anyone disobeyed, he would behead them.

Accordingly, lamps were lit in every Shiva temple in the kingdom of Kalinga. Through this virtuous and noble practice, King Dama obtained great wealth and led a peaceful existence. He eventually became Kubera, the Lord of Alaka. Alaka shines with many lamps of jewelled flames. The *Skanda Purana* thus explains that the smallest of offerings made to Shiva, even if made without knowledge or intent, even if made with the wrong intent, can bear auspicious fruit at the appropriate time.

The attendants explained to Shivasharman how this Gunanidhi, who became King Dama, attained the loyal friendship of Shiva. King Dama, who was a gambler in his past life, became a donor of wealth and performed severe penance through the lighting of lamps in devotion to Shiva. Described metaphorically, Dama went to Kashika, the abode of Shiva, and he ignited the lamp of his mind—the *chittaratna*—having Shiva as its only wick, and devotion as the supply of oil. The flame was motionless due to the steadfastness of his meditation upon the splendour of Shiva. The lamp itself was the union with Shiva. Fireflies like lust, anger, greed, and other obstacles dared not disturb it. There was no draft to disturb the lamp, because the prana of Gunanidhi had itself been stopped and was freed from impurities through the purity of his darshana.

King Dama then installed a Shivalinga, adorned with the flowers of devotion. He performed penance for ten thousand centuries until his body was reduced to nothing but skin and bone. Shiva then appeared, in the form of Vishveshvara, accompanied by Devi in the form of Vishalakshi. Shiva commanded the lord of Alaka to stop his penance and asked him to request a boon.

Dama opened his eyes and was blinded by the vision of Shiva, whose radiance outshone a thousand suns. He then spoke to Shiva:

'O Bhagavan! Give unto me the capacity of the eyes to see your feet. O Bhagavan! This alone is my boon that I am able to see you directly. Of what use is any other boon? Obeisance to you, O Moon-crested One!'

Shiva touched him with his palm, granting him the ability to see.

He opened his eyes and immediately saw Vishalakshi. Stunned by her beauty, he could not keep from looking at her greedily. His left eye burst open from the impropriety of looking at her with such lust.

Shiva commanded him to look upon Devi as his mother and to fall at Her feet. He granted him the boon of becoming the Treasurer of the Devas and the overlord of the Guhyakas, the king of the Yakshas, Kinnaras, and kings, too. He was designated as the lord of the Punya yajnas and the bestower of wealth upon all. He promised him constant friendship and that he would stay near him and Alaka. Kailasha is thus situated nearby to Alaka. Shiva then asked Devi to bless him, too.

Devi blessed him that his devotion to Shiva would always be steady. He would be the one with a brownish eye for his lost left eye. He would thereafter be known as Kubera—one with an ugly body—because he had momentarily been jealous of her beauty. She promised that the linga he had installed would thereafter be known by his own name and would bestow siddhi on all practitioners who prostrated before it. Thus, the linga became known as Kubereshvara Linga. Devi proclaimed that any man who visited the linga would never be without wealth, friends, or kinsmen. The Kubereshvara Linga was thus installed in the southern side of Vishveshvara. Shiva and Devi then entered Vishveshvara.

This is a particularly fascinating episode and a beautiful gloss added to the story of Kubera and Shiva's friendship. In each of these stories, Shiva blesses the individual Devas with that which is inherently in their *samskaras*: Varuna Deva attains mastery over all water bodies because of his abduction from a lake in his boyhood;

Kubera who had been addicted to wealth and gambling previously becomes the treasurer of the Devas. Shiva does not judge or show any partiality—whoever approaches him in whichever way, he accordingly reciprocates with affection and grace.

The Worlds of Dikpalakas and Planets

Proceeding from Alaka, Shivasharman and the attendants arrived at the city of Ishana. The sages devoted to Shiva reside here, engrossed in thinking about Shiva and observing holy vows and worshipping Shiva. Those who perform penance with the desire for enjoying Swarga assume the form of Rudra and reside here in the city of Rudra. The eleven *rudras*, bearing tridents in their raised hands, chief among them Ajaikapat and Ahirbhudhnya, govern the city. They protect the eight cities from the enemies of the Devas and constantly bless the devotees of Shiva.

In Kashi, the Rudras installed the great linga renowned as Ishanesha that accords splendour and auspiciousness to devotees performing great penance. Due to the blessings of Ishanesha, they became the lords of the Quarter of the Northeast. The eleven *rudras* move together in a cluster, adorned with a crown-like mass of hair. They have a third eye in the middle of their forehead; their throats are blue; their limbs are fair and pure; and they bear the emblem of the bull. The *rudras* on the surface of the earth are innumerable.

The merit of worshiping Ishaneshvara in Kashi and in other locations results in the devotee being reborn in the city of Ishana as a priest. Anyone who stays awake all night in the presence of Ishaneshvara, after observing a fast on any Chaturdashi—the fourteenth day of the moon—is liberated from samsara.

After hearing this story, as they continued on their journey, Shivasharman saw a place where there appeared to be moonlight even during the daytime. He marvelled at the beautiful sight and asked the attendants of Vishnu to tell him about this world that gave him such delight and filled him with admiration.

The attendants explained that this was Somaloka, the world of the Moon. Atri, one of the mind-born sons of Brahma, had performed a penance so great that it was known as Anuttara—other than which there is nothing greater—for three thousand years, as measured by the scale of Devaloka, where time passes much more slowly than on the mortal plane. Atri's penance caused his semen to flow upwards and become the Moon. It oozed out of his eyes in ten directions, brightening all the quarters.

Commanded by Brahma, the ten Devas of the ten directions tried to retain in their womb the semen so that they could conceive collectively. But they were unable to do so. Incapable of conception, Soma (the Moon) and the Devas of the ten directions fell to earth. Brahma was distressed at the sight of the fallen Soma. For the wellbeing of all the worlds, Brahma placed him on a chariot. He then took that chariot in a circumambulation of the earth twenty-one times.

The resplendence of the moon touched all corners of the earth. Herbs were born that sustain the world. Soma regained his brilliance and performed penance for a hundred *padma* years. A single padma year is one thousand billion years. In the course of his penance, Soma went to Kashi and installed an immortal linga known as Chandresha. He became the king of seeds, herbs, waters, and the Brahmanas. He dug a well, known as Amritoda, drinking the waters of which or bathing in which delivers a person from ignorance.

Delighted by his penance, Shiva bore Soma on his own head. Because he worshiped both Shiva and Uma, he became known as Soma (Sa + Uma, or, with Uma). In front of the Chandreshvara Linga, Soma Deva performed an excessively difficult penance as well as the *Rajasuya yajna*, which is an elaborate rite of consecration performed by kings to become established as the emperor or the king of kings.

He attained the status of becoming the eye of Mahadeva. Shiva, pleased by the devotion of Soma Deva, gave delight to all three *lokas*.

He told Soma Deva that he was his minor form. During his rise, joy would increase in the world, touched by his rays full of nectar. Shiva further blessed him by assuming the form of Ardhanarishvara—taking Uma Devi in half of his body, since Soma Deva worshiped them both—and resided in that linga named after Soma Deva. He promised that while Shiva was omnipresent, he would reside there in that linga on the fifteenth day in the bright half of every month—meaning, purnima, the day of the full moon—for the whole day and night, bringing with him all the prosperity of the three worlds.

Thus, it is said that whichever *sadhana* is performed in front of that linga on purnima, be it japa, homa, archana, dhyana, or dana, will bear great fruit. Just as doing *pitra tarpana* at Gaya releases man from the karmic obligation of pitra tarpana for the rest of his life, so also is he released from that karmic debt by offering *pinda* at Chandroda. Shiva remarked sadly that in Kali Yuga, the greatness of Chandresha would not be understood by the unfortunate ones. Time has proven the truth of this prophecy, not just about Chandresha, but so many of our sacred sites which have become neglected and forgotten or misunderstood.

Shiva revealed that the area where the Chandreshvara Linga had been installed is also known as Siddhayogishvara Peetha, a site that bestows siddhi on *sadhakas*. As they were talking, Shiva revealed that seven crore *siddhas*, among them Devas, asuras, gandharvas, nagas, vidyadharas, rakshasas, guhyakas, yakshas, kinnaras, and humans, were in front of them. He explained that one who meditates on Vishveshvari, the consort of Vishveshvara, after being on a strict diet for six months, would be able to see the siddhas who come to worship the Chandreshvara Linga. Siddhayogishvari would then grant boons directly to such siddhas. Shiva explained that there is nothing else on earth that bestows siddhi as quickly as Yogishvari Peetha, and that this was a site invisible to people who lack discipline or discrimination. Only individuals who have overcome lust, anger, covetousness, desire, egotism, and arrogance, can have darshana of Yogishvari, Shiva's Shakti, who is extremely benevolent.

With these final words, Shiva disappeared into the Vishveshvara Linga. Thereafter, Soma Deva filled the ten directions with the light of his rays spreading everywhere. Those who observe the Somavara vrata imbibe Somarasa and attain Somaloka, whisked there by a chariot with the lustre of the moon.

From there, the attendants and Shivasharman journeyed to the world of the Nakshatras. Once when the sixty daughters of Daksha Prajapati performed a severe penance at Vishveshvara, Shiva appeared before them to offer a boon. They requested a husband with beauty equal to Shiva's and someone who would be able to remove the distress of worldly existence.

The daughters established the Nakshatreshvara Linga by the bank of Varana near Sangameshvara. They performed a terrible penance, known as Purushayita, which cannot be performed even by men. The penance lasted for a thousand divine years. Greatly pleased, Shiva blessed them with mental steadiness and to be the wives of a husband of their desired specifications.

Shiva told them that never before had such a severe penance been endured by women. He granted them the ability to become male at will. He proclaimed that they would become the foremost among the system of constellations and be the source of the original zodiacs. They were promised to be wed to Soma Deva, the lord of herbs, nectar, and the Brahmanas. Through worshiping the linga that these women established, any man would be able to visit their world, and those who worship and observe the vows of the Nakshatras, would reside in their world with a lustre similar to that of the stars.

The attendants then told Shivasharman about how Soma Deva abducted Tara, the wife of Brhaspati, the guru of the Devas. The Devas and rishis tried to dissuade Soma Deva, but he persisted in pursuing and capturing Tara, proud as he was of his own ravishing looks. When he refused to give up Tara, Shiva took up his bow made of goat's horn and stood against him. They fought a tough battle, so fierce that Brahma feared the cosmos would be annihilated. He asked Shiva to desist and bestowed Tara on Brhaspati once more.

Tara was pregnant at this time, but nobody knew who the father of the child was. At her husband's instruction, Tara discharged the foetus upon a cluster of Ishika grass. The baby came to life and immediately the brilliance of his body eclipsed that of all the Devas. Once again, they asked Tara who the father was.

Tara was shy and did not respond.

The child was about to curse her for not revealing his paternity when Brahma intervened. Brahma asked Tara to resolve the doubt, and she admitted that the child's father was Soma Deva. Gladdened, Soma Deva sniffed the head of the boy and named him Budha, for he was intelligent.

Budha decided to undergo penance and took leave of his father to travel to Kashi. He installed the Budheshvara Linga and meditated upon the *ugra*—fierce—form of Shiva for ten thousand years. Shiva offered him a boon. Budha could not think of a boon to seek, other than to have unparalleled devotion to the feet of Shiva.

Pleased, Shiva blessed him with a world above the world of Nakshatras. He would be greatly honoured among all the planets, and the linga installed by him would bestow wisdom upon all and remove all evil intentions, granting residence in his world to those who worshiped it. This linga is established to the east of Chandreshvara in Kashi.

Then, the chariot bearing Shivasharman and the attendants of Vishnu reached the world of Venus, or Shukra who is the guru of the *danavas*. Once, as penance, Shukra inhaled the smoke of burning rice husks for a thousand years, an unbearably difficult penance. Through this, he acquired the *Mrtyusanjivini vidya*—the knowledge that enables one to revive the dead—from Shiva. Even Brhaspati, the guru of the Devas, does not know this *vidya*. It is said in the *Skanda Purana* that only Shiva, Skanda, Ganesha, and Parvati are privy to this vidya.

Once, there was a battle between Andhaka and Shiva. Andhaka approached Shukracharya and asked him to use the vidya to revive all the danavas. Shukracharya gave a small smile and consented. He had, after all, attained this knowledge for the benefit of the danavas. After reciting the mantra, all the danavas arose with their weapons.

The ganas, the associates of Shiva, witnessed this and Nandi reported back to Mahadeva.

Shiva laughed and told Nandi to quickly go and fetch Shukracharya, to pluck him from the midst of the danavas like a vulture seizing a quail. Nandi obeyed. He growled in his leonine voice, penetrating the opposing army quickly, and carried away Shukracharya who was being shielded by the danavas with nooses, swords, trees, boulders, and rocks in their hands. Nandi handed over Shukracharya to Shiva.

Shiva accepted him as if he were an oblation offered by a devotee and put the sage into his mouth, as if he were a piece of fruit. The asuras cried out in grief, losing all hope of victory. Andhaka lamented that they had been deceived by Nandi, who had carried away their preceptor by force. He vowed revenge and resumed the battle.

The war raged on for some time. Andhaka routed the ganas. In the meantime, Shukracharya, searching for an exit, wandered around inside Shiva's body. He saw the seven worlds and their guardians, the worlds of Brahma, Narayana, Indra, the Adityas, and the apsaras. For a hundred years, he kept looking but could not find any hole, any vulnerability in the body of Shiva that would allow him to escape. Eventually, he dropped out of Shiva's body in the form of semen. When he bowed down to Shiva, Shiva regarded him as his son and allowed him to leave with his blessing.

Shukracharya then re-entered the battle.

The attendants narrated to Shivasharman how Shukracharya had obtained this special vidya. Once, he had gone to Kashi and, installing the linga of Sri Shambhu, had dug a well before it.

There he performed penance for a long time and meditated upon Vishveshvara. He showered the linga with different kinds of flowers, adoring each one separately. He added one hundred thousand leaves to these flowers, in worship of Shiva. Then he bathed the linga one hundred thousand times with panchamrta. For five thousand years, he performed such austerities.

Seeing Shiva unmoved, Shukracharya undertook an unbearable vow. He inhaled the smoke of rice husks for one thousand years. Pleased with his devotion, Shiva emerged from the linga to bless him and offered him a boon of his choice. Shukracharya offered a beautiful litany of prayers in praise of Shiva.

Shiva lifted him up from the ground with his own hands. Shiva smiled, illuminating all the quarters through the moonshine-like radiance of his teeth. He told Shukracharya, the descendant of Bhrigu, that he considered him of the same status as his two sons because of the fierce unprecedented penance and the purity and steadfastness of his offerings, sanctified by being in the environs of Avimukta.

Shiva then blessed him that he would, someday, enter his belly, and then come out from his vital organs, thereby attaining the status of his son. He then bestowed upon him the *Mrtyusanjivani Vidya*, which had been concealed even from Vishnu and Brahma. He blessed him to be foremost amongst the planets, that all holy rites, all pious activities, taking place after the rising of Venus would become fruitful; that all inauspicious lunar days would become auspicious through association with him; and that his devotees would be blessed with virility and prolific progeny. Those who worshiped the Shukresha Linga would achieve success. Then Shiva disappeared into the linga.

Thus was Shukresha Linga established to the south of Vishveshvara in Kashi.

The World of Angaraka

Once, Shiva was undergoing penance as he mourned being separated from Sati. A drop of sweat fell from his forehead onto the ground. From this, a boy, red in limbs, was born from the surface of the earth. The earth lovingly nourished and raised the boy. Eventually, he became known as Angaraka and also known as Mangala (Mars), one of the Navagrahas. He performed penance in Kashi at the conjunction of the Asi and Varana rivers. There he installed the Angarakeshvara Linga. His penance lasted till a coal-like brilliance blazed out of his body. Shiva, satisfied with his unwavering commitment, granted him the status of a planet.

Shivasharman and Vishnu's attendants proceeded to the city of Guru (Jupiter). Angiras was one of the three primary mind-born sons of Brahma, and Angirasa was his son. Angirasa was a renowned scholar, gentle in speech and pure in mind. He, too, performed penance in Kashi and installed a Shivalinga there after meditating for ten thousand divine years. Vishveshvara manifested himself from the linga and commanded him to speak aloud the boon he had already contemplated in his mind.

Angirasa eloquently eulogized Shiva. The Adideva blessed that he would become the preceptor of the Devas by merits of his extensive penance. He was eventually turned into a great planet, worthy of adoration. He came to be known as Jiva throughout the worlds, for he had become the vital life of Shiva, through his affection. For his brilliant eulogy he came to be known as Vachaspati (Brhaspati), the lord of the world of words.

Shiva summoned Brahma, all the Devas, and the Yakshas, nagas, and Kinnaras. He commanded Brahma to anoint the virtuous Brhaspati as the preceptor of the Devas and pronounced that he would remain a great favourite of Shiva forevermore. Shiva also proclaimed that the linga established by Brhaspati would become known as Brhaspatishvara. This linga is said to be guarded by Shiva during Kali Yuga. Merely laying eyes upon the linga bestows one with intellectual gifts. Given its great powers, Shiva determined that the Brhaspatishvara Linga should be well-guarded and its details not be shared with all.

Shivasharman, escorted by the attendants of Vishnu, passed through the world of Shani (Saturn). Shani Deva, too, established a linga in Kashi known as the Shanaishchareshvara, lying to the south of Vishveshvara and north of Shukresha. Worship of this linga brings one joy. Shani Deva also gained the status of a planet.

The World of the Saptarishi

Next, they reached the world of the Saptarishi, the seven great sages. Shivasharman asked the attendants to explain the nature of this unrivalled and brilliant world. They revealed that the Seven Sages, or the *sapta* rishi, were directed by Brahma to create subjects. The attendants named them as Marichi, Atri, Pulaha, Pulastya, Krata, Angiras, and the illustrious Vasishta. They are also known as the mind-born sons of Brahma and have also been described as the Seven Brahmas in the Puranas. Their wives, respectively, are Sambhuti, Anasuya, Kshama, Preeti, Sannati, Smrti, and Arundhati; they are known as the mothers of the world.

The three worlds are upheld by the penance of the Saptarishi. When commanded by Brahma to engage in creation, they resolved to undertake penance. After prostrating to Brahma, their father, they went to Avimukta and installed the lingas named after them. Shiva bestowed the region of Prajapatya upon them.

It is said that those who visit the Atrishvara Linga on the western banks of the lake of Gokarnesha in Kashi stay in the Prajapatya realm. The *kunda* of Marichi is in the northeast of Karkotavapi; by bathing there with devotion, a man radiates brilliance like the sun. The Marichishvara Linga has been installed there. Pulahesha Linga and Pulastyesha Linga are on the west of Swargadwara. The Angiraseshvara Linga is in Harikeshavana. The Vasishtheshvara Linga is found on the banks of the Vanara, along with the Kratvishvara Linga.

These lingas bestow all that is desirable in this world and the other.

Arundhati also stays here. The *Skanda Purana* says that merely by remembering her, one attains the benefit of bathing in the Ganga. Narayana himself praises Arundhati to his consort, Lakshmi, pleased by her chastity and great virtue.

Enlightenment of Shivasharman

Then they came across the world of Dhruva, the Pole Star. Shivasharman inquired from the attendants about the person who was skilfully whirling multiple strings on the tips of his fingers, standing on a single foot and keenly observing everything. Shivasharman noticed how similar this being was to the pillar holding up the three worlds. He appeared to be meticulously measuring the boundless expanse of the stars, constellations, and planets. The strings he held seemed to gauge the vastness of the universe.

The attendants narrated to him the story of Dhruva and his devotion to Narayana. Since this episode is well-known from various Puranic tellings, I will not repeat it here. In short, after the child Dhruva meditated upon Vishnu, repeating his japa incessantly, Vishnu appeared before him and proclaimed that Dhruva would become the pivot of the entire group of planets, nakshatras, and other celestial bodies forever. He would control them with aerial strings, holding them together till the end of the *kalpa*. Vishnu revealed that he had acquired this position from Shiva in the past, and now, due to Dhruva's great penance, he was passing it onto him. Vishnu explained that some such positions were occupied for a period of four *yugas*, some for the period of a manvantara, but Dhruva would keep his for the entire duration of a kalpa.

Vishnu took Dhruva with him to Kashi in the month of Karthika. Dhruva was delighted to be riding on the back of Garuda with his beloved Bhagavan Vishnu who descended from Garuda's back at the outskirts of the Panchakroshi—the fifteen-kilometre perimeter of the city of Kashi—holding Dhruva's hand. He bathed at Manikarnika and instructed Dhruva to install a linga in Avimukta. Vishnu left Dhruva after explaining that if anyone were to repair the ruins of a temple or other sacred sites, he or she would receive benefits that would not expire even upon Pralaya.

Dhruva duly installed a linga near Vaidyanatha and built a great palace with a holy pit dug in front of it. After worshiping Vishveshvara, he was contented and went back home. It is said that by worshiping Dhruveshvara and offering water in the

Dhruvakunda, one attains the world of Dhruva replete with celestial pleasures.

Heavenly Realms

Shivasharman and the attendants then reached Maharloka, one of the seven heavens. The attendants explained that by meditating on Vishnu and practicing the great yoga of self-realization, the Devas see this world and reside here.

From there, the chariot took them, in a flash, to Janaloka. The mind-born sons of Brahma, great yogis, and others who have sublimated their sexual drives reside there. The chariot took them to Tapoloka at the speed of thought. The Vairajas, a class of Devas created by Hiranyagarbha with their minds and hearts devoted to Vishnu, reside there. Those who have mastered their senses and worshiped Govinda reside there, free from ambition or desire.

The World of Brahma

On arriving at Satyaloka, the world of Brahma, the attendants hurriedly disembarked from the chariot along with Shivasharman, and they all prostrated before Brahma. Brahma lavishly praised Kashi, acknowledging that nowhere in the entire Cosmic Egg of the universe was there a city like Kashi or a linga equivalent to Vishveshvara. After Brahma finished speaking, Shivasharman hesitantly mentioned that he had something to ask but was timid to speak up.

Brahma responded that he already knew what was on his mind—he wanted to inquire about mukti. Brahma assured Shivasharman that the two attendants were well-versed in all matters and would provide answers to all his questions. With that, Brahma sent them on their way toward Vaikuntha.

As Shivasharman and the attendants continued their journey, he inquired about the distance they had covered so far and how much further they had to go. He additionally expressed what had been weighing on his heart for a long time. He mentioned that he had visited all seven cities that grant mukti, the Saptapuri, yet he was puzzled by why he had not attained mukti yet.

The attendants promptly answered him as if they were waiting for this question. They explained that the sun is two hundred thousand yojanas above earth and the moon is one hundred thousand yojanas above the sun; the region of the Nakshatras is one hundred thousand yojanas above the moon; the abode of Budha is two hundred thousand yojanas above that region; the abode of Shukra is two hundred thousand yojanas away from Budha; the abode of Bhauma (Mars) is two hundred thousand yojanas away from Shukra; the abode of Brhaspati is two hundred thousand yojanas above Bhauma; the abode of Shani is two hundred thousand yojanas above Brhaspati; the region of the Saptarishi—what in astronomy we would call the Great Bear—is one hundred thousand yojanas away from Shani; and the abode of Dhruva, the Pole Star, is one hundred thousand yojanas away from the Saptarishi. All that can be covered by foot on earth is known as Bhurloka. The space extending from Bhurloka to the sun is known as Bhuvarloka. The space from the sun extending up to Dhruva is known as Svarloka.

Maharloka is ten million yojanas above earth. Janaloka is calculated to be twenty million yojanas above Bhurloka. Tapaloka is forty million yojanas from earth. Satyaloka is said to be eighty million yojanas above Earth. Vaikuntha is above Satyaloka, calculated to be one hundred and sixty million yojanas above earth.

The attendants also proclaimed that what is Shiva, so is Vishnu; what is Vishnu, so is Shiva; there is no difference at all between Shiva and Vishnu.

Finally, they addressed Shivasharman's most pressing concern: how and when he would attain mukti. They explained to him that he would spend one year (measured according to the time scale of Brahma) in Vaikuntha, due to the merit acquired by dying in a holy place—in this case, Haridwara. He would then ascend the throne of Nandivardhana in the south. The kingdom would be without rivals or enemies. It would prosper and thrive and be known for its fertility. The kingdom would be peopled by noble and healthy subjects. The land would be adorned with many rows of numerous gleaming temples, and each village would bear sacrificial posts.

The attendants foretold that he would be a righteous and heroic king. He would be handsome and would father three hundred sons by ten thousand queens. He would gain fame throughout the land as Vrddhakala. His hair would remain damp through the continued performance of sacred ablutions after concluding sacrifices. He would constantly meditate on the lotus feet of Govinda within his heart, discussing the glories of Vishnu day and night.

One day, sages draped in red garments would arrive from Varanasi to the assembly of kings to congratulate Vrddhakala. They would bless him by wishing Vishveshvara's beneficence upon him. They would explain to him that he had attained this kingdom through his merit and wish for him to employ his remaining merit to deepen his devotion towards Vishvanatha.

On hearing this benediction, Vrddhakala would remember his present journey with the attendants of Vishnu. He would bestow great wealth upon those sages and then, entrusting his kingdom to his son, he would set out for Kashi, accompanied by his chief queen.

He would install a linga named after himself, one that would be the cause of salvation—mukti. He would build a mansion and dig a well. One day, with body emaciated and fatigued from austerities and vratas, he would chance upon a sage at midday in a secluded spot. That sage would have tawny matted hair and emerge from the sanctum sanctorum, his slender body leaning on a staff.

Wobbling, he would come and sit next to Vrddhakala and put him to the test by asking him the name of the one who constructed the mansion and established the linga. Vrddhakala would reply that it was only Shiva who both accomplishes deeds and makes others accomplish deeds, and then Vrddhakala would fall silent.

The sage would ask for water, and Vrddhakala would draw it from the well. Upon the sage drinking the water, he would immediately transform into a young man, with the lustre of the full moon.

The sage would then tell Vrddhakala that he knows about the past lives of his wife and him. His wife, in a prior life, was a widow who observed holy vows and died in Ujjain. Due to the merits of her vows, she was married to Vrddhakala in this lifetime; the sage would promise that she, too, would attain mukti.

He would then recount Vrddhakala's past life as Shivasharman and praise him for not boasting about installing the linga or building the mansion. The sage would then elucidate that the Vrddhakaleshvara Linga had been in existence since time immemorial, yet the king's actions served as the instrumental cause of its manifestation. The sage would further reveal that worshiping this linga would fulfil one's every desire, and that the Kalodaka well would dispel old age and sickness. Moreover, by drinking its waters, one would be liberated from samsara. Whoever bathes in its waters and worships the Vrddhakaleshvara Linga would find their desires fulfilled within a year. The sage would finally proclaim that the Vrddhakaleshvara Linga to the north of Krttivasa should be visited by those who wish for mukti.

Saying this, the sage would take Vrddhakaleshvara and Anangalekha, his queen, by the hand, and they would all merge into the linga.

On hearing this, Shivasharman experienced horripilation due to being overcome with bliss and beheld Vaikuntha, resplendent with the radiance of ten million suns.

In time, all that was foretold by the attendants of Vishnu came to pass.

Thus, Agastya Muni explained to Lopamudra the importance of the Saptapuri and the special status of Kashi amongst the seven holy cities, as illustrated by the story of Shivasharman and his journey through the various worlds in search of mukti.

CHAPTER 5

The Manifestation of Kaala Bhairava and Dandapani

Presently, as Agastya Muni and Lopamudra continued on their way, they came to the forest of Skanda. Agastya Muni prostrated in front of Skanda, the son of Shiva, in delight and reverence. Skanda sensed that the separation from Kashi weighed heavily on the sage's mind, and he reassured him that all was well in Kashi. Agastya Muni was eager to hear more about Kashi and, at his request, Skanda began recounting the glories and history of Kashi to the sage just as he had heard it narrated by Shiva to his mother, Parvati.

Select ones of these stories elucidating the significant aspects of Kashi follow in these chapters as a condensed summary of the rest of the contents of the Kashi Khanda. There is no substitute, though, for reading the original text from the *Skanda Purana*.

We begin with the story of the manifestation of Kaala Bhairava.

Kaala Bhairava

Kaala Bhairava is known as the *kotwal* or the 'police chief' of Kashi. The *Skanda Purana* places his temple on the bank of the Kapalamochana Tirtha in the Omkareshvara area north of Maidagin. However, that site was destroyed during Muslim invasions. His temple is now located in the lanes of the old city.

Once, Brahma and Vishnu were in vain pursuit of the ends of the colossal primordial Linga, the pillar of light that embodied

Shiva. Brahma falsely claimed to have found the upper limit of the linga. He had, in reality, caught a fleeting glimpse of Neelalohita, which is the fourth of the eleven manifestations of Rudra. White in colour, Neelalohita had three eyes and four arms. Draped in white clothing, he stood erect. He held the trident in his hand, had several snakes draped around him, and bore the crescent moon as an ornament.

Brahma, in his fury and arrogance, addressed him: 'I know you. In the past, you had emerged from my own forehead as Rudra. Since you were born with a cry, I had named you Rudra then. Oh, my son, seek refuge in me alone, and I shall protect you.'

To cure Brahma's arrogance, Shiva created a *Purusha* of terrifying appearance and said to him, 'O, Kaala Bhairava, Brahma deserves to be chastised by you. Since you shine like Time itself, you shall be known as Kaalaraja. Since you are capable of bearing the entire universe, you shall be known as Bhairava (the one who can bear (bharana) the universe). Even Time and Death shall be afraid of you. Hence, you will be called Kaala Bhairava. Since, through your anger, you will suppress wickedness, you will be renowned as Amardaka. Since you eat up the sins of your devotees in a moment, you will be known as Papabhakshana. O, Kaalaraja, forever shall you be the overseer of Kashi, which is mine, the city of mukti, greater than all the others.

'Only you can admonish and punish those who perform ill deeds here. Even Chitragupta cannot record their deeds and misdeeds.'

After Shiva concluded speaking, Kaala Bhairava plucked one of Brahma's five heads with the tip of a fingernail from his left hand. He reasoned that since it was Brahma's fifth head that had censured Shiva, it was appropriate for only the fifth head to be cut off.

Vishnu and Brahma then sang hymns of praise to Shiva. Shiva bestowed his blessings upon them and commanded Kaala Bhairava to undertake the penance of carrying the skull of Brahma and begging as reparation for the great offence of slaughtering a Brahmana. Sent by Shiva, the spirit of Brahmahatya—a grotesque feminine entity with lolling tongue, incessantly drinking blood, carrying a knife and a shattered vessel—relentlessly pursued Kaala Bhairava. Even Kaala Bhairava was terrified of her.

Her presence turned Kaala Bhairava black. He journeyed through the three worlds, offering guidance to people. Yet the shadow of Brahmahatya continued to cling to him. Only on reaching Varanasi did the stain of Brahmahatya vanish.

The skull of Brahma effortlessly slipped from his hand, and Kaala Bhairava burst into ecstatic dance. This site came to be known as Kapalamochana. As the tale goes, Kaala Bhairava stood there, consuming the accumulated heaps of sins of his devotees.

The Story of Dandapani

Next comes the story of Dandapani. As the 'sheriff' of Kashi, he expels undesirable people from the city and protects the pious residents of Kashi. Sambhrama and Vibhrama are his assistants. Dandapani is an assistant to Annapurna Devi, and he feeds the needy citizens of Kashi.

Today, the modest shrine of Dandapani stands in the Vishvanatha lane, to the west of the Gyanvapi Mosque. His club, the *danda*, is a fragment from the Mahashmashana pillar at Lat Bhairava, near the Kaala Bhairava Mandir.

This is the origin story of Dandapani. Once, a virtuous yaksha dwelt on Gandhamadana Parvat. He consistently engaged in righteous acts. His son was named Purnabhadra. Meditating on Shiva, the father attained lasting peace and tranquillity. Following his father's departure, Purnabhadra revelled in all earthly pleasures. But the one thing he could not attain was a son.

Purnabhadra confided his sorrows to his wife, Kanakakundala, who was renowned as an excellent *yakshini*. With utmost sincerity, he asked her whether there existed a method for them to conceive a son. In response, she elucidated that by directing one's intelligence and concentration towards Ishvara, all desires and aspirations can be realized. She reprimanded him, asserting that only ignoble individuals blame fate for their fortunes. Destiny merely stems from the karma one has previously enacted. She concluded,

> Hence, one should resort to manliness and for the sake of subduing karma one should seek refuge in Ishvara, the cause of all causes. Acquisition of child, wealth, wife, ornaments, mansions, horses, elephants, all pleasures and even heaven and liberation is not far from devotion to Shiva. [...] Hence, if you wish for a dear son who is the most excellent of all persons, seek refuge in Shankara by all means. (Tagare 1950, Chapter 32)

Purnabhadra was an expert musician, and he worshiped Shiva through music. In a matter of days, his wife conceived and eventually gave birth to a son. They named the child Harikesha. By the age of eight, Harikesha's devotion was unwaveringly directed towards Shiva alone. He would skilfully mould Shivalingas out of specks of dust and worship them with leaves and blades of grass. He affectionately nicknamed his friends with the various names of Shiva, like Chandrashekhara, Bhutesha, Mrtyunjaya, Trilochana, and Bharga. Only the names of Shiva graced his tongue; only the names of Shiva met his ears. Not a morsel of food or a sip of water would pass through his lips without first being offered to Shiva. Awakening in the depths of the night, he would cry out, 'O, Trilochana! Wait for a moment. Where did you go?'

Purnabhadra became anxious due to his son's condition. He tried to distract him with worldly pursuits, attempting to entice him with the promise of horses, silk clothing, rare gems, crystals, livestock, and various other forms of wealth. Purnabhadra urged him to acquire the knowledge that would lead to material success and to avoid the activities, as he put it, of poor people who were always soiled with dust. Furthermore, Purnabhadra proposed that as he approached the end of his life, he could then resume the path of Bhakti yoga.

This mindset is quite common nowadays. We often turn to Ishvara when we encounter challenges, and once those difficulties are resolved, we sink back into the trivialities of samsara. We consider divine contemplation or self-realization as a pursuit for the elderly, those who have exhausted all other sources of enjoyment.

Harikesha, however, displayed greater discernment than his father and disregarded his well-intentioned counsel. As Purnabhadra's frustration mounted, Harikesha fled from home. He called out to Shiva, asking for guidance. He recalled a moment from his childhood, nestled in his father's lap. In that moment, someone had remarked to his father that Kashi should be sought by those who have been abandoned by their parents, those without alternatives, the aged, the disabled, and the destitute. Reflecting on this, Harikesha set forth towards Kashi.

Harikesha embraced a life of austerity. After a while, Shiva came to watch him and pointed him out to Parvati. Harikesha was engaged in penance under the roots of an ashoka tree. Dried tendons and sinews bound his bones together. Ants, moles, and worms had drained his veins of blood. Yet, he glowed with a crystalline radiance, like the moon. The trees of the forest surrounding him seemed to be bathed in the stream of nectar pouring from his gentle eyes.

Parvati was moved by compassion for Harikesha. She asked Shiva to bestow boons upon him. Shiva and Parvati descended from Nandi's back and approached Harikesha. Shiva gently laid his hand on Harikesha's body.

Overwhelmed with joy, Harikesha choked out his words of praise to Shiva.

Shiva granted him the esteemed position of the permanent Dandadhara—wielder of the staff of justice—at the sacred site of Kashi, beloved to Shiva. He named him Dandapani and entrusted him with authority over the ganas. He bestowed upon Dandapani two companions, Sambhrama and Udbhrama—those who invoke immense excitement.

Shiva gave him an exquisite appearance—a blue mark on his neck, serpents adorning his wrists, a third eye, an elephant hide for clothing, and a left side always adorned by the presence of a beautiful woman. His head would be crowned with tawny, matted hair and his body would be perennially smeared with ash. He would shine with the radiance of the crescent moon and move with a measured, graceful gait.

The residents of Kashi would receive nourishing sustenance and knowledge from the sage words flowing from his lips. He would establish Kashi as a steadfast haven for devotees. Having entrusted Kashi's guardianship to him, Shiva decreed that his followers must first appease Dandapani before they could worship Shiva.

Shiva further proclaimed that only he who, after performing the rites in the Gyaanavapi well, propitiates Dandapani would be considered to have fulfilled his duties. He commanded Dandapani to remain always in the southern direction, directly before Shiva's gaze. Dandapani's role would involve administering just punishment to those deserving it and bestowing liberation from fear upon devotees.

CHAPTER 6

The Story of Gyaanavapi

The Description of Gyaanavapi

Agastya Muni requested Skanda to narrate to him the greatness of the Gyaanoda Tirtha. Thus unfolds the origin story of Gyaanavapi, merely hearing which cleanses one of all transgressions.

Gyaanavapi is literally the wisdom well of Kashi, dug by Ishaana, a manifestation of Shiva, using the trishula. Traditionally, devotees on the path of their tirtha yatra to Kashi would start and end their journey with a sip of water from this well. It is a deep well, ten feet in diameter, and situated near the mosque built by Aurangzeb after destroying the earlier Vishvanatha Temple.

In Satya Yuga, Ishaana, an embodiment of Rudra's formidable aspect, was wandering across the world. This was at a time when there was no rain and so no rivers or other freshwater bodies were to be found. Water for drinking and bathing did not exist, nor was it needed. Water could only be found in the salty seas. This was a time when people roamed across the world as nomads.

Once, Ishaana reached Anandakandana, the forest of bliss, situated within Kashi. He entered the grove, the lustre from the pure rays of his blazing trishula illuminating the entire forest. There, he saw the Vishveshvara Linga, which had manifested earlier during the intense rivalry between Brahma and Vishnu. Adorned by flowers and ceaselessly venerated by Devas and rishis, the linga was covered with flowers and received the incessant mellifluous melodies of the gandharvas. Naga women waved lamps set with luminous gems before the linga.

Upon beholding the linga, Ishaana was moved to bathe the linga with vessels brimming with cool, pure water. With his trishula, Ishaana swiftly dug a deep pit. This pit was situated to the south of Vishveshvara, very near to the linga. Immediately, colossal columns of water, ten times the size of Earth itself, surged forth, inundating the mortal world from all sides.

With these ice-cold waters, Ishaana ritualistically cleansed the Vishveshvara Linga. The waters sparkled like the minds of virtuous people, azure like the sky, radiant like moonlight. Their sanctity and purity equalled that of the names of Shiva. Their fragrance was incredible, surpassing the allure of lotuses, captivating all.

These waters were more pleasing to Shiva than even the tender touch of Parvati. They held a more profound purifying essence than the final bath after a yajna. Ishaana continued to bathe the Vishveshvara Linga one thousand times through pitchers that poured forth thousands of streams of nectarine water onto the Linga.

Shiva's heart brimmed with delight as he spoke to Ishaana. He said,

> O, Ishaana, practitioner of excellent rites, I am pleased with this great rite of yours which has never been performed by anyone else. O, great ascetic with matted hairs, you who undertook this endeavour with utmost dedication, tell me what boon shall I grant to you. There is nothing that cannot be given to you today.

Ishaana humbly requested that this tirtha, where he had excavated the well, be named after Shiva.

In the divine form of Vishveshvara, Shiva replied, 'This tirtha surpasses all the tirthas situated within the three worlds. Those who contemplate the essence of words say that Shiva signifies knowledge in the form of wisdom. Due to my powers, that knowledge has merged into the waters with which you bathed me. Therefore, this tirtha has become renowned in all the three worlds as Gyaanoda. The mere sight of this Linga grants absolution from all sins.

'Listen to my words carefully. By merely touching the Gyaanoda Tirtha one gains the merits of an Ashvamedha Yajna, and that of a Rajasuya and an Ashvamedha Yajna by rinsing the mouth with these waters.'

Shiva continued to describe the powers and blessings bestowed by the Gyaanoda Tirtha. He explained,

> If the devotee observes a fast on the eleventh day and drinks three handfuls of water from here, undoubtedly, three Lingas will arise in his heart. The devotee should sanctify himself by taking a bath in this Tirtha, particularly on a Monday, appease the Devas, the rishis, and the pitrs, and make gifts for public welfare in accordance with his capacity. Then, by worshiping the Linga, he will have fulfilled all of his duties. Finally, by performing *sandhya vandanam* in Gyaanoda, a Brahmana shall instantly dispel all sins and attain wisdom and erudition.

Shiva further explained that this tirtha was variously known as Shiva Tirtha, the resplendent Gyaana Tirtha, the Taraka Tirtha, and certainly Moksha Tirtha—the tirtha that grants moksha.

He concluded, 'Multitudes of sins shall dissolve by remembering Gyaanoda. By visiting it, touching it, bathing in it, and drinking its waters, a state of purity is instilled within a person. Malevolent spirits, *dakinis*, *shakinis*, evil planets, epileptic fits, recurring fevers—all these are subdued by seeing the waters of this Shiva Tirtha.'

Shiva further promised that he, in the form of Gyaana, having assumed this liquid manifestation, would destroy *jadya*—meaning sluggishness or ignorance—and impart knowledge. Shiva then vanished. Ishaana considered himself fully blessed, drank the waters of the tirtha that he had dug up, and acquired the great knowledge that led him to the realization of Brahman.

The Glories of Gyaanavapi and Queen Kalavati

Skanda then recounted an ancient tale of wonder that took place in Gyaanavapi.

In Kashi, there once lived a Brahmana named Harisvami. To him was born a daughter called Susheela. She stood as the epitome of beauty. She possessed exquisite charm and displayed exceptional mastery over all the arts. Her melodious voice was sweeter than the cuckoo's. No other female, be it among the gandharvas, the nagas or even the asuras, could match her qualities. There were many young men whose eyes were always riveted on her heavy hips.

But she was oblivious to it all. She bathed in the waters of the Gyaanavapi every day and swept the temple of Shiva attentively. Neither did she look at anybody nor did she hear anyone's words. Her father, too, found it impossible to hand her over in marriage, for none could equal her glory or virtuous conduct.

Because of her close association with Gyaanoda Tirtha, Susheela perceived everything within and without as if pervaded only by Shivalingas.

Once, while Susheela slumbered in the courtyard of her home, a vidyadhara, captivated by her beauty, abducted her. As he was carrying her through the skies to his mountainous abode, a rakshasa named Vidyunmali saw them and desired to end both their lives. He was a formidable rakshasa, adorned with skulls for earrings and limbs smudged with suet and blood.

Susheela trembled with fear as the rakshasa relentlessly attacked the vidyadhara. Despite his graceful appearance, the vidyadhara was powerful and fought back valiantly. The rakshasa struck him with his trident, shattering the vidyadhara's chest. With an adamantine fist, the vidyadhara struck the rakshasa, killing him. However, the vidyadhara was crippled by the trident's blow.

His eyes rolling, the vidyadhara spoke in a faltering voice, 'Sush, my beloved, you have been brought here in vain.' Choking on these words, the Vidyadhara died, his final thoughts immersed in loving remembrance of Susheela.

Susheela, moved deeply by his valour and devotion, considered the vidyadhara to be her husband and consigned her body to the fire of grief. So great was her character, that simply through dying in her proximity, the rakshasa attained a divine embodiment and entered Swarga. The vidyadhara was reborn as the son of Malayaketu, and Susheela was reborn as his wife.

Due to samskaras, even in her next life, Susheela, now Kalavati, remained devoted to the worship of lingas. She would always collect and offer sandal powder and *vibhuti*, the holy ash, for worship. Eventually, she gave birth to three sons.

Once, there was a painter from the north who exhibited a canvas painting to King Malayaketu. The king then presented that painting to Kalavati. She was thrilled by the image containing her revered Shiva and kept gazing upon it, entranced. She resembled a *yogini* engrossed in meditation.

She spoke to herself as she beheld the painting, recalling the charming confluence of Varana and Asi near Lolarka. She vividly described to herself the painted site of Manikarnika, recollecting the glories of the tirtha and pointing out to herself the place where Harishchandra had sold himself. Her gaze then turned to the Kulastambha, the unwavering pillar, where Kaala Bhairava punishes those who deserve punishment. She noted that while a sin committed elsewhere may perish on seeing Kashi, transgressions committed in Kashi warrant extreme penalties and torture as a deterrent.

Her attention shifted to Kapalamochana, where one of Brahma's five skulls had fallen from the hand of Kaala Bhairava. She then looked at the image of the Rnamochana Tirtha, which radiated sanctity and purity. Bathing in its waters absolves one from the three karmic debts to the Devas, the rishis, and the pitrs. She then observed Omkareshvara where the Pranava shines eternally in the five abodes of A, U, Ma, Nada, and Bindu.

She beheld the Matsyodari river, which at that time, was a small tributary of the Varana flowing by the Omkareshvara Mandir.

She gazed upon Kameshvara, the fulfiller of the desires of the virtuous ones at whose shrine even Durvasa found fulfilment. She looked upon Skandeshvara, Vinayakeshvara, and the Parvatishvara Linga, where Shiva eternally abides with Parvati, bestowing liberation upon devotees. Bhrngishvara also met her sight, where Bhrngi attained liberation.

She looked upon Chaturvedeshvara, the guardian of the four Vedas; Yajneshvara; and Puraneshvara, eighteen *angulas* (finger's breadth) long and wide, worshiping whom a devotee shall become the receptacle of the eighteen vidyas. There was Dharmashastreshvara installed by the Smrtis themselves. The Sarasvata Linga, bearing the power to dispel sluggishness and ignorance, was also present along with the Sarvatirtheshvara Linga, which bestows instant purity. She looked upon the Shaileshvara Linga, adorned with the splendour of all varieties of jewels. Her attention then shifted to the Saptasagara, where one's visit yields the merit of a sanctifying dip in the seven seas.

Next, her eyes fell upon Mantreshvara, who bestows the benefit of reciting mantras. In the Krta Yuga, this linga was installed by the seven crores of great mantras themselves. She observed the kunda in front of Tripuresha Linga, which had been dug by the Tripura, the three cities, in ancient times—a site cherished by Shiva. She looked at Baneshvara Linga, worshipped by Bana of a thousand arms who attained nine hundred and ninety-eight arms through devotion to that linga. She looked upon Vairochaneshvara in front of Prahladakeshava. She turned to Adityakeshava to the east of Adikeshava, Bhismakeshava, and Dattatreyeshvara. To the east of Dattatreyeshvara stood Adigadadhara. She looked upon Bhrgukeshava and Vamanakeshava. She recognized Yajnavarahakeshava, Vidaranarasimha, the renowned Gopigovinda, and the palace of Lakshmi-Narasimha. She saw Kharvavinayaka, who bestows great spiritual powers upon devotees and Sheshamadhava, originally consecrated by Shesha. Alongside, stood Shankhamadhava, who took residence here after killing Shankha. She gazed upon the convergence of the Sarasvati and Ganga rivers.

She looked upon Bindu Madhava, the great form of Vishnu. It is said that the one who venerates Bindu Madhava with unwavering faith will be free from rebirth and poverty. Even Yama Deva bows down to Bindu Madhava. The essence of the Pranava is represented by Bindu Madhava assuming the form of Nada and Bindu. He is the unembodied Brahman.

She looked upon Mangala Gauri, the one who bestows auspiciousness here and in the hereafter. She looked at Mayukhaditya, the sun with garlands of rays that dispel the darkness. She looked upon the Gabhastisha Linga that bestows divine radiance. The son of Mrkandu had performed rigorous penance at that spot. And there Markandeya had enshrined a great linga, which thenceforth was named after him, granting longevity to devotees.

She beheld the Kiraneshvara Linga, famed in all the three worlds, believed to bestow the boon of guiding one to the abode of the sun, Kiranamalin, with just a single bow. She observed the Dhutapapeshvara Linga that purifies all sins. Nirvananarasimha, the bestower of Nirvana upon devotees; and Manipradipanaga, adorned with great jewels, the linga that guards against serpent attacks—all these were seen by her in that painting.

Her eyes fell upon Kapilesha Linga, consecrated by Kapila. Even monkeys attain liberation after visiting this linga once. She perceived the Priyavrateshvara Linga radiantly shining, worshiping which a creature attains the love and favour of all creatures. Her gaze turned to Kaalaraja, the abode constructed with rubies and other jewels. She gazed upon the Mandakini, who had come here to perform penance. She saw the Ratneshvara Linga, which had become the crest-jewel of the myriad jewels present in Kashi.

Her eyes stopped to scrutinize the lofty mansion of Krttivaseshvara. Of all the lingas, Krttivasas is the head, hailed as one of the most ancient lingas in Kashi. With Krttivaseshvara as the head, Omkaresha is known as the tuft of hair; Trilochana as the three eyes; Gokarna and Bharabhutesha as the two ears. Vishveshvara and Avimukteshvara are the two right hands. Dharmesha and Manikarnesha are the two left hands. The two feet are Kaleshvara and Kapardisha. Jyestheshvara is the waist, and Madhyameshvara is the navel. Mahadeva is the matted hairs; Shrutishvara is the crest-jewel; Chandresha is the heart. The Atman is the great Vireshvara. Kedara is the linga and Shukreshvara is the semen. Millions and billions of other lingas should be considered as the nails, hairs, and the ornaments of this body.

Among all these lingas, it is the two right hands, Vishveshvara and Avimukta, which perpetually bestow enlightenment on all creatures after granting them freedom from fear. Here, too, we see the unparalleled significance of Vishveshvara/Vishvanatha and the special relationship this manifestation of Shiva shares with Avimukteshvara, which we will delve into in greater depth in Chapter 23.

Her gaze shifted to Durga and the great Pitr Linga, Chitraghanteshi, Ghantakarna, Lalitagauri, Vishalakshi, Ashtavinayaka, Dharmakupa, Vishvabhuja Devi, and Bandi Devi. She observed the Dashashvamedhika Tirtha, where simply by offering three *ahutis* one can attain the benefit of maintaining Agnihotra.

She looked upon Manikarnika. Surrounding it were so many tirthas that no space the size of a sesame seed remained vacant. It is said that twenty-seven generations of ancestors are liberated by one who offers *pitr tarpana* in Manikarnika.

Finally, to the south of Vishveshvara, Kalavati spotted Gyaanavapi, its waters guarded against evil by Dandapani, Sambhrama, and Vibhrama. Gyaanavapi is the aquatic physical manifestation of the eight-formed Shiva. After seeing Gyaanavapi, Kalavati's entire body trembled like the flowers of the kadamba tree. She became impervious to everything around her and lost consciousness.

Kalavati's attendants grew concerned at the sight of her senseless body. Some surmised that she must have seen the object of her love from a previous life. They speculated that as the reason behind her sudden unconsciousness. They tried to revive her through various methods, including fanning her and sprinkling flower petals on her body.

One of her attendants, Buddhi-sharirini—her name literally meaning the embodiment of intellect—observed with distress their treatment of Kalavati. She instructed them to immediately place the painted canvas in front of her, asserting that its touch would revive her.

The attendants heeded her wisdom and followed her instructions.

'Look here, Kalavati. Your beloved deity is depicted here.'

At the mention of her 'beloved deity', Kalavati regained consciousness. She touched the image of Gyaanavapi on the canvas. Through that simple touch, she acquired knowledge of her previous birth and all that had transpired.

Contemplating the remarkable greatness of Gyaanavapi, she shared her past life as Susheela with her attendants. Delighted by her story, the attendants bowed down to her in reverence. They became eager to visit Gyaanavapi and personally experience the power she had described.

They asked, 'How can we attain Gyaanavapi with the powers you describe? Those of us who have not seen Gyaanavapi lead a futile existence! From this day onward, this shall be our primary sadhana—to experience for ourselves the glories of Gyaanavapi and the immense joy you have described feeling there. It must truly live up to its name. After all, the mere sight of it painted on a canvas granted you insight into your past life!'

Kalavati was pleased by their enthusiasm and words. She embraced the idea of visiting Gyaanavapi again. Being a spiritually attained woman, she composed her emotions and approached her husband, the king, with the proposal of visiting Gyaanavapi.

She spoke sweetly, 'O, lord of my life! Nowhere do I find anything more pleasing than you. Having you as my husband, O king, has bestowed upon me everything desirable. I have a humble request, my dear. Pondering over it, I am certain that it will be conducive to your welfare as well. If my being alive serves any purpose then grant me my desire. Otherwise, I will cease to live.'

The king replied tenderly, 'O my beloved beautiful lady, I do not see anything that cannot be given to you. Even my vital breaths belong to you by virtue of your noble qualities and skills in the arts. Do not delay any further. Reveal to me your desire and it shall be carried out. Nothing is unattainable for a chaste lady like you. My dear wife, our relationship is not an ordinary one. This entire realm, the treasury, the vast army, the fort, and everything else is yours to command. O, goddess of my life, the kingdom is but a blade of grass to me that I shall cast off in an instant, if you so desire.'

Kalavati was moved and responded solemnly, 'A life bereft of the Purushartha, the four pursuits of human life, is futile. Those acquainted with the ancient traditions have affirmed that the aims of life are fulfilled through the bond of affection between a husband and wife. O, my beloved, all that you possess is a blessing from Vishveshvara. Send me immediately to Vishvanatha. My vital breaths have already departed.'

The king contemplated this for a moment. 'My dear Kalavati, if you leave, what purpose does this royal glory serve? A beloved queen is the glory of the kingdom. This kingdom remains unthreatened by enemies. After relishing years of pleasure, our senses have been sated. We are content. We have had children. There is nothing further to accomplish here. Both of us shall certainly go to Kashi.'

He summoned *jyotishas* and honoured representatives of his subjects to seek their guidance. He entrusted the kingdom to his son.

Upon arriving in Kashi, the king trembled in bliss and Queen Kalavati recognized the various lanes of the city from her past life. They immersed themselves in the waters of Manikarnika and offered their wealth as gifts to Vishveshvara, including jewels, elephants, horses, cows, silken clothes, and utensils. After circumambulating the shrine, the king entered the Mukti Mandapa and listened to discourses there. After performing the evening puja, he remained awake the entire night, festively celebrating with instrumental music.

The next morning, guided by his wife, he walked along the path to Gyaanavapi. He and Kalavati bathed there and extended alms to the needy. Kalavati renovated the Gyaanavapi well with steps paved with jewels. Together, they devoted the remainder of their lives to austere living at this sacred place. Sometimes she would take a meal only once in every six days or once every two weeks. Occasionally, she observed month-long fasts. She performed the Chandrayana and Krcchra rites, too.

Once, following their morning bath in Gyaanavapi, as they rested, someone with matted hair came and offered them *vibhuti* (holy ash). He blessed them with a beaming face and instructed them to arise as they would be receiving the Taraka mantra momentarily.

As he spoke these words, a vimana with jingling bells descended. The moon-crested Shiva stepped down from the chariot and softly whispered the secret mantra transcending all words into their ears. The vimana ascended swiftly, casting a luminous trail across the sky as Shiva returned to his abode, accompanied by Kalavati and her husband.

Skanda concluded, 'Ever since, Gyaanavapi is considered unique and superior to all important holy tirthas. O sage, it is the bestower of direct knowledge. It is excellent, full of perfect knowledge, identical with all lingas. Gyaanavapi is the cosmic form of Shiva himself. It generates *gyaana*, perfect knowledge. There are many tirthas that sanctify devotees immediately. But they are not equal to even one-sixteenth of Gyaanavapi. If anyone listens to the origin of Gyaanavapi with great attention, his knowledge does not become extinct even upon death. This great narrative is meritorious. It is destructive of great sins. It increases the delight of Mahadeva and Gauri. By reading or causing to be read or listening to the auspicious narration of Gyaanavapi, one is honoured in the world of Shiva.'

Agastya Muni was elated by Skanda's recounting of the magnificence of Gyaanavapi.

He remarked, 'O delighter of Gauri's heart, after hearing this profound account of Gyaanavapi, I cannot help but reflect that despite Gyaanavapi's negligible size in the middle of Kashi, it is the most honoured tirtha. In its conduciveness to moksha and the fulfilment of one's desires, it never fails. How many holy places exist on this earth? Yet, can any truly compare to even a miniscule portion of Kashi? How many rivers in this world flow into the sea? Yet, which river can be as holy as the Ganga at Kashi? O Six-faced One, how many kshetras can grant moksha on earth? But none contain even a ten-millionth of the power of Avimukta in them. Is there any wonder that the glory of liberation is achieved where Ganga, Vishveshvara, and Kashi awaken and unite?'

We see in this couple's story the sublime bond between a devoted husband and a virtuous wife; they consult each other before making joint decisions, and as a good king, he ensures that the kingdom will be well-provided for and governed properly in his absence before leaving for Kashi. The power of Gyaanavapi is such that just the touch of the image from the canvas is enough to awaken the queen's memories of her past life. From these passages in the Kashi Khanda, we can see how exalted the status of Gyaanavapi has been since ancient times and the irony of the Gyanvapi Mosque appropriating its name.

CHAPTER 7

Separation of Shiva from Kashi

Avimukteshvara

Avimukta is the site of the Avimukteshvara Linga. Relying on the authority of the *Linga Purana*, Lakshmidhara pinpoints the location of Avimukta to the north of Gyaanavapi, where the mosque stands today and Vishveshvara stood previously (Tagare 1950, Chapter 39). According to the Kashi Khanda of the *Skanda Purana* and local tradition, Avimukteshvara is the guru of Vishveshvara as Vishveshvara had previously worshipped Avimukteshvara. A trace of the Avimukteshvara Linga remains, it is said, on the northern side of the Gyanvapi Mosque. It is said to be hidden among three Muslim graves. Devotees are said to be given access to sprinkle flowers on the Linga fragments every Magha Shivaratri, the significance of which is explained below.

Turning back to the Kashi Khanda, Skanda then narrated the glories of Avimukta to Agastya Muni, proclaiming it to be the means of attaining moksha. He described how Shiva grants liberation to beings at Avimukta. In other places, beings must practice *yoga*, partake in *dana*, or undergo *tapasya*. However, in Kashi, Shiva bestows mukti freely without the need of such external aid.

Skanda narrated the story of Divodasa, which begins in Avimukta. During the Svayambhuva Manvantara, the epoch of Padma Kalpa, when the universe was conceived and brought forth within the navel lotus of Vishnu, a prolonged drought plagued all the worlds and living beings. This drought lasted for sixty years.

The earth transformed into a desolate wilderness and cannibalism became widespread. Many resorted to thievery. To endure the scarcity of resources, everyone turned carnivorous. As the population dwindled, yajna and other offerings decreased in number. Consequently, the powers of the Devas, reliant on these offerings, was also depleted. Brahma was deeply concerned.

One day, Brahma saw the virtuous king, Ripunjaya, who was engaged in penance at Avimukta. Brahma approached him with a request to protect the earth with all its oceans, mountains, and forests. In return, Brahma pledged that Vasuki, the sovereign of the nagas, would bestow upon him Anangamohini, a virtuous naga maiden, as his bride. He would become known as Divodasa, the recipient of divine favours from the pleased Devas.

The king propitiated Brahma and then insisted, 'If I am to be lord of the earth, O Grandfather of the worlds, let the Devas return to their celestial realm. With the Devas in Devaloka and me in the mortal plane, the subjects will thrive under my reign as my kingdom will be without rival.'

Brahma consented.

Beating upon war drums, Divodasa proclaimed, 'Let the Devas return to Swarga. Let not the nagas tread here. Let my kingdom be peaceful and calm. As I govern Earth, let the celestial beings remain within their own domains.'

In the meantime, Brahma proceeded to Vishveshvara. Before Brahma could speak, Shiva urged that they proceed to Mount Mandara as the mountain was performing a rather difficult penance and Shiva was inclined to grant him a boon.

Shiva mounted Nandi, and, accompanied by Brahma, visited Mandara. When offered a boon, Mandara sought to become the equal of the Avimukta Kshetra. He asked that Shiva and Parvati reside on his head.

As Shiva reflected on this, Brahma recounted to him his encounter with Divodasa and the condition that the king had placed upon him. Brahma implored Shiva to maintain the veracity of his words and grant Mandara his heart's desire. In other words, he requested Shiva and Parvati to renounce Kashi and reside on Mandara.

Compassionately resolved to uphold the word of Brahma, Shiva acquiesced. So it was that for a long period of time just as Kashi bestows mukti in Jambudvipa, so also did Mandara in Kushadvipa.

Before departing for Mandara, Shiva consecrated his own linga, representing one of his cosmic forms, in order to bestow all powers and blessings, all glories, and all protection to those who live and die in Avimukta. He kept this a secret from Brahma. Consequently, Avimukta was never truly abandoned by Shiva, although he went away to Mandara. For this it is known as Avimukta.

Skanda explained that Avimukta used to be known as Anandavana, the forest of bliss, but since that time it became well-known as Avimukta. He also explained that while all adore Vishveshvara, Vishveshvara himself worships Avimukteshvara. This was the first linga. No linga existed before Avimukteshvara, nor did the world know what a linga was prior to the existence of Avimukteshvara. Only after having darshana of Avimukta were Brahma, Vishnu, and others able to install lingas.

For this reason, the great Avimukteshvara Linga is hailed as the primordial linga. Simply hearing its name rids a mortal of all sins acquired throughout his lifetime. Remembering the Avimukteshvara Linga instantly rids one of the sins committed in two lifetimes. By visiting the Avimukteshvara Linga, one discards the sins of three lifetimes and becomes meritorious. By touching the Avimukteshvara Linga, the sins from five lifetimes are destroyed. Devotion to the Avimukteshvara Linga begets blessings and contentment. One will never be born again. One who praises, prostrates to, and adores the Avimukteshvara Linga according to his or her own intellect and capabilities will himself become praised, prostrated to, and adored.

This linga is adored by Vishveshvara himself. On the fourteenth day of the dark half of Magha, known as Magha Shivaratri, all other lingas from the many holy locations converge to pay homage to Avimukteshvara Linga. On this day, all the lingas of all the different holy sites serve Avimukteshvara. If one holds vigil before Avimukteshvara on this night, then one attains the powers of a yogi who never sleeps.

Skanda concluded, 'Those who have not seen the excellent Avimukteshvara Linga in Avimukta, presided over by Vishveshvara, are deluded. On seeing from afar a person who has visited Avimukta, Yama Deva bows to him.'

As described in greater detail later in the book, particularly in Chapter 23, Avimukteshvara, the first of the lingas, was once perhaps the most important linga in Kashi, eclipsing even Vishveshvara in glory. Over time, through repeated cycles of destruction, its prominence declined and was replaced by Vishveshvara. Now most Hindus do not even have access to the fragments of the original Avimukteshvara Linga believed to be within the Gyanvapi Mosque compound.

Shiva's Longing for Kashi

Moved by the story of Shiva's separation from Kashi and recalling his own exile from his beloved Kashi, Agastya Muni asked Skanda how Shiva reclaimed Kashi from Divodasa.

Skanda resumed the story. When Shiva departed for Mandara, all the other Devas also accompanied him. Their departure from their respective abodes on Earth allowed Divodasa to govern the world unimpeded. Choosing Kashi as his capital, he protected his subjects. He was a great king, impressing even the Devas. He surpassed the excellence of all classes of beings—he was superior to the Vasus in wealth; assuming the form of the planets, he prevented them from turning malignant; he outshone the Ashvin twins in handsomeness; he was the most learned among the vidyadharas; his singing robbed the gandharvas of all their pride. In his court, his scholars won all debates on shastras. In the battlefields, his warriors remained unconquered.

It is worth noting in this context the special relationship between the Devas and the mortals. The Devas were not jealous or covetous of ruling over and residing on the earthly plane. They did not lord their power over the mortals but instead calmly complied with the wishes of Divodasa to reign over Earth unimpeded and without the presence of the Devas. This shows that the Devas are not greedy for power or to be acknowledged by us. Rather, they will appear when we welcome and invite their presence; otherwise, they are fine to leave us to our own devices in recognition of our own free will even when it is not in our best interests to do so.

In the meantime, Shiva began to yearn for Kashi. He rubbed sandalwood paste all over his body to soothe the pain of separation. The sandalwood turned to ash on his skin. The cool moon that had once been lifted out of the Ksheera Sagara, the Ocean of Milk, withered due to the waves of heat radiating out of Shiva's head, scorched by the fire of separation. Yet, Shiva's impeccable self-control concealed his inner turmoil from others.

Only Parvati discerned Shiva's emotional state. Again, we should understand this in the spirit of the divine leela that Shiva was exhibiting this bhava to bring glory to his abode of Kashi and help mortals understand the greatness of Kashi and the importance of honouring Kashi. It is not that Ishvara is subject to feelings of loss or depression in the conventional sense.

Parvati addressed him gently, suggesting they visit Kashi, the city that she described as being the lotus held on his trident at the time of the great deluge. She said that even the Himalayas, the abode of her father, the Lord of the Mountains, did not delight her nearly as much as Kashi, which was not part of Earth although it stood on the earth. She, too, missed Kashi.

Shiva found solace in her words. He explained that the predicament lay in King Divodasa's virtues and benevolence towards his subjects. Therefore, displacing him from Kashi would be inappropriate, especially as that would involve revoking Brahma's word. As the king was so virtuous, he would not be afflicted by old age or death.

While conversing with Parvati, Shiva noticed a group of yoginis of great maturity and attainment clustered nearby, easily capable of accomplishing difficult tasks. He beckoned them forth and urged them to hasten to Kashi to ascertain whether the king would be susceptible to being dislodged from Kashi by their yogic powers.

The yoginis accepted his command with bowed heads and departed for Kashi.

CHAPTER 8

Origin Stories of Various Sacred Sites and Deities in Kashi

Sixty-Four Yoginis

The yoginis were delighted. They travelled faster than thought, moving through the skies, whispering to each other. They rejoiced at having darshana of Shiva and also having the opportunity to visit Kashi.

Soon, the sixty-four yoginis arrived at Kashi. They concealed their divinity. Some assumed the form of female ascetics garbed in red. One donned the disguise of the wife of a gardener; another, someone adept in medicine; yet another, a beautiful midwife. One took the form of a snake charmer and another the guise of a female merchant. One appeared as a specialist in the art of seduction, and another a maker of pearl necklaces. One was expert in creating fragrances; another specialized in the game of dice; another was a conversationalist; and another was a Chatvaracharini, a mendicant woman roaming in quadrangles. One was a ropewalker, another a prankster; another clothed herself with rags picked from the roadside; one lived in the city as one capable of blessing the childless with children; another was an expert palmist. One yogini captivated audiences through her skill in drawing, another bestowed supernatural powers through pills; one was able to bestow *anjana siddhi* (the ability to view great treasures) through the use of kohl;

another was an alchemist; another bestowed *paduka siddhi*, the ability to transport to a desired place by touching one's sandals. One of them taught the art of *agnistambha* (stopping fire), *jalastambha* (stopping the flow of water), and *vakstambha* (stopping the power of speech); another offered the power of *khecharitva* (the ability to walk in the sky); and another offered the power of being invisible.

One offered the *akarshini siddhi* (the power to attract a desired woman or man); another offered *ucchatana* (disturbing stable individuals); a certain one used the beauty of her limbs to ensnare the minds of young men. One could bestow anything one thought of; another was an expert astrologer.

In this way, the yoginis assumed many various disguises, entered every house, and pervaded the entire city. For a year, they roamed the city ceaselessly. Their intent was to sow confusion in the mind of the king, but they found no vulnerability to exploit in him. They pooled their insights and strategized, but to no avail. Unable to accomplish their mission, they never returned to Mandara. They could not face Shiva. How could they go back to Shiva, having been entrusted with a task that they could not carry out when they had not even been wounded or killed?

They deliberated further and thought that perhaps they could live without Shiva, but they could never abandon Kashi. Since then, the sixty-four yoginis have never left Kashi, although they are free to wander through all the three worlds. Enveloped by an indescribable Maya, they can still be found in Kashi today.

At one time, there may have been or likely were separate temples for each of the sixty-four yoginis. Today, however, there is only one Chaumsathi Devi Temple remaining in Kashi, high above the Chaumsathi Ghat (Tagare 1950, Chapter 45).

The Twelve Temples of Aditya in Kashi

Now unfolds the account of the twelve Aditya temples in Kashi, dedicated to Surya Deva. The most prominent of these is Lolarka.

When the yoginis failed to return, Shiva sent Surya Deva after them to ascertain their fate. Shiva urged Surya Deva, too, to try to dissuade Divodasa from remaining in Kashi. But Shiva warned him, 'Do not underestimate that king. If one insults or disrespects one who is walking the path of piety, it will surely backfire and result in one's own suffering. It is a great sin to do so. If through your influence he swerves from the path of virtue, O seven-horsed One, you can devastate the city with your fierce rays. You, the eye of the universe, witness the deeds of all creatures. Proceed, then, to accomplish this task.'

Assuming a form capable of traversing the skies day and night, Surya Deva advanced towards Kashi, eager to reach that sacred city. After entering Kashi, in the form of the sun, he moved both within and without Kashi's confines. At times, he took the guise of a guest seeking something elusive, or a beggar, or a bestower of abundance. Sometimes he appeared wretched; sometimes an astrologer; sometimes a performer of rites beyond the pale of the Vedas. At times, he established the philosophy of the materialists. Sometimes he appeared with matted hair and sometimes he appeared as a nude mendicant; sometimes he was a snake doctor and an expert in antidotes against poisons. Sometimes he played the role of an expert in heretical doctrines and at others, a Vedantin. Sometimes he was a juggler and at other times he incited virtuous women with advice on various vows and observances. An entire year passed, but Surya Deva could not find a chink in King Divodasa's armour of virtue, nor a single vulnerability in the people of the kingdom.

He chastised himself for his failure and pledged to abide in Kashi forever, establishing his hermitage there. This was the only way he could think to redeem himself.

Surya Deva divided himself into twelve entities and manifested his presence throughout Kashi. The twelve Adityas to be found in Kashi are (i) Lolarka (ii) Uttararka (iii) Shambaditya (iv) Draupadaditya (v) Mayukhaditya (vi) Khakholka (vii) Arunaditya (viii) Vrddhaditya (ix) Keshavaditya (x) Vimaladitya (xi) Gangaditya and (xii) Yamaditya. These twelve Adityas protect Kashi from tamasic influences.

Lolarka

Surya Deva's intense eagerness (*lola*) to behold Kashi earned him the moniker 'Lolarka'. Lolarka is established in the southern part of Kashi, at the confluence of the Asi and Ganga rivers. In this form, Surya Deva makes the inhabitants of Kashi achieve and preserve the good.

It is said that whatever sacred rite is performed at Lolarka—like dana, homa, and archana offered to the Devas—such rite is capable of providing never-ending benefits. Those who visit Lolarka on Sundays or take the water of Lolarka will never have misery or skin disease. It is said that Lolarka holds the paramount position among all the holy tirthas in Kashi; the others are subsidiary as they are watered by its holy waters.

Uttararka

The site of Uttararka Kunda lies near Bakaria Kunda. The original temple was destroyed and its ruins transformed into Islamic structures. M.A. Sherring uncovered a Sun disc with relief carvings at this location, thus confirming the ancient site of Surya Deva (Tagare 1950, Chapter 47).

Skanda described to Agastya Muni that the excellent holy pool, or *kunda*, is situated in the northern side of Kashi named Arka, thus becoming known as Uttararka. Uttararka scorches and dispels the clusters of miseries that otherwise would plague the inhabitants of Kashi. With his rays, Surya Deva makes good people flourish. It is said that Uttararka, the Sun of great splendour, ever protects Kashi.

Once, a Brahmana named Priyavrata resided in Kashi. He was born in the lineage of Atri. Priyavrata demonstrated unwavering devotion to guests and invested himself in only splendid endeavours. His wife, Shubhavrata, was extraordinarily charming.

They bore a daughter who possessed both beauty and modesty. They named her Sulakshana. As she matured, her father pondered over who would be a worthy match for her. His anxiety resulted in him becoming afflicted with a terrible fever that could not be treated with medicine. He eventually succumbed to this fever and his wife followed him in death, leaving behind their orphaned daughter. This shows the danger of allowing oneself to be overcome with unnecessary worry and tension; then the very thing we fear the most happens.

Sulakshana was engulfed in sorrow at the loss of her parents. Soon after the funeral rites were completed, she was approached by many young men for marriage. Yet, she did not allow anyone access to her inner thoughts and had no interest in marriage. She resolved to perform severe penance, maintaining unwavering celibacy in close proximity to Surya Deva in his embodiment as Uttararka.

She conquered her senses and steadied her mind. During her penance, a small kid goat would come and stand placidly before her, every day. In the evening, the baby goat would eat some grass and drink the water from the pool then return home.

Several years transpired in this manner. On one occasion, Shiva and Parvati arrived there in the course of their wanderings. They watched Sulakshana performing penance, steady as a stone pillar. Parvati, moved by pity, asked Shiva to bless this orphaned girl.

Sulakshana sat, with her eyes closed, in meditation.

Shiva spoke to her. 'O, Sulakshana! Your penance has pleased me. O maiden of admirable vows, choose your boon.'

She opened her eyes and bowed down to Shiva and Parvati, overcome by their grace. As she contemplated over which boon to choose, she saw the young goat before her.

She spoke. 'Who in this world does not live for his own sake? He who lives for others truly lives. For many years, I have been attended to by this small goat. If a boon is to be given to me, then may this kid goat be blessed. She has the same absolute devotion to me as I do to you but cannot speak of it for she is an animal.'

Shiva was extremely pleased. He said to Parvati, 'The intellect of noble individuals is like this—all the more powerful as a result of helping others. Those who endeavour to help others with sincerity are the blessed ones. Worldly objects do not last long, my beloved, but rendering help to others lasts for a long time. Devi, tell me, what boon shall be given to this blessed Sulakshana? And what boon shall be granted to the kid goat?'

Parvati said, 'May Sulakshana become one of my companions. For her lifelong celibacy, she shall hold a special place in my affection. May she continue to inhabit her current form, with divine limbs and adorned with ornaments, attires, fragrance, and knowledge. Let her be near me forever, holding the moving chowries (a yak-tailed whisk for fanning). As for the young goat, may she be born as the princess of the king of Kashi. After enjoying her life in Kashi, she will attain mukti. May she emerge as a princess of exceptional vision, due to the merit accrued by bathing in Arkakunda on the Sundays of the Pushya month [mid-December–mid-January] before sunrise, despite the cold."

Shiva granted these boons.

Parvati concluded, 'In recognition of the profound penance performed by this young goat, let this Arkakunda also be known as Barkari Kunda, given the great penance practised by the kid goat. The annual pilgrimage of Uttararka shall be performed on a Sunday in the month of Pushya by devotees desiring the benefits of Kashi.'

There exists speculation that the name Bakaria Kunda might suggest Islamic influence, and that these could have been subsequent additions to the lore of Kashi to explain the secondary nomenclature. Such is the essence of Sthala Purana—to evolve and adapt in response to the flow of history, ensuring the tradition remains vibrant and dynamic.

It is believed that by absorbing the tales of Lolarka and Uttararka, one would be safeguarded from disease and poverty.

Shambaditya
Today, the Shambaditya shrine is situated near the Surya Kunda. The remnants of the temple's foundation suggest its former grandeur.

Two sun discs beneath a tree, amidst the ruins, bear witness to what must have once been an ancient impressive temple (Tagare 1950, Chapter 48).

Skanda proceeded to recount to Agastya Muni the history of Shambaditya. Once, Narada visited Sri Krishna in Dwaraka. While the Vrshnis humbly bowed to Narada, Sri Krishna and Jambavati's son, Shamba, refrained from bowing to the great rishi.

Narada, angered by Shamba's arrogance, resolved to retaliate against him. One day, he tricked Shamba into entering the inner chambers of Sri Krishna where he was spending time with his wives. Longing for their husband, the women were stirred with desire. Narada accused Shamba of intruding upon Sri Krishna and his wives, interrupting their time together, and trying to seduce them with his handsomeness and charm.

In reality, Shamba looked upon every woman as his own mother. Yet, fate could not be averted.

Sri Krishna cursed Shamba with leprosy. Realizing the truth shortly after, Sri Krishna directed his son to go to the city of Vishveshvara for a cure. He told Shamba that by propitiating Surya Deva, he would regain his health.

Meanwhile, Narada Muni, having accomplished his task, departed from Dwaraka and returned to his abode. Shamba left for Kashi, appeased Surya Deva, regained his health, and returned to Dwaraka.

Ever since that time, Shambaditya has become the dispeller of all ailments. It is believed that bathing in the waters of Shambakunda at dawn on a Sunday safeguards against disease. Skanda told Agastya Muni that by circumambulating this deity of Surya Deva in the western quarter of Vishveshvara eight times, one is freed of sins and attains the benefit of staying in Kashi.

Draupaditya

Presently, Draupaditya is to the west of the Kashi Vishwanath Temple, under a tree.

During the narration of the *Skanda Purana*, Suta said to Vyasa, 'O Sage Vyasa, descendant of Parashara Muni, at the time Skanda recounted this tale to Agastya Muni, Drupada had no daughter.'

Veda Vyasa replied, 'The Purana Samhita recounts all three aspects of time: past, present, and future. No doubt should be entertained in the matter.'

What this means is that the wisdom of the Puranas is beyond the ken of time, and there is therefore an element of omniscience of past, present, and future in the Puranas.

Skanda's exposition of the twelve Aditya shrines of Kashi continued. He told Agastya Muni that once Shiva divided himself into the five bodies of the Pandavas and Parvati manifested as Draupadi.

Amidst the hardships faced by the Pandavas and Draupadi in the forest, Draupadi visited Kashi, beseeching Surya Deva for blessings upon her five husbands.

Touched by her reverence, Surya Deva gave Draupadi an *akshaya patra*, an inexhaustible vessel and a ladle. Pleased with the purity of her mind and the intensity of her devotion, Surya Deva said, 'O blessed lady, as long as you do not consume food, all those who seek sustenance from you, irrespective of their number or how big their appetite, all of them will be satisfied. This vessel, brimming with cooked food, will become empty only after you have eaten.'

He conferred another boon, proclaiming, 'If a person propitiates me while positioned to the right of Vishveshvara and keeps you [Draupadi] before them, he will never face hunger. Those who revere your deity, the virtuous wife of Yudhishthira, positioned near me in the vicinity of Dandapani to the south of Vishveshvara, will never experience the anguish of separation from their loved ones.'

Mayukhaditya

This shrine is now housed within the Mangala Gauri Temple.

In the past, Surya Deva undertook a rigorous penance at the site of Panchanada in Kurukshetra. There, he installed the Gabhastishvara

Linga and a deity of Mangala Gauri. He worshiped Shiva and Parvati in these forms for a hundred thousand celestial years. His penance intensified his radiance, emitting scorching rays that the other Devas found unbearable. They hesitated to travel across the firmament, fearing incineration by Surya Deva. The sun's rays alone filled the interstellar expanse, evoking fear among all.

Observing the predicament of the Devas and the inhabitants of the universe, Shiva approached Surya Deva, intending to persuade him to temper his fervour. Upon encountering Surya Deva, deeply engrossed in meditation, radiating brilliance, Shiva was wonderstruck by the intensity of his penance.

Shiva asked him to choose a boon. So absorbed was Surya Deva that he could not understand what Shiva was saying. After repeating himself thrice, Shiva realized Surya Deva had become as inert as a log of wood.

He touched Surya Deva, reviving him with nectar. Surya Deva, Vishvalochana, the Eye of the Universe, opened his eyes like blooming lotuses at sunrise. Surya Deva, overcome with bliss, blossomed like drought stricken vegetation after rainfall. He then composed and recited an eight-versed *stotra* in honour of Shiva and another eight-versed stotra in reverence for Mangala Gauri Devi.

Shiva blessed Surya Deva: 'O Mitra, I am pleased. You dwell within my gaze, through which I see the mobile and immobile beings. You are my cosmic form. Be omniscient and omnipresent, the knower of all the activities of everyone. Any man will attain devotion to me by reciting the prayer you composed. The eight verses dedicated to Mangala Gauri will be known as Mangalashtaka. By reciting this stotra, one will attain auspiciousness. Anyone living in exile in far-away lands should recite this thrice a day to purify themselves and attain Kashi. This pair of prayers shall accord the blessing of mukti in Kashi.

'The Linga named Gabhastishvara will yield all siddhis. Let it be forever known as Gabhastishvara, O Sun, as you venerated it through your clusters of rays resembling *champaka* and lotus flowers. Any devotee, man or woman, should worship Mangala Gauri on the third lunar day in the bright half of Chaitra Masa. This entails worshipping the deity, keeping awake all night through dance, bhajans, and spiritual discourse. The next morning, twelve maidens should be honoured and fed. At dawn, one hundred and eight offerings of sesame seeds and ghee shall be made into the fire. A Brahmana couple shall be fed and clothed, accompanied by the recitation of the mantra to please Mangala and Ishvara. Only then should the fast be broken. Adhering to this ritual prevents widowhood and ensures that a man will never become separated from his wife. It shall avert physical unattractiveness, ensuring a maiden shall attain an excellent husband and a bachelor will obtain an excellent wife.'

Shiva concluded, 'During your penance, O son of Aditi, only your rays were visible and not your body. Henceforth, you shall be known as Mayukhaditya.'

After granting these boons, Shiva vanished, while Surya Deva remained humbly standing.

Khakholkaditya
The story of Khakholkaditya originates from the renowned tale of Kadru and Vinata from the Mahabharata. Following a consequential wager, Vinata resolved to cleanse herself of the sin of enslavement by visiting Kashi. On revealing this intention to her son, Garuda, he vowed to accompany her. They both performed severe penance there. Garuda installed Shambhu's linga and Vinata installed Khakolka Aditya.

Shiva and Surya Deva were pleased.

Shiva granted many rare boons to Garuda. 'O Lord of Birds, you will acquire knowledge. All my secrets not known to the Devas will be understood by you. The linga you have installed will become known as Garudeshvara. It will bestow perfect knowledge on devotees. Listen to one thing more, O Lord of Birds. I shall tell you something beneficial. You should not see Vishnu and me as being different from each other."

Saying this, Shiva vanished.

It is important to reiterate this point. Even within Kashi, the worship of Vishnu is paramount just as is the worship of Shiva. Bindu Madhava and many tirthas in Kashi are particularly sacred for Vishnu. The other Devas, too, like Surya Deva, Ganesha, Devi, and others have important temples dedicated to them. This is an inclusive vision of pluralistic worship within the Hindu fold.

Then arrived Surya Deva. He granted Vinata the boon of destroying all of her sins and also bestowed upon her the knowledge of Shiva. Surya Deva obliterated the sins of the residents of Kashi. Thus, he became renowned as Khakholka Aditya, the destroyer of darkness and obstacles in Kashi.

Arunaditya

In the story of Kadru and Vinata, Kadru bore a hundred sons, while Vinata bore three: Uluka, Aruna, and Tarkshya. The eldest Kaushika, Uluka, claimed dominion over the birds. However, since he was bereft of virtues, he was dethroned by the other birds, who decided to live without a king.

Desiring another son, Vinata prematurely broke open an egg, which was supposed to hatch one thousand years later. But Vinata cracked it after eight centuries, delivering a child who had only developed limbs above the thighs. Emerging from the egg, he cursed his mother, the splendour of his face Aruna—red—with rage. He cursed her to become the slave of the children of Kadru, her co-wife.

Trembling with fear, Vinata implored her son, 'O Anuru (thigh-less one), tell me how to end this curse. I am your mother.'

Anuru advised, 'Do not break open the third egg. The one born from it shall redeem you from slavery.'

Anuru then flew to Anandakanana, seeking blessings from Vishveshvara. He was known as Anuru because he had no thighs; he was also known as Aruna because his face had become red from anger. He performed penance at Kashi and propitiated Surya Deva.

Pleased with his devotion, Surya Deva granted boons to him and took on the name of Arunaditya for himself.

He told the son of Vinata, 'O Aruna, stay forever in my chariot in front of me, dispelling the darkness for the welfare of all the worlds. Those who worship the deity of me installed by you will have nothing to fear from anywhere or anyone.'

Thus Anuru/Aruna became the charioteer for Surya Deva.

Vrddhaditya

Once, an old sage named Harita propitiated Surya Deva. When Surya Deva offered him a boon, the sage requested the ability to regain his youth. He did not want this out of vanity, however. He lamented that since he had become old, he was no longer capable of performing penance. By regaining his youth, he would perform wonderful penance.

Harita emphasized his thoughts by saying: 'Penance alone is the greatest virtue. Penance alone is the greatest wealth. Penance alone is the great love. Penance is certainly liberation. Even death is preferable to old age. Death is painful for a moment, but the pain of old age occurs at every moment.'

Surya Deva acquiesced, rejuvenating the old man and granting him vibrant youth. Harita then performed fierce penance in Kashi. As result, this deity of Aditya began to be known as Vrddhaditya, because he had been propitiated by the old sage.

It is said that many have attained supernatural abilities by propitiating Vrddhaditya, the destroyer of old age, wretchedness, and ailments.

Keshavaditya

Surya Deva once witnessed Adi Keshava (Hari) worshiping a Shivalinga. Surya Deva descended from the firmament and watched in amazement as Vishnu completed his worship.

After he was done, Surya Deva asked him why he, Vishnu, worshiped Shiva.

Vishnu stopped Surya Deva with a motion of his hand, as if rejecting the question itself as invalid. Vishnu explained to him the glories of the Shivalinga and the importance of worshiping it. He instructed Surya Deva to also worship the Shivalinga in order to increase his effulgence and glory.

Inspired, Surya Deva established a crystal linga and began worshiping it incessantly. He chose Adi Keshava as his guru and performed his worship of the linga to the north of Adi Keshava under his protective gaze. For this reason, the linga came to be known as Keshavaditya.

On the Rathasaptami day, the seventh day of the bright half of Magha, coinciding with a Sunday, a devotee should bathe in the waters of the Padodaka Tirtha in front of Adi Keshava and silently worship Keshavaditya. Instantly, he will be free of the sins incurred in the course of seven births.

Vimaladitya

In the mountainous Uccha Desha, there once lived a Kshatriya named Vimala who suffered from leprosy due to past-life karma. Forsaking his home, family, and wealth, he came to Kashi and worshipped Surya Deva with wonderful flowers and exquisite offerings.

Surya Deva promised to remove his leprosy and offered him another boon. Vimala requested that there be no leprosy in the whole family of those who remained steadfastly devoted to Surya Deva, that such a family not face any other ailments or poverty, and that no distress ever come to his devotees.

Surya Deva agreed. He further promised to always remain near the deity worshiped by Vimala and named it after him. Vimala then returned home.

Gangaditya

Gangaditya stands to the south of Vishveshvara. One attains purity merely by having darshana of this deity. When Ganga Devi arrived in Kashi, Surya Deva stationed himself there to eulogize and worship her. To this day, Surya Deva faces Ganga Devi night and day and constantly reveres her, delighted by the sight of her.

Yamaditya

Yama Deva performed penance in Yama Tirtha and installed the Yamesha Linga and the Yamaditya deity. Both bestow supernatural powers. Yamaditya alleviates the torments linked to Yama Deva. One is absolved of the karmic debt owed to one's pitrs by offering rice balls in Yama Tirtha on the fourteenth lunar day, on a Tuesday, in the presence of Bharani Nakshatra.

Skanda thus concluded the account of the twelve Aditya deities in Kashi. He explained that many other Adityas have been installed in Kashi by various devotees of Surya Deva, like Guyakarka.

Dashashvamedha Ghat

Meanwhile, back at Mandara, Shiva awaited word from the yoginis and Surya Deva. He eventually invited Brahma to visit, expressing his reluctance to attack Divodasa, who was abiding by Dharma. Shiva sent Brahma to see what, if anything, could be done.

Riding a white swan, Brahma, departed for Kashi. He took on the form of an aged Brahmana and visited the king. The king honoured him and asked after the purpose of his visit.

Disguised as the Brahmana, Brahma said, 'O King, I am an aged person staying here for a long time. You may not know me, but I recognize you as Ripunjaya from your previous birth. Many monarchs have crossed my path, yet your exceptional qualities stand out: you consider your subjects as members of your family; you consider Brahmanas as your deity; and you have performed great austerities. Afraid of you, even the Devas do not dare go astray. Now to the matter at hand, O King, I wish to perform a sacrifice and seek your help.'

The king replied graciously, 'O Brahmana, I have grasped your words in my heart. I am at your service. Take what you need from my treasury. Consider your desires fulfilled. Selflessness guides my reign. My entire family and I are at the service of others. The sole duty of kings is to safeguard their subjects. This duty is more important than the performance of sacrificial rites and pilgrimage to tirthas. The fire arising from the suffering of subjects is more devastating than the thunderbolt, wrecking the kingdom, family, and the physical body of the king.'

Brahma was moved by these words. With the king's patronage, Brahma performed a sacrifice of ten great horses in Kashi. These were conducted at the tirtha then known as Rudrasarovar. Due to Brahma's ten sacrifices, it became known as Dashashvamedha. Brahma's presence in Kashi has endured ever since. Sukul, however, claims that Dashashvamedha Ghat has been so named to represent the set of ten Ashvamedha sacrifices conducted by the Bharashivas rulers, not those attributed to Brahma, the site of which is marked by the Ahilyabai Ghat on the banks of which Brahma's yajnas were performed (Sukul 1974, 271).

The Ganas

Subsequently, Shiva dispatched his ganas to Kashi one by one. None returned or reported back to Shiva, nor were they able to disturb Divodasa's rule. While in Kashi, each gana also established lingas.

Pingala established Pingalakhyesha to the north of Kapardisha. Veerabhadra, the great favourite of Shiva, established the Veerabhadreshvara Linga behind Avimukteshvara. A visit to it confers heroic powers. Worshiping this linga ensures victory and wards off obstacles and defeat. By worshiping Veerabhadra accompanied by his auspicious and splendid consort, Bhadrakali, one obtains the benefit of residing in Kashi.

Keerata established the Keeratesha Linga to the south of Kedara. It bestows freedom from fear. Chaturmukha is meditating steadily, even today, upon Chaturmukheshvara Linga near Vrddhakalesha. The devotees of Chaturmukhesha are honoured by the Devas, including Brahma, and enjoy all pleasures.

Nikumbha established the Nikumbheshvara Linga. After visiting this linga, a successful journey back home is assured. After adoring Panchakesha, the great linga to the south of Mahadeva, one shall attain the ability to remember one's previous birth. By meditating on Bharabhuteshvara Linga installed by Bharabhuta, at the northern gate of Antargrha, a devotee secures residence in Shivapura. Even today, Tryaksha meditates upon the great Tryakeshvara Linga. Devotees of this linga become three-eyed upon death.

Kshemaka, the leader of the ganas, maintains unwavering meditation on Vishveshvara. Worshiping Kshemaka in Kashi removes all obstacles and ensures wellbeing at every step. For someone in a distant land, worshiping Kshemaka ensures their safe return.

By visiting Langalishvara Linga, on the northern side of Vishveshvara, one never falls ill. This linga also endows a devotee with riches. Propitiating Veeradheshvara, established by Veeradha to the southwest of Dandapani, one attains freedom from crimes they might have committed in the past. By visiting Sumukhesha, one is rid of all sins. By bathing in Pilipila Tirtha and visiting Sumukhesha, one is assured to always see the pleasant face of Yama Deva and not the terrifying one. Devoutly visiting Aashadheeshvara Linga on the new-moon day in the month of Aasadha absolves one of all sins. This linga was established by Aasadha to the north of Bharabhutesha.

Ganesha Brings Everyone under His Spell

Pondering how best to facilitate Shiva's arrival in Kashi, Ganesha journeyed from Mandara to the holy city on a swift chariot, assuming the guise of an old astrologer. He visited every house in Kashi. He injected dreams into the minds of the inhabitants during the night and would visit them with explanations the next morning. This mesmerized them. By often sharing the evil forebodings from these bad dreams, Ganesha, the Lord of Obstacles, expelled numerous inhabitants from Kashi.

Utilizing his Maya, he accomplished similar feats within the women's quarters. Eventually, he won the favour of the queens, who began to praise him to the king. Once, Leelavati, the chief queen of King Divodasa, spoke to him about this Brahmana. She urged the king to meet with him. The king granted permission for the meeting.

When he arrived, the king was delighted by the sight of him. He immediately felt that good qualities are present where excellent form and features are found. The king and the Brahmana conversed. The second time they met, the king asked the Brahmana what would be most conducive to the king's welfare.

Ganesha was waiting for this opening. He replied, 'Even the smallest duty of kings should be explained by a wise man when asked privately. What is conducive to your wellbeing is known to me. On the eighteenth day from today, a Brahmana will come to you from the north and advise you. His advice should be unhesitatingly carried out by you, O King.'

Saying this, Ganesha departed.

CHAPTER 9

Enlightenment of King Divodasa

Vaishnava Tirthas in Kashi

Agastya Muni was curious to know what Shiva did in Mandara while Ganesha was in Kashi. Skanda explained that after the departure of Ganesha, Vishnu, too, accompanied by Lakshmi, set out for Kashi. Vishnu washed his hands and feet at the confluence of the Ganga and Varana and bathed in the waters there. Hence, this site became known as Padodaka Tirtha. Offering shraddha there with water and sesame seeds pleases the ancestors as much as offerings made in Gaya. Bathing a *shalagrama* inscribed with a discus in the waters of the Padodaka Tirtha and drinking the water thereof will grant immortality.

After performing his daily rites, Vishnu withdrew his form pervading the three worlds and fashioned a stone image with his own hands. This deity became known as Adi Keshava, worshiped by Narayana himself. Those who worship Adi Keshava reside in Shveta Deepa, the abode of Vishnu.

In front of Adi Keshava is another tirtha known as Ksheerabhdhi. One who performs rites at this site will reside on the shores of the Ocean of Milk. By offering cows here, one will be able to make all of his ancestors sleep comfortably with quilts. To the south of Ksheerabhdhi is the Shankha Tirtha. One who offers water there to the pitrs is honoured in Vishnu Loka. To the south of Shankha Tirtha is the Chakra Tirtha. One who performs shraddha here is freed from debt to the ancestors. The Gada Tirtha nearby destroys all mental anguish and causes the redemption of the pitrs. Beyond that is Padma Tirtha. After bathing in the waters of Padma Tirtha, one never lacks wealth.

Lakshmi herself bathed in the water of the Mahalakshmi Tirtha. The deity of Lakshmi Devi there is adored by all the three worlds. Prostrating to her, one never suffers from sickness.

The Tarkshya Tirtha, near Tarkshyakeshava, saves one from the serpent in the form of worldly existence. At the nearby Narada Tirtha, Narada Muni was instructed in Brahmavidya. One who bathes there will obtain perfect Brahmavidya from Adi Keshava. Like that, many Vaishnava Tirthas are described in the *Skanda Purana*.

The Adi Keshava Temple overlooks the Ganga and Varana, located in a grove of trees on the banks of the Rajghat plateau. The other Tirthas cited are not visible for the most part today, while some, such as the Prahlada Tirtha, can still be found (Tagare n.d.[b]).

After entering into the deity of Adi Keshava, Narayana emerged gradually, determined to do something for Shiva. For his stay, Vishnu created Dharmakshetra to the north of Kashi. Lakshmi took the form of an exquisitely beautiful female mendicant. The entire universe became motionless, gazing upon her.

Garuda took on the guise of their disciple and began expounding on *dharma* and *ahimsa* to the populace of Kashi. He proclaimed that there is no other virtue on par with compassion for living beings as all embodied beings are equal and all embodied beings suffer from the fear of death. The people of Kashi were drawn to his talks.

In the meantime, Lakshmi, disguised as the mendicant, deliberately encouraged women to become materialistic. King Divodasa grew concerned about these developments and anxiously awaited the eighteenth day and the promised arrival of the Brahmana, as foretold by Ganesha.

Finally, on that awaited day, Vishnu approached the king in the guise of a Brahmana. Taking Vishnu into his private chambers, the king confided his concerns, revealing a waning interest in ruling. All his enemies had been vanquished and the subjects were fully protected and cared for. He acknowledged that his arrogance, born of pride in his penance, had caused him to slight the Devas, but insisted that it was for the benefit of the kingdom. He requested Vishnu to become his guru.

Pleased with the king's words, Vishnu commended Divodasa's unique reign but pointed out his singular mistake: he had kept Shiva away from his beloved Kashi. He instructed the king to expiate for that wrong by installing a Shivalinga. After meditating for some time, Vishnu spoke again.

'O Divodasa, because of your presence and proximity, we are highly blessed. Among mortal beings, those who utter your name are also blessed. O! The purity of this one is excellent. O! The destiny of this king cannot be obtained by anybody else. What is far away from even us is not far away from him!'

Then, Vishnu, still in the guise of the Brahmana, described to the king that which he had seen during his meditation. He told him that the tree of his cherished desire had borne fruit today and that he would be attaining the highest position with his own body. A divine vimana, aerial chariot, of Shiva would come in seven days to take him away. This merit was all due to the king's service to the city of Kashi. He said that even if one takes care of a single resident of Kashi, that individual would attain the same benefit at the time of his or her death.

The king, delighted by these words, blessed the Brahmana, none other than Vishnu in disguise. After leaving the palace, Vishnu saw the whirlpool, *Panchanada Hrada*, and decided to make that his abode. In the meantime, he sent Tarkshya to convey the news about the king.

Panchanada

Panchanada, otherwise known as Panchaganga, is one of the five most sacred tirthas on the Ganga. Before Ganga's descent through the efforts of Bhagiratha, the Dhutapapa and Kirana streams merged into the Dharmanada pool. At Prayaga, Ganga unites with the Yamuna and Sarasvati rivers. Coming from Prayaga, these three rivers intermingle with the Dhutapapa and Kirana. This confluence of the five rivers became renowned as the Panchaganga Tirtha, home to Panchaganga Ghat (Tagare n.d.[c]). Today, to the north of the ghat, is a trickle of water called Dhutapapa and, to the south, a kunda called Kirana.

Agastya Muni asked Skanda to elucidate the origin and sanctity of Panchanada Tirtha within Kashi. Skanda explained that it is through the power of Prayaga that all the tirthas remove sins. In the month of Magha, all the tirthas come in contact with Prayaga, and their impurities are eliminated. It is due to the power of Panchanada that Prayaga is able to get rid of all the impurities dumped into it by all the other tirthas and its own devotees as well. Throughout the year, Prayaga gathers together all the sins poured into it and the other tirthas. Then, in the month of Karthika, by a single dip in Panchanada, all the sins are destroyed.

Once, there was a great sage named Vedashiras, born in the family of Bhrigu. While he was performing penance, Shuchi, one of the apsaras, appeared before him. He expelled a stream of semen, frightening Shuchi. It was a great wrong to disturb the penance of a sage, and she did not want to be blamed for an inadvertent mistake.

Vedashiras curbed his anger and said, 'O Shuchi, you are indeed *shuchi* (pure). Neither of us are at fault. It is said that young women are like fire and men are like butter. Do not fear. When free from lust, the emission of a sage's semen, unlike a person's outburst of rage, is harmless. Rage, on the other hand, is inimical and blinding. How can wealth and the wellbeing of humans flourish should there be anger, the cause of ruin and disaster? When fury grips the mind, how can love survive?

'O fair lady, semen should never be wasted. Should you accept it and take care of it, an extremely pure girl will be born to you.'

The apsara was moved and swallowed the semen of the sage. In time, she gave birth to a baby girl and left her in the hermitage of Vedashiras. Shuchi then left and went about as she pleased.

Vedashiras affectionately brought up the girl, feeding her the milk of a doe from his hermitage. He named her Dhutapapa, one who has shaken off all sins.

One day, he asked her, 'O, my blessed daughter, to whom shall I marry you?'

Dhutapapa replied, 'He should be the holiest of men. He should be one whom all love, from whom all happiness originates, who never perishes and always exists. He must be one with whom marital bliss will increase day by day. He should be one with whose support the fourteen worlds remain steady and stable. For your wellbeing and mine, dear father, give me unto that *vara*, that excellent bridegroom, who possesses these and other good qualities."

Her father was extremely pleased and said that his ancestors were blessed to have a daughter like her in their family. He concentrated for a while, visualizing through his spiritual powers the appropriate husband for his daughter.

Vedashiras informed her that while such a man existed, he could not be won over through physical beauty, intellect, or valour. Rather, in order to win him as her groom she needed to undertake rigorous penance, through *dama* (controlling the senses), *dana* (meritorious offering of gifts), and *daya* (compassion).

Dhutapapa embarked on severe penance in Avimukta, enduring extreme conditions. Even ascetics could not easily perform such *tapasya*. The girl with soft limbs spent many stormy, windy nights on a large stone. She performed the penance of five fires without even feeling thirsty. The intensity of her horripilation in the cold season was such that the goosebumps on her skin appeared to be a shawl. Her mind remained steadily engaged through spring and summer, undisturbed by the call of birds. Just as a jewel whetted on a stone becomes more radiant, so also her body, whetted through penance, shone all the more brightly.

Her penance caught Brahma's attention, who approached her and asked her to choose a boon.

She asked him to make her the purest of all. Delighted, Brahma promised that the purity of three and a half crore pure tirthas in the worlds would reside in every pore of her body and that she would be the most sanctifying of all.

Having fulfilled her penance, Dhutapapa went back to her father's hermitage.

Eventually, Dharma sought her hand in the Gandharva form of marriage. He approached her several times. She rejected him, explaining that she wanted her father to perform the kanyadana. Dharma was not dissuaded. Undeterred, he kept professing his love. For his insensitivity, Dhutapapa cursed him to become a river. Enraged, he cursed her to become a rock, for her hard-heartedness.

Dhutapapa returned home and revealed everything to her father. He comforted her, recognizing her suitor as Dharma. He advised her to transform into a lunar stone, melting into a river at moonrise. In this way, she would have two forms, one solid, the other liquid. There would then be two forms of her: the original body she was in and the liquidized form of her in the Dhutapapa river. Due to their mutual curses, Dharma became the Dharmanada river and Dhutapapa became the Dhutapapa river. Ever since, the still pond has become famous as Dharmanada, and in its liquid form, Dharma is the destroyer of great sins. Dhutapapa, the splendid river, contains all the tirthas and strips away sins like trees from the riverbank.

Before Ganga's descent, Surya Deva had performed penance at that tirtha, worshiping Gabhastishvara and Mangala Gauri. The sweat from his body became the holy river, Kirana. Initially, Dharmanada joined Dhutapapa, and later, Kirana, enhanced by the Sun, joined Dhutapapa, merging into the auspicious Dharmanada. Bhagirathi later brought down the Ganga and Sarasvati also descended.

Thus, this tirtha came to be known as Panchanada since five glorious rivers meet here—Dhutapapa, Dharmanada, Kirana,

Ganga, and Sarasvati. By bathing a single time in the waters of the Panchanada, one gains a whole month's worth of bathing in the waters of Prayaga in the month of Magha. After bathing here, one should worship Bindhu Madhava so as to never be reborn.

There is a folk song performed by ancestors in regard to Panchanada, a line of which goes as follows: 'Will someone belonging to our family come to Panchanada at Kashi and perform shraddha to liberate us?'

It is also said that if one bathes a deity of one's choice with the waters of the Panchanada, filtered through a cloth, the devotee will attain great benefit. In Krta Yuga, this tirtha is known as Dharmanada; in Treta Yuga, it is known as Dhutapapaka; in Dvapara Yuga, it is known as Bindu Tirtha; and in Kali Yuga, it is known as Panchanada.

By listening to this account of Panchanada, and by making others listen with devotion, one becomes purified and is honoured in the world of Vishnu.

The Liberation of Divodasa

Divodasa summoned all of his subjects, vassals and their ministers, the keeper of the treasury, cavalry and elephant army, along with other officials. Also present were his eldest son, Samaranjaya, and five hundred other sons, priests, guards, princes of the vassal kingdoms, cooks, physicians, foreigners present on various missions, the queen and others from the inner apartments, elders, cowherds, and all other children. He shared with them, in a humble and deferential way, what the Brahmana had told him.

They were sad at the thought of losing their beloved king. Afterward, the king took Prince Samranjaya to the royal palace outside of Kashi. He crowned him as king and bestowed gifts and favours upon the citizens and residents of the surrounding districts. After returning to Kashi, the king built a palace on the western bank of the Ganga. He spent the remainder of his wealth won from battle in building a shrine to Shiva. He installed the

Divodasheshvara Linga and considered his duties completed. That auspicious site became known as Bhupalashri.

At the appointed time, when the king was worshiping that Shiva Linga, a vimana descended from the skies. The chariot was surrounded by tridents and *khatvangas*—skull-topped clubs—borne by attendants. The attendants had three eyes and matted hair, their limbs shining like pure crystal. They were adorned with the jewelled hoods of serpents and had blue-tinged necks. The vimana was further surrounded by hundreds of *rudrakanyas*, maidens whose fingers whisked yak-tailed fans.

The attendants garlanded the king, perfumed him with divine fragrances, and draped him in silk robes. His forehead became three-eyed; his throat became blue; his limbs whitened; and his body developed four arms and became ornamented with serpents. A crescent-shaped moon hovered above his head.

The attendants took him away.

It is said that if anyone enters a battlefield after listening to the account of Divodasa, he need not fear his enemies. Reading this narrative removes obstacles and fulfils desires.

This tale teaches that some things must ripen on their own and in their own time, without manipulation. Even the Devas and rishis cannot always hasten the process; more precisely, they are not inclined to do so. As the story shows, while the Devas and yoginis and ganas appeared in Kashi and catalysed certain situations, they did not coerce the king or the citizens of Kashi; they did not deprive them of their own free will. If the king had not independently cultivated dispassion and a willingness to relinquish the throne, Shiva would have remained apart from Kashi. Like the famous Mrtyunjaya mantra proclaims, may moksha come as easily and smoothly as the ripe cucumber is plucked from the creeper—i.e., such things happen naturally and easily when the causes and conditions are ripe and the ground is ready.

It is because Divodasa had lived out his karma, enjoying the kingdom and working for his people, that a natural *vairagya* had overtaken him. The messages of wisdom from Ganesha and Vishnu came to him only when he was ready. Prior to that, the yoginis, Surya Deva, and the ganas prepared the ground, purifying the city of Kashi. Also, nowhere do the Devas, the most powerful ones in the universe, exert force or extortion against Divodasa. They defer to his righteousness and dharmic conduct. They do not want to falsely manipulate him. They let time and destiny work their own spells. They stand ever ready to advise him, support him, and help him, as well as the kingdom of Kashi.

Like Divodasa, we are the masters of our own karma and fate, and it is up to us to realize that we need the presence and support of the Devas in our lives and in our abodes. Shiva belongs not only in Kashi but also in our hearts and homes.

CHAPTER 10

The Story of Bindu Madhava

The former site of the Bindu Madhava Mandir, atop the summit of the Panchaganga Ghat, must have been incredibly majestic. Sri Tulsidas Maharaj documented its splendour during his stay in Kashi in the sixteenth century. Jean-Baptiste Tavernier had also noted its grand appearance, likening it to a large pagoda. Subsequently, the temple was torn down under Aurangzeb and rebuilt into a mosque complex that now towers over the skyline of Kashi against the backdrop of the Ganga. The Bindu Madhava deity was relocated into a nondescript building in the shadows of the mosque, where it still resides today.

Narayana left Mandara, evicted King Divodasa from Kashi, and briefly stayed at the Padodaka Tirtha and the Panchanada Tirtha. One day, near Panchanada, Vishnu encountered an emaciated sage, Agnibindu, performing penance. He approached Vishnu and prostrated to him. He eulogized Vishnu profusely. Vishnu offered him a boon of his choosing with a movement of his eyebrows.

Agnibindu requested, 'For the wellbeing of all creatures, particularly those who desire enlightenment, stay here in Panchanada, and grant me devotion to your lotus-like feet. I do not desire anything else.'

Vishnu consented, pleased with the request. He promised to stay at Panchanada forever, confessing that he was desirous of doing the same. He told Agnibindu to choose another boon.

The sage, overwhelmed with joy, experienced horripilation, so great was his delight. He said, 'O, Consort of Lakshmi, stay here in Panchanada Tirtha and adopt my name. Grant liberation to devotees as well as non-devotees. Grant liberation even to those who bathe in the waters of Panchanada but die abroad. Let your consort, who has the twin forms of being steady and unsteady, not forsake those men who worship you after bathing in the waters of Panchanada.'

Vishnu inclined his head in consent. 'My name shall be a combination of half of your name and half of Lakshmi's. Henceforth, I shall be known as Bindu Madhava. If people keep me in their hearts as being stationed in Panchanada always, Lakshmi in the form of wealth and in the form of liberation shall always be by their side. O, Agnibindu, this tirtha shall be known as Bindu Tirtha after your name. If, in the month of Karthik, a devotee follows the vow of celibacy and bathes in the Bindu Tirtha before sunrise, he would have no reason to fear Yama Deva.

'Dharma stays firm in the body purified by vratas. Artha, kama, and moksha also reside there. Those vratas that contribute to the attainment of Dharma should be observed by men who desire the Purushartha (the four principal aims of life: dharma, artha, kama, and moksha). At the very least, vratas should be performed during Chaturmasya (the four-month period during the monsoon months when the Devas sleep in *yoga nidra* and devotees undertake a period of increased austerity and retreat). Some examples of vrata are lying down on the bare ground, celibacy, abstaining from eating certain foods, subsisting on one meal a day, providing dana every day according to one's abilities, listening to the Puranas and acting in accordance with their values, maintaining *diyas* in front of deities, and worshiping the deity of one's choice. Especially during the month of Karthik, one should perform vratas. In the month of Karthik, one should stick to a diet of vegetables, milk, fruit, and cooked barley.

'One who observes the vow of lying down on the bare ground will never touch the earth again. One who maintains the continuous unextinguished light of sacred lamps with ghee-soaked wicks will never be blinded by delusion. On Prabodhini Ekadasi, the eleventh day in the bright half of Karthik, one should bathe in Bindu Tirtha and keep awake the whole night. He should light as many lamps as he can after worshiping me. He should listen to the Puranas. There should be great festivities until the day is over. He should make gifts of cooked food.

'O sage, in Satya Yuga, I am worshiped as Adi Madhava. In Treta Yuga, I am known as Ananta Madhava, the bestower of all siddhis. In Dvapara Yuga, I am known as Sri Madhava, the one who brings about the fulfilment of the greatest aim. In Kali Yuga, I shall be known as Bindu Madhava, the destroyer of the impurities of the Kali Yuga.

'In Kali Yuga, men do not attain me, engrossed in debating their differences. Let it be known that those who perform many devotional rites in my honour will still be my enemies if they are inimical to Vishveshvara. They will become pishachas and spend thirty thousand years in the ocean of misery at the whim of Kaala Bhairava. Only by the Vishveshvara's grace will they be liberated. Criticizing Shiva and his devotees brand one as my enemy, condemning them to fall into hell.

'In this Panchanada Tirtha, during Karthik month, Vishveshvara himself bathes in Dhutapapa, along with his ganas, attendants, and Skanda. Brahma, the Vedas, Yajnas, the seven oceans, the rivers, and the mothers—all these bathe in Dhutapapa in the month of Karthik.'

Once Vishnu finished speaking, Agnibindu asked in how many forms did Vishnu manifest within Kashi.

Vishnu, as Bindu Madhava, said, 'I am Adi Keshava at Padodaka Tirtha, the bestower of liberation; to the south, at Shveta Deepa, I impart knowledge as Gyaanakeshava. I am Tarkshyakeshava in Tarkshyatirtha. Those who worship me there become dear to me like Garuda (Tarkshya). As Naradakeshava in Narada Tirtha, I am the instructor of Brahma vidya. In Prahlada Tirtha, I am Prahladakeshava and increase the devotion of those who worship me there.

'In the Ambareesha Tirtha, as Aditya Keshava, I destroy dark sins. To the south of Dattatreyeshvara, as Adi Gadadhara, I remove all illnesses. In the Bhargava Tirtha, as Bhrgukeshava, I fulfil the desires of my devotees. At Vamana Tirtha, as Vamanakeshava, I bestow all forms of auspiciousness. In the Naranarayana Tirtha, devotees attain identity with Naranarayana.

'In Yajnavarahatirtha, I bestow the fruits of yajna. At Vidaranarasimha Tirtha, I remove obstacles from Kashi. By worshiping me as Gopigovinda in the Gopigovinda Tirtha, one can remain untouched by Maya. At the Lakshminarasimha Tirtha, I bestow liberation. As Shesha Madhava at Shesha Tirtha, I fulfil all desires. Bathing my Shankha Madhava form at the Shankha Madhava Tirtha with water poured through a conch shell grants one the treasure of Shankhanidhi. Worshiping me as Hayagriva Keshava at Hayagriva Tirtha, one attains the realm of Vishnu.

'To the west of Vrddhakalesha, I am Bhishma Keshava, dispelling torments and calamities. To the north of Lolarka, I am Nirvana Keshava, guiding devotees to liberation and dispelling fickleness of mind. To the south of Trilokasundari, I am Tribhuvana Keshava, granting moksha. In front of Gyaanavapi, I am known as Gyaana Madhava, bestower of eternal wisdom. Beside Vishalakshi, I am Shveta Madhava. To the north of Dashashvamedha, I am Prayaga Madhava. Bathing in Prayaga Tirtha yields tenfold benefits compared to a visit to Prayaga in Magha.'

He told Agnibindu that the tirthas in Kashi do not go anywhere; if they go anywhere, they go to the three excellent tirthas in Kashi. He explained that in the month of Karthik, they come to him in the Panchanada Tirtha. In the month of Magha, all the tirthas bathe near Prayagesha after Vishnu bathes there. And in the midday period, all of the tirthas bathe every day in the waters of

Manikarnika. Not only that, every day, at midday, Vishveshvara with his consort bathes at Manikarnika and Vishnu journeys from Vaikuntha every day to bathe along with Lakshmi there. Brahma, Indra, the Guardians of the Quarters (the Dikpalakas), the nagas as well as rishis and all the sentient ones come to take their holy bath at midday in the waters of Manikarnika.

Manikarnika, in her physical form, appears as a twelve-year-old Devi with four arms, large eyes, and a sparkling third eye in the middle of her forehead, standing facing west with palms joined together. She holds a garland of blue lotuses in her right hand. Her left hand is lifted in a boon-granting gesture, bearing a pomegranate. She is always in the form of a kanya, shining like crystal with glossy, dark blue hair and lips the colour of coral. She is adorned with pearl necklaces and lotus garlands, dressed in moon-white silk.

Manikarnika is the abode of Nirvana Lakshmi. The Bhakta-Kalpadruma mantra associated with her bestows the eight siddhis upon a devotee. The *Skanda Purana* provides further details on this puja *vidhi*.

Vishnu explained that he had personally installed the Manikarnishvara Linga. To the south lies Pashupata Tirtha, presided over by Pashupatishvara, where Shiva had imparted the teachings of Pashupata Yoga. A special yatra is performed here on the fourteenth day of the bright half of the month of Chaitra.

In front of Pashupata Tirtha is Rudravasa Tirtha. To the south thereof is the Vishva Tirtha, gathering all the tirthas worldwide. After bathing here, devotees should visit Vishvanatha and ardently revere Vishvaa (Gauri), identifying themselves with the entire cosmos. Subsequently, at Mukti Tirtha, worshipers should bathe and venerate Moksheshvara to attain enlightenment. Avimukteshvara Tirtha lies beyond Mukti Tirtha. Beyond that is Taraka Tirtha, where Shiva utters the Taraka mantra. Nearby is Skanda Tirtha, where devotees transcend the six *koshas*, or sheaths, of the physical body—skin, flesh, blood, semen, bone, and marrow. Beyond that is the Dhundhi Tirtha, where worship ensures freedom from obstacles. To the south of Dhundhi Tirtha is Bhavani Tirtha, granting salvation to the devotees of Kashi. Bhavani and Shankara should be worshiped with great devotion together. One who bathes in Ishaana Tirtha near Bhavani Tirtha is freed from rebirth.

Gyaana Tirtha, bestowing wisdom, is nearby. One who worships Gyaaneshvera will never lose wisdom, even upon death. North of Gyaana Tirtha is Shailadi Tirtha, visiting which one becomes a gana and attains wealth and glory. South of Nandi Tirtha is Vishnu Tirtha, to the south of which lies Paitamaha Tirtha where ancestors should be honoured. One who worships with devotion the Pitamaheshvara Linga there, stationed above Brahma Nala, will attain Brahma Loka.

Nabhi Tirtha is the navel of the cosmic egg at Manikarnika. The cosmic egg emerges from here. Brahma Nala is a great Tirtha, bathing in the waters of which one shakes off the impurities of ten million births. If even a bone of a person were to fall into Brahma Nala, that person would never enter samsara again.

South of Brahma Nala is Bhagirathi Tirtha. The Bhagirathishvara Linga is near Swargadwara. If one's ancestors met an inauspicious end, one should make offerings to them at Bhagirathi Tirtha. To its south lies the great Khurakartari Tirtha. It is named so because cows from Goloka Vrndavana made the ground here uneven with the tips of their hooves. One who performs worship here will attain Goloka Vrndavana.

Further south, Markanda Tirtha promises a long life, splendour, and great renown to those who visit it. Vasishtha Tirtha destroys great sins. Adjacent is Arundhati Tirtha, enhancing marital bliss for women. Even an unchaste woman will become purified by plunging into the waters of that tirtha; this is the power of the great *tapasvini*, Arundhati. By worshiping Vasishtha and Arundhati together, a woman does not become a widow and a man does not become separated from his wife.

To the south of Vasishtha Tirtha is Narmada Tirtha. Generous offerings here ensure the perpetual favour of Lakshmi. East of

Trisandhyeshvara is Trisandhya Tirtha. Offering *sandhya vandanam* here safeguards against the demerits of its omission or irregularity in performance at other times. One who performs sandhya vandanam three times a day here will attain the merit of reciting the three Vedas.

Beyond Trisandhya Tirtha is Yogini Tirtha, granting yogic siddhis to visitors. One who visits the Yogini Peetha there will attain yogic siddhi. Agastya Tirtha is also there, named after Agastya Muni. One who offer libations to the ancestors in Agastikunda and bows down to Lopamudra with her consort, Agastya Muni, shall be rid of all distress and go to Shiva Loka along with his ancestors.

Vishnu said that he is the Vaikuntha Madhava, east of Vairochaneshvara. To the west of Viresha, he is Veera Madhava. In the vicinity of Kaala Bhairava, he is Kaala Madhava. Neither Kali nor Kaala affects his devotees. South of Pulastishvara, he is Nirvana Narasimha. To the east of Omkara, he is Mahabala Narasimha. East of Chanda Bhairava, he is Prachanda Narasimha. To the east of Dehalivinayaka he is Giri Narasimha, the tearer of elephantine sins. To the west of Peeta Maheshvara, he is Narasimha, the remover of fears. West of Kalasheshvara, he is Atyugra Narasimha. Near Jvaalamukhi, he is Jvaalamali Narasimha burning down the grasses in the forms of masses of sins. As Kolaha Narasimha, the subduer of *daityas* and *danavas*, he creates chaotic noise among the evil ones when his very name is uttered.

Behind Neelakantheshvara, he is known as Vitanka Narasimha. By worshiping him there, a man becomes fearless. Near Ananteshvara, he is Anantavamana. He is also named Dadhivamana because he bestows yogurt rice on devotees. Merely by remembering this name of his, one is rid of poverty.

To the north of Trilochana, he is Trivikrama. East of Balibhadreshvara, as Balivamana, he increases the strength of devotees. South of Bhava Tirtha, he is Tamravaraha, the bestower of desires. He is Dharanivaraha in the vicinity of Prayageshvara. He grants immense benefits in exchange for a small offering of cooked food. In the vicinity of Kiteeshvara, he is known as Kokavaraha.

Vishnu concluded, 'There are six million ganas in my form with the discus and club upraised. They all keep watch over the holy site of Kashi.'

Delighted, Agnibindu asked for a description of Vishnu's various deity forms. Vishnu then mentioned twenty-four different forms of his, beginning with Keshava. While he was narrating this, Garuda arrived with the news of Shiva's impending return.

Vishnu saw from a distance Shiva's bull-emblemed chariot approaching. The faces of the quarters of the firmament were brightened with the splendour of ten million suns. The entire sky was covered by the chariots of the Devas. The mountains echoed with the sounds of great musical instruments and became fragrant with the flowers scattered by Vidyadhara girls. Vishnu desired to arise and greet Shiva.

He instructed Agnibindu to touch the Sudarshana Chakra with his right hand, thus transforming Agnibindu into Sudarshana, one of excellent knowledge and wisdom.

Skanda explained to Agastya Muni that one should always stay in Kashi; one should always visit Bindu Madhava; and one should always listen to this story of Bindu Madhava and Agnibindu. The story of the origin of the Panchanada Tirtha is conducive to merit, as is the story of Bindu Madhava, as is residence in Kashi. Those who read Agnibindu's prayer before Bindu Madhava shall attain their desires and mastery over their salvation.

CHAPTER 11

Kashi Pravesha: The Arrival of Shiva in Kashi

Mounted on Garuda and accompanied by Ganesha, the ganas, Brahma, Surya Deva, and the yoginis, Vishnu approached Shiva. He descended from Garuda's back and they all prostrated to Shiva together.

Brahma bowed his head, but Shiva prevented him from bowing further. Ganesha placed his head at Shiva's feet, and Shiva kissed his head, smelling the crown of his head with great affection. Shiva made Ganesha sit on his own seat.

The other ganas bowed, prone like logs of wood, before Shiva, while the yoginis, after bowing, sang auspicious songs in his honour. Surya Deva also bowed down to Shiva. Shiva sat Vishnu to the left of his throne and Brahma to the right. He glanced kindly at all the ganas and nodded at the yoginis. He gestured to Surya Deva to take a seat as well.

One by one, Brahma, the ganas, the yoginis, and Surya Deva expressed their remorse for not having fulfilled Shiva's mission and apologized for staying on at Kashi. Shiva blessed them graciously, pleased with their service to the city's devotees.

Five cows appeared from Goloka. Shiva glanced at them benevolently, causing their udders to release streams of milk spontaneously, flowing like a second Ksheera Sagara, the Ocean of Milk. Shiva named that tirtha the Kapila Hrada. He declared that offering rice balls as shraddha offerings here would please one's ancestors at Shiva's behest. He explained that in Kapiladhaarika Tirtha, those who died in fires, those not cremated, those denied last rites or the sixteen samskaras, those who suffered unnatural deaths, or committed misdeeds, including suicide, would find solace. Shiva explained that this tirtha is full of milk in Krta Yuga, honey in Treta Yuga, ghee in Dvapara Yuga, and water in Kali Yuga. He pledged to stay at this site as Vrshabhadhvaja, with the bull-emblemed flag, in the company of Brahma, Vishnu, Surya Deva, and various attendants.

Soon, Nandi arrived to inform Shiva about the preparations for the victory procession. The chariot would be pulled by eight lions (the seven *tattvas* and Moola Prakrti) and eight bulls (the eight *dhaatus* or constituents of the body) as well as eight fast horses (*chitta, ahamkara, buddhi*, and the five sense organs). The controlling mind would sit upon the chariot, whip in hand. Ganga and Yamuna would be the poles of the chariot; the two wheels— the morning and the evening—would be presided over by Vayu Deva. The heavens would be the umbrella; the clusters of stars the nails; the serpents the binding cords; the Shruti of the Vedas the path finders; the Smrti the defenders of the chariot. Dakshina would be the firm yoke; sacrifices the guards; Pranava the seat; Gayatri the footstool; the Vyahrtis with the ancillaries the steps; the sun and the moon the perpetual gatekeepers; Agni Deva, the snout-like projection in the front, shaped like an alligator; the moonlight the chariot ground; the Mahameru the flagstaff; the lustre of the sun the banner; and Vak Devi the holder of the chariot.

Thus informed, Shiva rose, supported by the hands of Vishnu. Beings from all worlds gathered, including the thirty-three million Devas, the one million and two hundred thousand ganas, the nine million *chamundas*, and the one million *bhairavis*. Eight million six-faced followers of Skanda arrived on their peacock mounts. Seven million elephant-faced gods, large-bellied, wielding shining axes hurried in—those renowned for being obstacles to obstacles.

Eighty-six thousand Vedic sages came, alongside an equal number of householders. Three million serpents from distant worlds, and two million each of the danavas and the daityas joined the assembly. Eight million gandharvas, five million yakshas and rakshasas, and two million and one hundred thousand vidyadharas arrived. Sixty thousand apsaras, eight hundred thousand mother cows, and six hundred thousand mother birds also joined.

The seven seas, bearing numerous jewels, and fifty-three rivers attended. Eight thousand mountains, three hundred *vanaspatis* (varieties of trees and herbs), and eight *diggajas* (elephants supporting the quarters), came.

Accompanied by them all, with Parvati at his side, a contented Shiva rode in the chariot and finally entered Kashi.

Even today, Annakut, the day after Deepavali, is celebrated grandly at the Kashi Vishwanath Mandir. This celebrates Shiva's return to Kashi after being exiled by Divodasa (Sukul 1974, 249).

Skanda informed Agastya Muni that listening to this meritorious narrative destroys the sins from ten million births. By reading it and making others read it, one shall become one with Shiva. This should be particularly read during the Shraddha period. Reading about the greatness of Vrshabhadhvaja Tirtha, in the presence of Shiva, every day for a year, grants a son to those without one. After joyously reading this narrative, one should enter a new house. There is no doubt that such a person will enjoy every kind of happiness.

This narrative is known as the Kashi Pravesha, an excellent *japya* or holy text to be recited.

Dhundhi Vinayaka and the Fifty-Six Vinayakas

Dhundhi Vinayaka, also known as Dhundhiraja holds a position of utmost importance at the heart of Kashi and is to be worshiped immediately upon entering Kashi. His name is derived from *dhudh*, meaning to search or find, because Shiva's re-entry into Kashi was facilitated through Vinayaka's orchestration.

The fifty-six Vinayakas of Kashi are arranged in seven concentric circles, with Dhundhiraja at the centre, near the Vishvanatha Temple, positioned at the eight directional points as follows: (i) Arka, Durga, Bhimachanda, Dehali, Uddanda, Pashapani, Kharva, Siddhivinayanaka (ii) Lambodara, Kutadanta, Shalakatantaka, Kushmanda, Mundavinayaka, Viktadvija, Rajaputra, Pranava (iii) Vakratunda, Ekadanta, Trimukha, Panchasya, Heramba, Vighnaraja, Varada, Modakapriya (iv) Abhayada, Simhatunda, Kunitaksha, Ksipraprasadana, Chintamani, Dantahasta, Pichandila, Uddandamunda (v) Sthuladanta, Kalipriya, Chaturdanta, Dvitunda, Jyeshtha, Gajavinayaka, Kalavinayaka, Nagesha (vi) Manikarna, Ashavinayaka, Srstiganesha, Yakshavighnesha, Gajakarna, Chitraghanta, Sthulajangha, Mitravinayaka, and (vii) Moda and others, Gyaanavinayaka, Dvaravighnesha, Avimuktavinayaka.

Skanda then described the entry of Shiva into Kashi. Accompanied by Parvati and Skanda, with Nandi and Bhringi proceeding ahead, surrounded by rudras, and attended upon by the rishis, Shiva entered Kashi. He was hailed with joy by the commanders of all the *ayatanas*, or the local shrines, and by the Guardians of the Quarters. All the tirthas displayed their holy waters. All the quarters reverberated with the deafening sounds of the Vedic chants by the rishis. Vimanas surrounded him everywhere.

Shiva, showered with the dried grains slipping through the fists of the ladies of Swarga, experienced joyous horripilation. Descending from Nandi's back, Shiva embraced Ganesha. He acknowledged the pivotal role that his son played in facilitating his entry into the challenging city of Kashi.

He announced, 'The fact that I have reached the auspicious city of Kashi, so difficult to access, is due to the favour of this child alone. What is difficult to be accomplished even by a father in all the three worlds can easily be accomplished by a son. By the powers of his gigantic intellect, the Elephant-faced One has achieved something remarkable in order to facilitate my entrance into Kashi.'

In recognition of Dhundhi Ganesha's contribution, Shiva composed a stotra named Sarvasampatkara—Giver of all prosperities—in his honour. He said that if anyone recites this stotra in the presence of Dhundhiraja, all the siddhis would stay near him always. The man who repeats this prayer will attain wives, sons, land, excellent horses, excellent houses, wealth, and food. If anyone desires to go anywhere for a specific purpose, he should go after reciting this stotra.

Then Shiva proceeded to describe all the places where Ganesha (Dhundhi) resides for the sake of guarding Kashi.

First Circle of Vinayakas

At the confluence of the Ganga and Asi resides Arkavinayaka. Paying homage to him on Sundays will subdue all distress. Durga, renowned for vanquishing wretchedness, occupies the southern region of Kashi. In the southwest, near Bhimachandi, stands Bhimachandavinayaka, removing great fears. Dehalivinayaka, to the west, eliminates all the obstacles. On the northwestern side is Uddanda, who strikes down massive groups of obstacles. To the north, Pashapani-Vinayaka always binds obstacles due to the devotion of the residents of Kashi. Kharavinayaka at the confluence of Ganga and Varana subdues even the most daunting obstacles faced by devotees. To the east and west of Yama Tirtha, Siddhivinayaka is always ready to protect Kashi and promptly bestows divine powers upon sadhakas.

These eight Vinayakas are on the outer ring of Kashi. They expel non-devotees and bestow all siddhis on devotees.

Second Circle of Vinayakas

On the western bank of the Ganga, north of Arkavinayaka, stands Lambodara Ganadhyaksha, the leader of ganas, who washes off all the mud of obstacles. To the west thereof and to the north of Durga-Vinayaka, is Kutadanta, the annihilator of difficulties and calamities. Slightly northeast of Bhimachanda Ganesha is

Shalakatamkata, worthy of adoration. Kushmanda, situated east of Dehalivighnesha, is to be worshipped for the suppression of great mishaps and calamities. Mundavinayaka, southeast of Uddanda, is extremely renowned and to be adored well. His body is stationed in Patala while his head remains in Kashi, earning him the name of Mundavinayaka.

One shall attain leadership of the ganas by worshiping Vikatadvija to the south of Pashapani. Rajaputra, located southwest of Kharva, can reinstate a dethroned king. Pranava, on the western bank of Ganga and south of Rajaputra, will lead a devotee to heaven.

These Vinayakas dispel obstacles for those who permanently reside in Kashi.

Third Circle of Vinayakas

Vakratunda, the remover of the mass of sins, is north of Lambodara, on the beautiful bank of the Ganga. Ekadantaka, north of Kutadanta, always protects Anandakanana from calamity. Trimukha, the monkey-lion-elephant–faced Vinayaka is situated to the northeast of Shalakatankata. He removes the fear of the people of Kashi.

Panchasya, in the eastern direction of Kushmanda, guards the city on a lion-drawn chariot. Heramba, southeast of Mundavinayaka, is like Devi in fulfilling the desires of all the residents of Kashi. Vighnaraja, stationed to the south of Vikatadanta, destroys all obstacles for the purpose of obtaining siddhi. Varada, slightly southwest of Rajaputra, bestows boons. Modakapriya, stationed to the south of Pranava, is worthy of being adored.

Fourth Circle of Vinayakas

The eight Vinayakas of the fourth circle destroy the obstacles of the devotees. Abhayada, the destroyer of the fear of all, is stationed on the bank of the Ganga to the north of Vakratunda. Simhatunda, north of Ekadanta, destroys the calamities of the inhabitants of Kashi. Kunitaksha, northeast of Trimukha, protects the city from the evil eye. Kshipraprasadana, east of Panchasya, swiftly bestows siddhis and safeguards the city. Chintamani, southeast of Heramba, grants devotees their wishes—whatever is thought of by them, like the Chintamani, the wish-yielding stone, after which he is named.

Dantahasta, south of Vighnaraja, commands thousands of obstacles to harass those inimical to Kashi. Pichindhila, southwest of Varada, protects the city day and night with the assistance of the fierce beings called *yatudhanas* that surround him. Uddandamunda, south of Modakapriya in Pilipeela Tirtha, fulfils all wishes of devotees when visited.

Fifth Circle of Vinayakas

The eight Vinayakas of the fifth circle protect the holy site. Sthuladanta, stationed on the bank of the Ganga to the north of Abhayaprada, bestows enormous siddhis for the people's benefit. Kalipriya, north of Simhatunda, creates discord among those who seek to harm the devotees of Kashi. Chaturdanta, northeast of Kunitaksha, obliterates obstacles. Dvitunda, east of Kripraprasadana, is equally majestic from the front and back, granting all glory and splendour to those who prostrate to him.

Jyeshtha, the eldest of the Vinayakas, resides southeast of Chintamani. Worshiping him on the fourteenth day of the bright half of the month of Jyeshtha grants excellence. Gaja-Vinayaka, south of Dantahasta, brings prosperity with elephants. Kala-Vinayaka, south of Pichindila, dispels the fear of Yama Deva. Those who visit Nagesha, south of Uddandamunda, are honoured in Naga Loka, the world of the nagas.

Sixth Circle of Vinayakas

Merely listening to the names of the Vinayakas of the sixth circle can grant one supernatural power. Manikarna destroys obstacles in the east. Asha Vinayaka, southeast of Manikarna, fulfils devotees' hopes and desires. Srshthiganesha in the south represents creation and annihilation. Yaksha Vighnesha in the southwest is the greatest destroyer of all obstacles. Gajakarna in the west brings wellbeing to all. Chitraghanta in the northwest protects the city. Sthulajangha represses the sins of those who control their minds. Mitravinayaka, located north of Yama Tirtha, protects Kashi in the northeast.

Seventh Circle of Vinayakas

In the seventh circle are Moda and others. The sixth one is Gyaanavinayaka, the seventh is Dvaravighnesha, the one before the great door, and the eighth is Avimukta Vinayaka, who removes all the distress from those with humble minds in Avimukta.

Those who remember these fifty-six forms of Ganesha, in the various guises he assumed while residing in Kashi, will attain knowledge upon death even if they are living in a far-off country. If one recites the names of the fifty-six Ganeshas, he becomes meritorious and obtains supernatural powers at every step. Wherever one may live, all these Ganeshas should be remembered.

Shiva was joyous after describing the fifty-six Vinayakas. He was coronated by Brahma and others, and he granted them all various boons. He then entered the royal palace built by Vishvakarma, the divine architect.

CHAPTER 12

The Manifestation of Various Lingas

The following section details the stories and lore behind the manifestation of various Shiva lingas that are situated in Kashi. These manifested after Shiva's return to Kashi once Divodasa had been expelled.

Jyeshtheshvara

Upon entering Kashi, Shiva, always affectionate towards his devotees, encountered the sage Jaigeeshavya, who was living in a cave. Ever since Shiva had left for Mandara, this sage had taken a vow to not eat or drink until he could see Shiva's feet in Kashi again. Against all odds, he had survived. Knowing this, Shiva immediately granted darshana to that sage, resulting in the manifestation of the Jyeshtheshvara Linga. It is said that men should perform great religious rites there on the fourteenth day in the bright half of the month of Jyeshtha.

Nearby, Gauri appeared as Jyesthaa and Shreshthaa in order to bestow all spiritual powers. A woman who bathes in Jyesthavaapee and bows down to Jyeshtha Gauri will attain wealth and familial bliss. It is said that a great festival should be celebrated there on the eighth day in the bright half of the month of Jyeshtha and the devotees should stay awake all night.

Since Shiva himself stayed there, the linga there has also become known as Nivaseshvara Linga, believed to bring abundance to those who visit. Jyeshtheshvara should be worshiped in Kashi for personal wellbeing followed by Jyeshtha Gauri for excellence.

Shiva instructed Nandi to take a small lotus, enter the cave and touch Jaigeeshavya's limbs with it. This revived the sage, who uttered a long prayer in honour of Shiva with Parvati standing by his side. Delighted by his devotion, Shiva asked him to choose a boon. The sage requested that he never again be far from the feet of Shiva and that Shiva should remain present in the linga he had installed. Shiva readily agreed and further granted another boon that he would pass onto him the Yoga Shastra; consequently, he would become the foremost *yogacharya* among all yogis. He promised that the sage would understand correctly the secret of Yoga Vidya and thereby attain liberation. He further promised that, like Nandi, Bhrngi, and Somanandi, he would be free from old age and untouched by death. He praised him that while there are many vratas, many varieties of holy observances, restraints, and dana, greater than everything else was the holy observance that he had practised, that is to consume food only after seeing Shiva.

Thus, it was that the Jaigeeshavyeshvara Linga in Kashi became highly revered as one of the most precious lingas of all. It is said that after serving that linga for three years, one will attain mastery of yoga. Shiva also promised that a devotee eagerly engaged in practising yoga will attain his desired objectives within six months after entering the cave of Jaigeeshavya. However, he cautioned that the Jaigeeshavyeshvara Linga should be carefully guarded, especially in the Kali Yuga, from those of perverted intellect. He also blessed the sage that the prayer he had uttered would be highly conducive to the achievement of yogic power for those who chant it.

Shiva addressed the assembled Brahmanas. In Shiva's absence, they had stopped accepting gifts and relied solely on bulbous roots for sustenance. They had dug the ground with thick sticks and created a beautiful pond named Dandakhata. They installed many lingas.

They came, shouting slogans of victory and reciting auspicious hymns, showering wet rice grains, *durva* grass, flowers, and fruits upon Shiva. He was pleased and offered them a boon. The Brahmanas requested that Shiva should never abandon Kashi and that no curse ever be an obstacle to moksha or bear effect in Kashi. Finally, they asked to remain in Kashi for the rest of their lives and requested Shiva's presence in the lingas they had installed.

Shiva gladly granted those boons and bestowed knowledge upon them.

Parashareshvaradi Lingas

Skanda shared with Agastya Muni the location of the five thousand lingas surrounding Jyestheshvara. Notably, the Parashareshvara Linga to the north of Jyesthesha is particularly powerful, and merely by seeing it, pure knowledge is attained. Nearby, the Mandavyeshvara Linga grants siddhi, as does the Jabalishvara Linga. The Sankaresha Linga bestows auspiciousness always, while Bhrgunarayayana Linga bestows spiritual powers.

The sage Sumantu installed the Shreshtha Aditya deity at this site, known to cure leprosy. Bhairavi taking the form of Bhishana there destroys everything terrible. The Upajanghani Linga liberates one from karma, bestowing spiritual powers within six months. The Bharadvajeshvara and Madrishvara Lingas are worshiped together. The linga installed by Aruni and the beautiful Linga, Vajasaneya, are also there.

Skanda elaborated on the various lingas around Jyeshtha Sthana. Kanveshvara, Katyayaneshvara, Vamadeveshvara, Authathyeshvara, Hariteshvara, Galaveshvara, Kumbhi, Kausumeshvara, Agnivarneshvara, Naidhruveshvara, Vatseshvara, Parnadeshvara, Saktuprastheshvara, Kanadesha—another great linga installed by Mandukayani—and Babhraveyeshvara; Shilavrttishvara, Chyavaneshvara, Shalankayanakeshvara, Kalindameshvara, Akrodhaneshvara, Kapotavrttisha, Kankesha, Kuntaleshvara, Kantheshvara, Kaholesha—the linga adored by Tumbaru—Matangesha, Maruttesha, Magadheyeshvara, Jatukarneshvara, Jambukeshvara, Jarudhisha, Jalesha, Jalmesha, Jalakeshvara, these and other lingas number around five thousand, said Skanda, advising that if one remembers, visits, touches, adores, bows down to and eulogizes these auspicious lingas, no sin arises in him or her.

Skanda then described to Agastya Muni a wondrous event that had occurred at Jyeshthasthana. As Shiva was enjoying himself, Parvati, too, was playing games with a ball. As bees hovered around her, attracted to her fragrant breath, her eyes became unfocused and her hair loosened. The garland of flowers fell from her neck, and the sweat on her face enhanced her radiance. Her upper cloth moved about as her palms reddened from continuously bouncing the ball.

As she was sporting like this, two *ditijas*, demons named Vidala and Utpala, saw her as they were traveling across the firmament. They were arrogant due to the boons they had received from Brahma. They used sorcery to try to abduct Devi, approaching her in the guise of Shiva's attendants. Shiva immediately recognized them, and Durga, who occupied half of Shiva's body, killed them with that very same ball. The demons whirled round and round before finally collapsing.

The ball itself became a linga, named Kandukeshvara. It wards off all evil-minded ones. Bhavani brings about *yogakshema*—acquisition of what one lacks and preservation of what one has—to those who are devoted to Kandukeshvara. Devi herself always worships this linga, and so her presence is particularly powerful here.

Another particularly wonderful occurrence took place near Jyesteshvara. While the Brahmanas were practising great austerities in Dandakhata, a daitya, Dundubhinirhrada, who was the maternal uncle of Prahlada, was plotting to destroy the Devas. He decided the continuous slaughter of Brahmanas would weaken the Devas, since they survive on yajna based on the Vedas, and the Vedas are in the custody of Brahmanas. Observing that Brahmanas were largely concentrated in Kashi, the daitya decided to start his murder spree there. He attacked and devoured many Brahmanas in Kashi.

On Maha Shivaratri, a devotee was meditating upon Shiva in his hut when Dundubhinirhrada transformed into a tiger and tried to seize him. The devotee, who was engaged in meditation with the unshakeable resolve to realize Shiva, was impervious to his attacks. Shiva then came to know the daitya's intention and decided to kill him.

Shiva emerged from the linga. The daitya grew to the size of a mountain, retaining his tiger form. Shiva defeated him simply by squeezing him within his armpit and pressed upon him. The daitya howled and roared, the sound of his cries filling all the worlds.

The sages from the area came out in the dark of the night and saw Shiva with the king of beasts trapped in his armpit.

They spoke as one: 'O, Preceptor of the Universe, stay here in this same form and take the name Vyaghresha.'

Shiva replied, 'So be it.'

He promised to destroy the mass of calamities of one who visits him faithfully in that spot and that if a man worships this linga and travels, he will not have any fear arising from thieves or tigers. He also promised that anyone would win on the battlefield after listening to this story.

Shailesha and Other Lingas

To the south of Jyesthesha lies the Apsaras Linga and the Saubhagyodaka well. Bathing in this well safeguards one from misfortune. Adjacent to the well is the Kukkutesha Linga. The auspicious Pitamahesvara Linga is on the bank of Jyeshthavapi. To the southwest of Pitamahesha is Gadadhareshvara Linga. In the southwest quadrant of Jyeshtheshvara is the Vasukishvara Linga. Bathing and performing rites in the Vasuki Kunda remove the fear of serpents. To the west of that kunda is Takshakeshvara Linga, which accords all spiritual powers to devotees. One who performs rites in the water there is never attacked by serpents.

To the north of Vasuki Kunda, one encounters Kapali Bhairava, who vanquishes fear, protects the devotees and cares for the entire holy site. Mantras and practises performed there bear fruit within six months. There, Chandi Devi destroys obstacles. To the west is Chatuhsagara Vapika, where the four oceans have consecrated lingas. Bathing there equals the merit of bathing in all four oceans.

Further north is the Vrshabheshvara Linga, installed by Nandi. Visiting it grants liberation within six months. To its north is Gandharveshvara and to its east is Gandharva Kunda. This pond promises the company of gandharvas, through worship performed there.

Eastward lies the serpent Karkota, a well called Karkotavapi and the Karkotakeshvara Linga. Worshiping there grants honour in Naga Loka and safeguards from poison. To the west lies Dhundhumareeshvara Linga, the worship of which dispels the fear of enemies.

To the north lies Pururaveshvara Linga, which should be visited with effort to attain fulfilment of the four aims of life. To the east of there is the Supratika Linga, adored by the elephant of the quarter, boosting fame and strength. The Supratika Lake has shining waters in front of the linga. By visiting this spot, a devotee attains the position of being one of the Devas of the Quarters.

Vijaya Bhairavi, stationed at the northern gateway, protects the devotees. On the banks of the Varana, the ganas, Hundana and Mundana, guard the site and eradicate obstacles. Visiting them, one becomes happy.

Skanda then proceeded to narrate a story of what had once happened on the banks of the Varana. One day, Mena, the mother of Parvati, was lamenting that she had no news of her daughter since her marriage. Himavan, the father of Parvati, consoled his wife and promised to go ask after her.

Himavan proceeded to Kashi and encountered a traveller who informed him that just days earlier Shiva and Parvati had arrived in Kashi and Divodasa had departed for Swarga. He also informed Himavan that Shiva was presently residing in Jyeshtheshvara Sthana and that Vishvakarma was building a large mansion for Vishveshvara and Devi. He described at length the opulence of the palace, and Himavan was humbled by the glories of his son-in-law.

After some time, the traveller went away. Himavan was left alone with his thoughts.

He realized the greatness of Shiva and considered that Shiva was younger to him yet also elder to him, that he was greater and older than the greatest and oldest one. Himavan realized that he may be the Lord of the Mountains, but his son-in-law was the Lord of the Universe. Himavan resolved to go home and return later.

He called together all the great mountains and ordered them to establish a temple before sunrise the next day. His followers built a beautiful temple, and Himavan installed the Shaileshvara Linga. This temple boasted of a grand pavilion, radiant with white moonstones. Himavan then bathed at Panchanada Tirtha, bowed down to Kaala Raja, donated his jewels, and left for his own abode. The other mountains followed.

In the morning, the two ganas, Hundana and Mundana, saw the temple and reported to Shiva. Shiva and Parvati visited the temple. Shiva entered the sanctum sanctorum and saw the linga made entirely of moonstone, sparkling and radiant.

Shiva said affectionately to Devi, 'See your own father's creation.'

Parvati was delighted. At her request, Shiva promised to remain present within the linga and the temple. He said that devotees should bathe in the Varana and then worship Shailesha and make gifts in accordance with their capabilities. Then they would never return to samsara. He also said that just as he was the son-in-law of Himavan, the devotees of Shailesha would verily be Shiva's own sons.

Ratneshvara Linga

Skanda explained to Agastya Muni the origins of the Ratneshvara Linga. The jewels initially gathered by Himavan to the north of Kaala Raja—also known as Kaala Bhairava—coalesced into a linga possessing the lustre of all the stones and splendour of the rainbow; this is also referred to as Indra's bow.

After visiting Shaileshvara, Shiva and Parvati encountered the newly manifested Ratneshvara Linga. The entire firmament was radiant with the multicoloured splendour of that linga.

Parvati enquired about its origin, and Shiva explained that her father had brought for her sake a huge collection of jewels and that whatever is offered with great faith at Kashi for her sake or for Shiva's will always bear fruit like this. He said that the influence of the Ratneshvara Linga would be tremendous, and it would be the crest-jewel of all the lingas in Kashi. He asked her to build a mansion for the linga with the gold that had been kept in a heap by her father.

Devi engaged numerous ganas to construct the mansion, which materialized within a *yaama*, or three hours. The building resembled Mount Meru. Parvati requested Shiva for further explanation regarding the origins of the linga. Shiva revealed that while the linga was eternal, its manifestation was a result of Himavan's merit. He said it is the greatest among great secrets in Kashi, just as a precious stone kept safely at home is not known to others. He said that those who worship Ratneshvara Linga without any desire will become one of Shiva's ganas and see him there.

Then, Shiva told Parvati the story about Kalavati, a dancing girl who lived in the area of the linga. Once, on the Shivaratri day during Phalguna, she kept awake throughout the night, danced, and sang very sweetly. She thus propitiated Ratneshvara Linga by means of a triple symphony and then returned to her homeland. She died and became the daughter of Vasubhuti, a gandharva king. She became famous as Ratnavali in that incarnation, one who was beautiful with exquisite form and features, expert in all the arts, and very sweet-spoken.

Her three female companions—Shashilekha, Anangalekha, and Chitralekha—and she meditated together on Vak Devi, the Devi of speech. Sarasvati granted them the knowledge of all the arts. Ratnavali vowed to speak only after visiting the Ratneshvara

Linga. Every day, she would visit the linga in silence, with her three friends, and not say a word until after she had darshana.

Once, Ratnavali sang a series of sweet songs to Shiva, and he granted her the boon that the man who would come to her with a similar name to hers that night would become her husband. She was delighted and shy at the same time.

She travelled back home and shared the news with her friends. The next morning, the friends met up again. Ratnavali confessed that the man had appeared and spent the night with her. But lost in a liminal state of pleasure, she could not recall his departure. Now she burned with the fire of separation.

Her friends sought to comfort her and revived her with the waters used to bathe the Ratneshvara Linga. Skanda explained that the water with which the feet of Mahadeva have been washed is always the preferred remedy for a devotee undergoing any calamity or torment, no matter how great. Ratnavali regained her intelligence and senses. She asked Shashilekha to draw pictures of all the male Devas, Anangalekha to draw the pictures of all the young mortal men moving about Earth, and Chitralekha to draw pictures of all those young males in the nether worlds. They praised her cleverness and immediately set out to do so. When they had completed the drawings, Ratnavali found the one she was seeking in the image of Ratnachuda, the king of the nagas, in the nether worlds. Her friends comforted her that since Shiva had promised him to her, surely, they would be reunited.

The four companions travelled across the skies but were abducted by Subahu, a danava. The girls were exceedingly terrified, as they had known nothing in their lives other than playing with toys, adoring Ratneshvara, and being virtuous children to their parents. As they were crying out in terror, pleading with Shiva to save them, Ratnachuda heard them.

He thought to himself, 'Who is uttering the name of my Lord Ratneshvara, the great Lord of the Lingas, the One who severs the bonds of Karma?'

He seized his weapons and set out to find the girls in distress. He saw the danava consuming human flesh and animal suet. Ratnachuda called out to the demon: 'O wretched one, O abductor of cultured girls, now that I have seen you, where will you go? At the time of danger or death, if people utter the name of Ratneshvara, they need not fear anyone, including someone like you.' He assured Ratnavali and the others to not be afraid.

Ratnachuda shot an arrow at the danava who retaliated with the throw of a huge iron bar, which Ratnachuda promptly split into two. He quickly killed the danava and rescued the four girls, who were still blinded by terror. The others of the girls introduced Ratnavali to him and explained that she was seeking the one whose image she had seen painted in a picture, although the name of his residence and family were unknown.

Feeling compassionate towards them, Ratnachuda offered to show Ratneshvara to them. He led them to steps leading to a tank of water. The steps were made of different-coloured gems. Swans and geese surrounded the place. At his instruction, the four female companions entered the tank and dipped in its waters, fully clothed, and then emerged after bathing. Once they were out of the water, they found themselves in Kashi. Presently, Vasubhuti, the father of Ratnavali, found his daughter there. He had been informed of their misadventure. He embraced his daughter fondly and brought her back home.

Skanda explained to Agastya Muni that Ratnachuda would daily come out from Naga Loka through the path of the tank to bathe in the waters of the Mandakini and worship Ratneshvara, offering eight handfuls of gems and eight golden lotuses each time to the deity. Once, in his sleep, Ratneshvara had informed Ratnachuda that one day he would rescue a girl abducted by a demon and that she would become his wife. Ratnachuda remembered that omen.

When Ratnavali's father, the king of the gandharvas saw the naga king, he was elated at the prospect of having him as a son-in-law. However, he took his time getting to know Ratnachuda and his family before offering his daughter to him in marriage. Shashilekha, Anangalekha, and Chitralekha informed their parents of their desire to woo him as their husband. Thus, Ratnachuda married all the four gandharva maidens.

Ratnachuda then took all four of his wives back to his palace, approaching his father like Pranava proceeds towards Shiva along with the four Vedas. His parents congratulated them and welcomed the brides to their family.

Shiva explained to Parvati the significance of Ratneshvara, his immobile linga that grants blessings to all and bestows everything upon everyone, a linga whose power is unparalleled. In front of this linga, thousands of siddhas had attained great power, and till that day, this linga had remained hidden until Himavan had catalysed its manifestation. He said that he loves this linga very much and that through the blessings of this linga many jewels are attained, like a wife and a son and moksha.

He then revealed that in her previous birth as Sati, Parvati had established the Dakshayanishvara Linga to the east of Ratneshvara. There she is known as Ambika and he as Ambikeshvara. Moreover, said Shiva, Skanda's image can be found there and by visiting all three, a man can avoid re-entering samsara.

It is said that one who reads the narrative of Ratneshvara is never separated from his sons, grandsons, or wealth. On hearing the story of the origins of Ratneshvara Linga, a bachelor will obtain an excellent bride and a girl will attain a suitable husband. On hearing this history, no one will face distress due to the fire of separation from loved ones.

Krttivaseshvara

The Krttivasas Linga stands in the northeast of Maidagin, being one of Kashi's most ancient lingas. Krttivaseshvara is one of the Pancha Linga of Kashi mentioned in the *Kurma Purana*, the others being Vishvanatha, Omkareshvara, Madhyameshvara, and Kapardishvara (Tirtha Yatra 2022). The original temple, unfortunately, was destroyed by Aurangzeb—the first he destroyed in Kashi—and replaced by a mosque built over it. The site, where the original linga is still believed to reside, is accessible to Hindus only on Maha Shivaratri (Tagare n.d.[d]; see also Tirtha Yatra 2022). Another temple was reconstructed next to the mosque compound in 1656 with another Krttivaseshvara Linga, believed to have been retrieved from the Narmada river in Madhya Pradesh after the original linga had been moved there during the times of destruction (Tirtha Yatra 2022).

Skanda continued, recounting another incident at Ratneshvara. While Shiva was narrating the tale of Ratneshvara to Parvati, an abrupt commotion arose, heralding the approach of Mahishasura's son, the demon Gajasura.

Realizing that only his trishula could vanquish Gajasura, Shiva swiftly struck the demon with the trident. Impaled on the trident, Gajasura proclaimed to Shiva that perishing on the tip of his trishula would be his blessing.

Shiva chuckled and extolled Gajasura's valour. He told Gajasura to request a boon. Gajasura asked that Shiva wear his hide always, if it pleased him to do so. He said it would be of the right size and smooth in texture. He requested that the hide may always have a pleasing odour and remain soft and pure, that it may always be an excellent decoration for Shiva. He said, had his hide not been meritorious, how could it have come into contact with Shiva's trishula in the course of battle?

Further, Gajasura beseeched Shiva to adopt the name of Krttivasa. Shiva agreed and granted the boon transforming his body into a linga known as Krttivaseshvara. It would be the most excellent of the lingas, likened to being the head among all lingas. He vowed to reside there with his kin and followers, for the wellbeing of all mortals. He said that people should worship Krttivaseshvara by chanting the Shatarudriya mantras and visiting the linga again and again. Particularly, on the fourteenth day of the dark half of the month of Magha, a devotee should fast, worship, and keep awake all night during Shivaratri in front of this linga to attain the great goal of moksha.

Shiva then accepted the great hide of Gajasura and wore it. There was a great celebration on that day when Shiva, the sky-clad one, wore the hide. When the trishula was lifted to impale Gajasura, a great kunda was also formed. It is said that a devotee should bathe in this pond and then visit Krttivaseshvara to be blessed.

Skanda explained to Agastya Muni how by the power of that tirtha, crows were transformed into swans. There used to take place a great religious festival at Krttivasa on Chaitra Purnima. Cooked rice that was offered at this time was kept in a heap by the priests. Birds would fight with each other over the cooked rice. The weaker ones were struck down by the strong. They fell into that kunda from the sky and were saved from death by being transformed into swans with black feet and beaks.

Ever since then, that kunda has become known as Hamsa Tirtha. All impure beings are immediately purified by performing rites in the waters of Hamsa Tirtha.

Skanda told Agastya Muni that while there are many lingas in Kashi, Krttivaseshvara Linga should be remembered as the head of them all. After worshiping Krttivasa with a devoted mind, one attains the benefit of worshiping all of the lingas in Kashi. Any japa, dana, tapasya, abhishekha, or homa performed in the vicinity of Krttivasa provides endless benefit. Around Hamsa Tirtha, said Skanda, are ten thousand and two hundred lingas installed by the rishis. These siddha lingas become concealed in the different yugas and manifest themselves again through the presence of Shiva.

The Lomashesha Linga was installed by Lomasha to the west of Krttivasas. The Malatisha Linga to the north of Krttivasa grants dominion over elephants. The Antakeshvara Linga further north eradicates sins. The Janakesha Linga bestows the knowledge of Brahman. To the north is the large deity of Bhairava with dark limbs. Shushkodari with terrible eyes is also to the north of Krttivasa. To the southwest thereof is the *vetala*, or spirit, Agnijihva, who fulfils all desires if worshiped on a Tuesday. The Vetala Kunda there eradicates all ailments, including cuts and tumours. A gana is present there with two arms, four feet, and five heads. He destroys all sins.

To the north thereof is Rudra, with the four Vedas as horns, the *savanas* as three feet, two heads—the Prayaniya as the introductory rite and the Udayaniya as the concluding rite—and the seven Vedic metres as hands. In the shape of the Dharma Bull, Rudra cries out, 'Those who are evil-minded in Kashi and those who bring obstacles to Kashi, I hold this dagger to cut them off. Those who are pious and remove obstacles in Kashi, I hold the *amrta* jar in my hand to make their families flourish.'

To the north of Rudra is Manipradipa, the naga deity. Beyond him is the Mani Kunda, the kunda that dispels poison. One who worships Manipradipa will obtain a kingdom full of jewels and rubies, abundant with elephants, horses, and chariots, with many wives and sons.

Assembly of the Sixty-Eight Holy Spots

Skanda proceeded to describe all of the lingas in Kashi that are conducive to liberation. The spot where Shiva wore the hide is known as Rudravasa. After he was residing there with Parvati, Nandi came and reported that sixty-eight mansions full of jewels had been constructed. He himself had brought all the holy temples from all of the three worlds to Kashi. He then described them in detail.

Sthanu had arisen from Kurukshetra, and one-sixteenth of it was now in Kashi. In front of it was the holy lake named Sannihati, located to the western side of Lolarka. To the north of Dhundhiraja was the Devadeva Linga, which bestows all spiritual powers, and beyond it the well known as Brahmavarta; these arose from Naimisharanya. From Gokarna came the Mahabala Linga near Shambaditya. The Shashibhushana Linga came from Prabhasa and had been installed to the east of Rnamochana. Mahakala came from Ujjain, and the Mahakala Linga was established to the east of the Pranava Linga. Ayogandheshvara Linga arose from Pushkara, along with the holy lake, in the northern side of Matsyodari. Mahanadeshvara Linga came from Attahasa to the north of Trilochana. Mahotkateshvara Linga came from Marutkota, to the north of Kameshvara. Vimaleshvara Linga came from Vishvasthana. The Mahavrata Linga came from the Mahendra Mountain and bestows the merit of great vratas.

During the Krta Yuga, when the rishis were reciting mantras, a great linga manifested after piercing the hard ground. The rishis proclaimed it to be Mahadeva, and it was through the power of that great linga that Kashi became holy. This is the presiding deity of Kashi, named Mahadeva.

The Pitamaheshvara Linga came from Gaya at the place where Dharma performed austerities for one million yugas, keeping as his witness the Dharmeshvara Linga. From Prayaga, Maheshvara came by himself, accompanied by the tirtha itself, staying to the south of the Nirvanamandapa. Maheshvara should be worshiped at the beginning in Kashi, it is said. From Shankukarna came the Mahatejas Linga. The Mahayogishvara Linga came from Rudrakoti. In the place it is located, known as Rudrasthali, those who die, whether they be worms, insects, locusts, birds, beasts, barbarians, or learned ones, become rudras. Krttivasas itself came from Ekambara. From Marujangala came Chandisha, armed with the noose. Neelakantha himself came from the Kalanjara mountain. The Vijaya Linga came from Kashmir and bestows success.

From Tridanda city arrived Urdhvaretas staying behind Kushmandaka, the officer of the ganas. Srikantha Linga came from Mandaleshvara. Kapardishvara manifested from the Chagalanda Tirtha. From Amratakeshvara came Sukshmesha. Devesha Jayanta arrived from Madhukeshvara. Tripurantaka manifested from Srishaila. Kukkuteshvara came from Saumyasthana. Trishuli came from Jaleshvara; Jati came from Rameshvara; Tryambaka came from Trisandhya; Hareshvara came from Harishchandra.

Sarva came from Madhyamakeshvara, and Yajneshvara Linga came from Sthaleshvara, bestowing the benefits of all lingas. Sahasraksha Linga came from Suvarna. The Harshita Linga came from Harshita. Rudra came from Rudramahalaya. Vrshesha came from Vrshabhadvaja. Ishaneshvara came from Kedara. Samhara Bhairavi came from Bhairava. The Ugra Linga manifested from Kanakhala. Bhaveshvara manifested from Vastrapatha. Dandi arrived from Devadaruvana.

The Bhadrakarnahrada pool came from Bhadrakarnahrada. The Kala Linga came from the Yama Linga. Pashupati came from what is now Nepal. Kapalisha came from Karaviraka. The Diptesha Linga came from Kailasha. Nakulishvara came from Kayarohana. Amaresha came from the confluence of the Ganga and the sea. Bhimeshvara came from Saptagodavari Tirtha. The Bhasmagatra Linga came from Bhuteshvara.

Hearing the news of Shiva's return to Kashi, Dharani Varaha came down from the Vindhya Mountain. He came accompanied by the ganas, rishis, and Devas. From Karnikara came Ganadhyaksha. Virupaksha came from Hemakuta. Himasthesha came from Gangadvara; Ganadhipa came from Kailasha. The Bhurbhuvah Linga came from Gandhamadana Parvat.

The Hatakesha Linga came from beneath the bottom of the seven nether worlds, accompanied by Bhogavati, the river of Patala Loka. That linga is made of pure gold and adorned with jewel necklaces.

From the world of the stars, Taraka, the Tarakeshvara Linga came and manifested itself in front of Gyaanavapi. *Taraka gyaana*—knowledge of liberation—is obtained by worshiping that linga. A man should bathe in the waters of Gyaanavapi, visit Tarakesha, perform all the rites at twilight, and then observe the vow of silence until the linga is visited. At the end of his life, he will receive the Taraka gyaana, which will liberate him.

From Kirata, where Shiva had assumed a hunter's form, arrived Kirateshvara Linga. The Marukeshvara Linga came from Lanka and eradicates fear of rakshasas. The Nairrteshvara Linga destroys all evils. Jala Linga appeared from the Ganga. The Shrestha Linga came from Kotishvara. The Analeshvara Linga came out of the mouth of Vadava—fire from under the sea. The Trivishtapa Linga of beginningless existence came from the Virajas Tirtha. Omkara arrived from Amarakantaka.

Nandi concluded by explaining that he brought all of these great holy spots, *ayatanas*, after leaving only a part behind in the original sites, pleasing Shiva. He instructed Nandi to appoint the nine crores of Chamundas, accompanied by their deities, *bhutas*, *vetalas*, and *bhairavas*, to guard the city.

CHAPTER 13

Origin Stories of the Other Special Lingas

Devi asked Shiva to explain what makes the lingas in Kashi so special and which of them have existed eternally. In which of these lingas does Shiva always remain with her, his beloved, even during Pralaya; by the power of which lingas has Kashi become well known as the city of liberation?

Shiva proceeded to enumerate the significant lingas in Kashi that grant mukti. He said that there are gross and subtle lingas, lingas crafted from gems and metals, many that are swayambhu and many that were installed by Devas and rishis. They are venerated by siddhas, charanas, gandharvas, yakshas, and rakshasas. There are even lingas installed by asuras, nagas, mortal men, danavas, apsaras, elephants, mountains, bears, monkeys, and birds. Some are visible, while others remain concealed. Some have been ruined by the ravages of time, but Shiva said they are all still to be worshipped.

There used to be one hundred *parardhas*—a parardha is one followed by seventeen zeroes—of lingas. Sixty crores lingas are in the Ganga alone. Those siddha lingas have become invisible in Kali Yuga.

Shiva then identified the fourteen lingas that bestow mukti: Omkareshvara, Trilochana, Mahadeva, Krttivaseshvara, Ratneshvara, Chandreshvara, Kedaranatha, Dharmeshvara, Vireshvara, Kameshvara, Vishvakarmeshvara, Manikarnishvara,

Avimukteshvara, and finally, the fourteenth, the great Vishveshvara Linga. The combination of these fourteen lingas is known as Muktikshetra.

The contemporary location of these fourteen lingas is as follows: (i) Omkareshvara (north of Macchodari; of which only partial remains can be found) (ii) Trilochana (between Macchodari and Ganga) (iii) Mahadeva (northeast of Trilochana) (iv) Krttivaseshvara (northeast of Maidagin; temple demolished and converted to a mosque) (v) Ratneshvara (in the middle of the road from Maidagin to Mrtyunjaya) (vi) Chandreshvara (west of Sankata Devi Temple) (vii) Kedaranatha (at Kedara Ghat) (viii) Dharmeshvara (east of Vishvanatha at Dharma Kupa) (ix) Vireshvara (south of Sankata Devi) (x) Kameshvara (east of Macchodari) (xi) Vishvakarmeshvara (northeast of Mrtyunjaya) (xii) Manikarnishvara (above Manikarnika Ghat) (xiii) Avimukteshvara (in the Vishvanatha area) (xiv) Vishveshvara (the centre of Kashi, today known as Vishvanatha Temple) (Tagare n.d.[e]).

Agastya Muni inquired if there were other lingas that bestow mukti. Skanda clarified that these lingas remain concealed during the Kali Yuga, and only those who are devoted to Shiva and know Kashi will be able to know of these lingas. The names of these fourteen lingas are as follows: Amrteshvara, Tarakeshvara, Gyaaneshvara, Karuneshvara, Mokshadvareshvara, Swargadvareshvara, Brahmeshvara, Langala, Vrddhakaleshvara, Vrshesha, Chandisha, Nandikeshvara, Maheshvara, and Jyotirupeshvara.

Another set of fourteen lingas was also described by Shiva to Parvati: Shailesha, Sangamesha, Svarleena, Madhyameshvara, Hiranyagarbha, Ishaana, Gopreksha, Vrshabhadhvaja, Upashanta Shiva, Jyeshtha, Nivaseshvara, Shukresha, Vyaghra, and Jambukesha. These fourteen, too, bestow mukti.

Shiva concluded that the names of these lingas constitute the Upanishad of the sacred site of Kashi. The unbounded greatness of each and every one of these lingas is known only to Shiva, he said.

Omkareshvara

Parvati then desired to know the origin stories of each of the fourteen lingas in the first set that Shiva had mentioned. Shiva began with the Omkareshvara Linga.

Brahma had once performed a great penance at this site for one thousand yugas. A supreme radiance sprang up before Brahma, piercing the seven lower worlds and illuminating all the skies. The sound of crackling and splitting emerging from that radiance roused Brahma from his *samadhi*.

As he opened his eyes, Brahma saw before him the letter A, endowed with *sattva*, the cause of the *Rg Veda* and the protector of creation, identical with Narayana and beyond the reach of *tamas*. Then, he saw the letter U, having the *rajasic* form, the source of the *Yajur Veda* and the creator of everything; it was Brahma's own reflection. Beyond it, he saw the letter M, the silent darkness of tamas, the source of the *Sama Veda* and the cause of dissolution, in the very form of Rudra. Then Brama saw the Nada, the cosmic form of Shabda Brahman endowed with and without attributes, the abode of Para, the subtlest sound, the embodiment of the supreme bliss, the cause of all verbal utterance. Above the Nada, he saw the subtlest ultimate form of Bindu, the cause of all causes.

Brahma saw these come together as AUM, that which protects and raises up the devotee, that which is formless and also endowed with form. This Aum is also known as the Taraka and glorified as the Pranava. It is from this that the Vedas emerge.

Brahma saw Shiva in the form of the linga embodying the five syllables of Om (A, U, M, Nada, and Bindu). Brahma then recited a longer prayer in praise of this Omkareshvara form of Shiva.

Pleased, Shiva offered him a boon. Brahma asked only that Shiva remain present in this linga.

Shiva agreed, saying that this great linga is identical with the Shabda Brahman. He said that if a creature bathes in Matsyodari Tirtha and then visits Omkareshvara, he will never be reborn. A mere glance at Omkareshvara will ensure the benefit of an Ashvamedha yajna. If Omkareshvara alone is visited, it is equivalent to visiting all of the lingas on Earth. The devotees of Omkareshvara should not be considered human; they are in fact rudras covered with human skin. The power of this linga is very rare, indeed.

Skanda told Agastya Muni that even today Brahma worships the Omkareshvara Linga through the chanting of the Brahmastava that he had composed.

One thousand years ago, Omkareshvara was one of the most important Shivalingas in Kashi. It was housed in a majestic and large temple on the bank of the Matsyodari lake. It consisted of a group of five temples representing the five components of the Pranava, Om: A, U, M, Nada, and Bindu. It was destroyed by the Muslims. Ahilyabai Holkar, the Maratha queen, rebuilt the main temple and appointed a Brahmana to look after it. Today, the temple complex is barely known and dilapidated, surrounded by a Muslim neighbourhood with Muslim graves in the front of the temple. The Nada and Bindu Temples have disappeared, and the others are in disrepair. (Tagare n.d.[e]).

Two further stories are associated with Omkareshvara. Once there was a Brahmana by the name of Damana, the son of Bharadvaja. This was during the Padmakalpa. In a quest for enlightenment, after *upanayanam* and learning the lore, Damana wandered from mountain to mountain, tirtha to tirtha, practising austerities. He stayed in all of the holy spots all across the world, but the peace of mind he was searching for was elusive. He could not find a suitable teacher who could guide him.

One day, that ascetic, Damana, saw the Amarakantaka Tirtha bearing the site of Omkareshvara. Immediately upon seeing it, his mind became steady. He saw there practitioners of the Pashupata tradition who worshipped the linga, subsisted on alms, and studied the Agamas. He bowed to them and sat in front of their preceptor. Their preceptor was the great sage, Garga. He was at that time considered the most excellent of ascetics.

Garga asked Damana who he was and from where he had come. Damana recounted his story and explained his quest. Garga told him he would narrate what he had directly seen in Avimukta and describe that which is the bestower of all siddhi on good people.

He spoke of the glories of Kashi, describing Manikarnisha in the east, Brahmesha in the south, Gokarna in the west, and Bharabhuta in the north. He said that if a devotee bathes in Manikarnika, visits Vishveshvara and circumambulates that holy spot, he will attain the fruits of a Rajasuya yajna. There is no holy spot on par with Avimukta anywhere in the cosmic egg, he explained. It is true, he said, certainly, it is true.

He went on to explain that the Mahaparishadas, the great attendants of Shiva, bearing noose and swords, always protect Kashi. Attahasa, surrounded by one crore ganas, protects the eastern gate, day and night. Bhutadhatrisha protects the southern gate. Gokarna, also surrounded by one crore ganas, protects the western gate. Ghatakarna protects the northern gate. Chagavaktra protects the northeastern corner. Bhishana protections the southeastern direction. Shankukarna protects the southwest direction, and Drmichanda protects the northwest.

Kalaksha, Ranabhadra, Kauleya, and Kalakampana are the ganas stationed on the other bank of the Ganga, protecting from the east. Veerabhadra, Nabha, Kardamaliptavigraha, and Sthulakarna are on the other side of the Asi. Vishalaksha, Mahabhima, Kundodara, and Mahodara protect the western gate. Nandisena, Panchala, Kharapada, Karantaka, Ananda, Gopaka, and Babhru protect from the banks of the Varana.

Garga then explained that five pashupatas—Kapila, Savarni, Shrikantha, Pingala, and Amshuman—became siddhas just by worshipping Omkareshvara Linga. Once, all five of them had performed their puja and begun dancing, making sounds like that of a bull, and in that moment, they all merged into that linga.

Garga recounted another wondrous event that had occurred there. Once, there was a she-frog who always circumambulated the

Omkareshvara Linga and ate the rice grains from the remnants of the puja offerings. Because she ate that *nirmalya*, she did not die there but rather died outside of the holy region. Later, she was born as a daughter in the house of Pushpabatu. She had an auspicious form, but her face resembled the face of a vulture due to the demerit of eating the raw rice grains from the puja materials for Shiva. Still, she had a sweet voice and was expert in music.

Since childhood, that girl named Madhavi worshiped Omkareshvara constantly, due to the samskaras of her past life. Her mind became as stable and steady as that of a noble sage due to the practice of yoga. She did not feel hunger or thirst during the day, nor did she feel sleepy at night. So absorbed was she by the darshana of the linga that she viewed even blinking as an obstacle. All day and all night, she chanted the names of Omkareshvara.

Once, on the fourteenth day of the month of Vaishakha, Madhavi fasted during the day and stayed awake all night. When those who had gathered for the festival left, she swept the temple premises and joyously worshipped the linga, singing sweetly and dancing gracefully. Meditating on Omkareshvara, she merged into the linga. So attained was she that her physical body itself merged into the linga, as Garga's own guru witnessed. A radiance emerged from the linga and pervaded the sky.

It is said that in front of the linga is the Srimukhi cave, which is the doorway to Patala. Siddhas stay there. Those who observe vratas and stay in that cave for five nights will see naga females who will recount auspicious and inauspicious things. By visiting this Nadeshvara Linga, one can hear all the sounds that exist. It is said that innumerable devotees serving Omkareshvara have attained siddhi with their physical body transforming into a divine one. While Avimukta is the greatest sacred place in the entire cosmos, even greater than it is Omkareshvara on the banks of the Matsyodari.

After narrating this story to Damana, Garga accompanied him to Kashi. Damana then worshipped Omkareshvara and merged into that linga.

Shiva said to Parvati, 'There is no linga like Omkareshvara anywhere in the world.'

Trilochana

Trilochana is one of the oldest and most famous of the lingas in Kashi. Skanda explained to Agastya Muni that three rivers have their confluence at Trivishtapa, where the Trilochana Linga is located. These rivers are the Sarasvati, the Kalindi (i.e., the Yamuna), and the Narmada. They bathe the linga thrice a day with pitchers held in their own hands. All around the Trilochana Linga, other lingas named after these rivers have been installed by them.

While Omkareshvara illuminates the path of liberation, Trilochana is the form of the ultimate *shreyas*, meaning welfare. It is said that all sins, save the slander of Shiva, can be expiated by bowing down to Trilochana Linga.

It is said that one with shraddha should make the following resolve: if they are desirous of making a beginning, if they are afraid of sins, if they consider the shastras to be true, then they should give up everything and go to Kashi, where Vishveshvara himself is present. If one enters the holy city of Kashi with this resolve, all will be attained.

At the time of Pradosha, if a devotee circumambulates the Trilochana Linga seven times, he attains the merit of circumambulating the entire Earth, said Shiva. He then told the secret behind the linga to Parvati. Once, when he was absorbed in yoga, this linga pierced through the seven nether worlds from beneath the earth and established itself before him. Shiva had then given to Gauri three eyes so that she could perceive the linga. Ever since that time, this linga has been known as Trilochana, the bestower of the vision of knowledge.

The devotees of Trilochana are themselves three-eyed; these attendants of Shiva are liberated ones even while living. Shiva said that the devotees should bathe in the Pilipila whirlpool on the third day in the bright half of the month of Vaishakha, fast, and keep awake all night. They should bathe again in the morning and worship the Trilochana Linga. They should then offer pots filled with cooked rice and monetary gifts, referred to as *dharma-ghatas*, to their ancestors. Then they should break their fast in the company of other devotees. After they die, they will become ganas of Shiva.

Shiva told Devi that every month, on Ashtami and Chaturdashi, all the tirthas come to visit Trivishtapa.

Next to the Trilochana Linga are many other lingas that are also powerful and bestow mukti. The Shantanava Linga, installed by Shantanu, was installed on the banks of the Ganga. To the south of it is the Bhishmesha Linga, upon seeing which one will never suffer from death or lust. To the west of it is the Dronesha Linga, worshipping which Drona assumed a celestial form once more. In front of it is the Ashvatthameshvara Linga, worshiping which the son of Drona, Ashvatthama, does not fear even Kaala. To the northwest of Dronesha is the great Valakhilyeshvara Linga, by visiting which one obtains the merit of performing all yajnas. To the left of that is the Valmikeshvara Linga, by seeing which a man is cleansed of all grief.

Shiva then narrated to Parvati an incident that occurred at Trilochana during the Rathantara Kalpa. Two pigeons had nested in the mansion of Trilochana, built out of rubies and other precious stones. The mansion had many windows of various shapes. When the wind fluttered the banners, it seemed as if the banners were warding off sins from entering. The pigeons circumambulated the mansion every day in the morning, afternoon, and evening.

The wind from the fluttering of their wings removed the dust from the mansion. The names of Trilochana and Trivishtapa, being uttered incessantly by the visiting devotees, entered their ears. The waving of the lights during aarti entered their vision every day. Absorbed in watching these activities, they did not fly elsewhere and therefore did not have the opportunity to eat. A long time elapsed this way.

Once, a cruel vulture saw them. He wanted to take the pigeons, but seeing that the pigeons were fearless, his eyes turned red with anger.

The female pigeon became anxious and alerted her husband to the presence of an enemy. The male pigeon scoffed, saying that there was no need to worry and that she should just enjoy herself with him. The female pigeon remained quiet. Like this, the vulture came and went a few times. Once, it came and sat for three hours, closely watching their nest. Then he flew away again.

The female pigeon urged her husband that they should go nest elsewhere. Again, the male pigeon counselled her not to be afraid.

The next day, the vulture came and obstructed the path of the pigeons. He stayed there for a few days and urged the male pigeon to fight. If he was just going to starve himself to death, he would surely fall into hell, said the vulture. He pointed out that there were two of them and just one of him, that victory and defeat are uncertain and in flux. Either heaven or the fort of the mansion itself could be attained by one who dared to fight.

The male pigeon then came out and tried to fight the vulture. Immediately, the vulture seized both pigeons and flew off.

The female pigeon then spoke to her husband. 'You considered me a mere female and took my words lightly. Hence you have come to this plight. If even now, my dear, you would heed a single request of mine, it would only be to your benefit. Even as I am held by this vulture in his beak, even as he continues to fly without touching the ground, bite his foot so that he at least lets you go.'

Her husband did so. Presently, the vulture, crying out with pain, released both of them. Thus, it is said that even in adversity efforts should not be abandoned by wise men.

After some time, the two birds died on the banks of the Sarayu. The male pigeon became a vidyadhara in Ayodhya, one of the Saptapuri. Even in childhood, he was deeply devoted to Shiva. He also took the vow to only have one wife, reasoning to himself that the attachment to other men's wives reduce fame, longevity, strength, and happiness, and that a sensible man should avoid this. Parimalalaya, that brilliant young man, also resolved to take refuge in Trilochana alone. He thus travelled frequently to Kashi to visit Trivishtapa.

The female pigeon was born as Ratnavali, the daughter of the naga, Rantadeepa, in Patala. She had two female companions who were inseparable from her: Prabhavati and Kalavati. She took the vow that she would break her silence every day only after worshipping Trilochana in the company of her two friends.

Once, during the month of Madhava, they fasted on the third day and kept awake throughout the night, dancing, singing, and narrating tales of Shiva. The next morning, they bathed in the Pilipila Tirtha and worshipped Trilochana. Then they slept in the pavilion of the temple.

As they slept, Shiva, limbs white as camphor, emerged from the linga, adorned with a serpent-like girdle. His throat was blue, and his serpentine ornaments shone. The left side of his body bore Devi. He wore a snake as his sacred thread.

He told the three girls to get up. Recognizing him as their lord, they eulogized him with a long, beautiful prayer. He told them that Parimalalaya would become their husband. He promised that after enjoying the pleasures of the vidyadhara world for a long time, they would become detached and attain what is worthy of being attained by staying in Kashi. All four of them would attain mukti at the end of their lives. He explained that Ratnavali was the female pigeon and Parimalalaya the male pigeon from their past lives.

By removing the dust through the fluttering of their wings, their circumambulations above and below as they flew around the courtyard, their bathing in the Chaturnada Tirtha, and the pleasing music of their chirps, they had served Shiva. Due to their merits, they died in Ayodhya, which is conducive to attaining Kashi in the next life. He also recounted the merits of the other two naga maidens.

The naga maidens were delighted. Shiva disappeared back into the linga. In the course of time, all transpired as he had said it would.

Kedara Linga

The Kedara Linga is a rough mound with a white line in the middle. It is said to resemble a mound of *khichari* cut in half, related to the time that King Mandhatr offered half his khichari to Shiva and the whole mound transformed into a stone linga. The temple of the Kedara Linga is at the top of the Kedara Ghat and was saved from Aurangzeb's onslaught of destruction. It is said that Kedareshvara and the entire Kedara section of Kashi is particularly ancient and sacred.

Shiva then narrated to Parvati about the Kedareshvara Linga. He said that if a man simply desires to go to Kedara and takes the sankalpa to do so, all his sins from birth perish. If he actually leaves his house with the intent to travel towards Kedara, the sins of two lifetimes are destroyed. Once he reaches the halfway point to Kedara, the sins of three lifetimes leave in despair, sighing grievously. One who continues to stay at home but repeats 'Kedara, Kedara, Kedara' thrice in the evening will attain the benefit of pilgrimage to Kedara.

By visiting the peak of Kedara and drinking the water of Kedara Tirtha, a devotee will eliminate the sins of seven lifetimes. By bathing in the Harapapa Hrada and worshipping Kedareshvara, a devotee will eliminate the sins acquired in ten million lifetimes. After prostrating once to Kedara and performing all of the rites, a devotee will fix the linga in his heart and attain mukti upon death.

Shiva told Parvati about an incident that had occurred during the Rathantara Kalpa. A son of a Brahmana had travelled from Ujjain to Kashi. After upanayanam, he took the vow of celibacy. He was awed to visit Kashi and see it filled with followers of Pashupati, adorned with matted hair and holy ash. All these devotees were contented to subsist on alms.

This young man was initiated into the Mahapashupata Vrata by Hiranyagarbha. He soon became the most excellent of the Pashupatas at the tender young age of twelve.

Once, a young man, known as Vashishtha, went on pilgrimage to Kedarnath in the Himalayas. When they reached the Asidhara Mountain, his guru, Hiranyagarbha, passed away. While the sages watched, Shiva's attendants came and joyously took him to Kailasha. It is said that one who dies halfway to Kedarnath will live in Kailasha for a long time.

After concluding the pilgrimage, Vashishtha returned to Kashi and resolved to visit Kedarnath on every Chaitra Purnima for so long as he resided in Kashi. He made sixty-one such pilgrimages. In his sixty-second year, again, he made preparations for the pilgrimage although he was aged and feeble. While others dissuaded him, he maintained his resolve, thinking that even if he died midway, he would go to Kailasha just like his guru.

Shiva appeared in his dream and offered him a boon. Vashishtha requested that all these people in Kashi along with their followers should be blessed. Pleased, Shiva offered him another boon. Vashishtha asked him to stay in Kashi in his Kedara form. Shiva obliged.

Once, two ravens fighting in the sky had fallen into the waters of the Hamsa Tirtha and transformed into swans. Because Devi herself had bathed in those waters, it became known as Gauri Tirtha. Shiva said that if one bathes in the Kedara Tirtha and offers balls of rice, or pinda, without hurrying through the rites, one hundred and one generations of his family will transcend samsara. He also said that in Kali Yuga, not everyone will understand the greatness of Kedareshvara.

Shiva further said that the Chitrangadeshvara Linga to the north of Kedara is very auspicious. To the south of Kedara is Neelakantha and to the northwest is Ambarishesha. If one visits the nearby Indradyumneshvara Linga, he will ascend to Swarga in a luminous chariot. The one who visits Kalanjareshvara Linga to the south will conquer old age and time. By visiting Kshemeshvara Linga to the north of Chitrangadeshvara, a devotee will be well in this world and all worlds.

Dharmeshvara

The Dharmeshvara Linga is located to the east of Vishvanatha Temple near Dharma Kupa.

Parvati asked Shiva to describe the glories of the Dharmeshvara Linga. Shiva explained that Devi was herself present in the form of Mukti here. When Shiva had wanted to attain victory in the battle over Tripura, victory was attained by the offering of many *modakas* here. This was the tirtha where Indra got rid of his sins after killing Vrtra. It was here that Yama Deva obtained Dharmadhikarana, the authority over matters relating to merits and demerits and their associated rewards and punishments. Even birds have attained mukti here. This site is also known as Dharmapeetha.

Shiva told Parvati that once Yama Deva, the son of Surya Deva, had performed a severe penance. During winter, he used to stand in water; in the rain, he used to stand under the thunderclouds; during summer, he used to stand in the middle of five fires. Sometimes he would stand just on the tips of his big toes for a long time. When he was thirsty, he would take just a few drops of water through the blades of *darbha* grass. Like this, he performed penance for four yugas to see Shiva four times.

Shiva appeared before him to bestow boons. Yama Deva was there under the golden-branched banyan tree known as Kanchana-shakha. That tree sheltered many birds and provided extensive shade.

Yama Deva had installed the great Dharmeshvara Linga made of crystalline solar stone. Shiva blessed Yama Deva that he would be known as Dharmaraja, and he alone would be employed by Shiva for the administration of dharma unto all embodied beings, mobile as well as immobile. He conferred upon him lordship over the southern direction and that he would be the witness of the karma of all creatures.

Yama Deva was overjoyed. Shiva offered him another boon. Yama Deva asked that he grant boons to these baby birds, the parrots who had witnessed his penance for a long time and been deprived of their parents. When they were born, the mother died of illness from delivery and the father was eaten by a hawk.

Pleased by Yama Deva's compassion, Shiva summoned them and offered them a boon.

The birds said that the greatest benefit they could have wished for was to have his darshana. They said that by witnessing Yama Deva's worship of the Dharmeshvara Linga, they were able to remember tens of millions of their previous births. Sometimes they were asuras; sometimes they were danavas, nagas, kinnaras, vidyadharas, or gandharvas. Many times, they were human kings; they had also been sea creatures and land animals. They had been protectors as well as murderers. They had been happy and miserable, triumphant and defeated, masters and servants both. But nowhere did they have tranquillity until they arrived at Dharmeshvara.

The birds said that if after all that, a boon was still to be given, to please grant the knowledge of liberation to creatures like them. They said that they do not covet the position of Indra or that of the moon. They desired only to die in Kashi.

On hearing the soft, sweet, articulate speech of the birds, Shiva was deeply pleased. He remarked, 'Among all the cities in the three worlds, Kashi is my royal place. By circumambulating this site, birds become liberated as do the Devas.'

Shiva further said that if one, without any personal desire, reads the Dharmashastras, the Puranas, or the Itihaasa at Dharma Peetha, they will stay in Shiva's abode. He further explained that in Gyaanavapi, he would always be sporting in the waters with Parvati and merely by drinking that water one would get pure knowledge. In front of that place is his Shringaramandapa, which should be known as Shree Peetha bestowing glory and wealth.

To the north of the palace called Mokshalakshmivilasa is the Aishvarya Mandapa, where Shiva bestows opulence. To the eastern side of his palace is the Gyaana Mandapa where he bestows knowledge. In the mansion of Bhavani is his culinary hall where he joyously accepts whatever is offered there. His floor of rest, the Vishramabhumika, is the mansion of Vishalakshi. There the ultimate rest, mukti, is granted. Chakrapushkarini is the tirtha for his midday bath that eliminates all impurities for all who bathe there. Manikarnika is where he redeems ignorant beings from the bindings of karma. In Kashi, that is the spot for granting mukti by Shiva.

Avimukteshvareshvara is the greatest site for adoring the linga. The evening Sandhya is performed in Pashupatishvara. The early morning sandhya is performed by Shiva at Omkareshvara. On every Chaturdasi, he stays in Krttivasa. He abides in the Trilochana Linga always. The Mahadeva Linga grants spiritual powers. Vrshabhadhvaja provides delight to the ancestors. Taking the form of Adi Keshava, he leads all the devotees of Vishnu to Shvetadeepa. In the form of Bindu Madhava, the greatest manifestation of Vishnu, he leads the devotees of Vishnu who bathe in the waters of the Panchanada Tirtha.

Shiva concluded that while there are many *peethas* in Kashi at every step, the power of Dharmesha Peetha is something unique and excellent. He said that those parrots would ascend to his abode in a divine chariot and would enjoy pleasures for a long time before acquiring the knowledge directly from Shiva. The chariot then appeared, and the birds left for Kailasha.

Vireshvara

Shiva then narrated the story of the Vireshvara Linga to Parvati. Once, there was a king named Amitrajit who was righteous and sattvic. He was devoted to Vishnu.

Once, Narada had come to visit him. He told the king that he had decided to help him. There was a daughter of a vidyadhara, named Malayagandhini, who was abducted by Kankalaketu, a powerful danava, from the Gandhamadana Parvat.

The girl had seen Narada and told him that the danava was destined to die by being struck by his own trident in battle but was invincible otherwise. She also told Narada that Devi had given her a boon that an intelligent, young devotee of Vishnu would marry her by the next Tritiya. She asked Narada to help make this boon come true.

That was why Narada had approached the king. The king was instantly eager to rescue the girl. The king asked Narada how to reach them at Champakavati. Narada told him to go to the ocean on Purnima and seated on a boat he would see a divine kalpa tree standing in a chariot. There he would see a celestial woman seated on a couch signing sweetly the following verse, while holding the veena: 'A karma, whether good or evil, done by one will certainly get its consequence experienced by the same person guided by the thread of fate.'

Narada said that she would then dive into the ocean along with the chariot, tree, and couch. The king would have to follow her unhesitatingly, after which he would see the city of Champakavati in Patala. The king followed the sage's instructions and found the vidyadhara girl in Champakavati. They awaited the arrival of the danava.

When the danava came, he tried to coax the vidyadhara girl to marry him. He rambled on, intoxicated with human flesh and suet. Then he went to sleep and kept the trident on his lap. The girl summoned the king and placed the trident in his hand, urging him to kill the danava quickly. With a joyous shout, the king kicked the demon with his left foot, remembering Hari.

The kick roused the danava, who quickly struck the king in the chest. The danava howled, his hand hurt. Protected by Hari, the king did not experience pain at all.

The danava recognized the king as a votary of Vishnu and told him that he had not violated the girl, and that she should be viewed as Lakshmi herself, being guarded by him for the king's sake. The danava then struck the king again. The king withstood the blow, and, balancing the trident in his hand, he took aim at the danava's chest. The danava died instantly. The couple got married and went to Kashi.

They led a happy life together. One day, the queen told the king that she intended to take up the vrata of Abhishta Trtiya to obtain a son. With his consent, she performed the vrata and gave birth to a son. The queen prayed to Gauri that her son be born of a part of Vishnu—that as soon as he was born, he would go to Swarga and then return; that he would be a great devotee of Shiva and become well-known to the entire world; that he would be born as a sixteen-year-old boy. Gauri blessed her accordingly.

Being born under a malignant star, the boy was abandoned and taken by the yoginis to the mothers: Brahmani, Vaishnavi, Raudri, Varahi, Narasimhika, Kaumari, Mahendri, Chamunda, and Chandika. They told the yoginis that the boy was marked with excellent signs and deserved to rule a kingdom. They asked the yoginis to take him to the place where Panchamudra Devi resides in Kashi. The boy would then attain siddhi.

The yoginis did so, and the boy practised austerities. Shiva manifested himself in the form of a linga and asked the boy to request a boon from him. The boy requested Shiva to remain there always, alleviating the distress of worldly existence, and to grant the devotees what they desire without the devotees having to undertake formal rituals. He asked Shiva to grant great siddhi to those who merely visit, touch, and bow to the linga, even without chanting the mantras. The boy asked that Shiva always bless those who are devoted to the linga mentally, verbally, or physically.

Shiva agreed and addressed him as Vira. He promised that the linga would be known after him as the Vireshvara Linga. At Kashi, it would bestow all the desires of the devotees. Shiva promised that if a devotee performs eight *namaskaras* in front of the Vireshvara Linga, he will attain the benefit of eighty million namaskaras. This linga, he promised, would be the bestower of all riches.

As they conversed, Shiva explained to Vira the various tirthas at the confluence of the Ganga and Varana. He expounded on the glories of Manikarnika. He said that those who dwell in the heavens recite the japa of Manikarnika during each of the three sandhyas. Shiva himself performs japa three times a day on behalf of those individuals who recite the japa of Manikarnika. If that five-syllabled mantra, *ma-ni-kar-ni-ka*, is uttered by anyone, it is as though they have performed many great yajnas. Shiva concluded by saying the glory of Manikarnika is the glory of moksha itself and that even Shiva does not know the entire greatness of Manikarnika. There is no tirtha on par with Manikarnika anywhere in the cosmic egg, said Shiva.

Kameshvara

Once the great sage Durvasa was wandering across the oceans, mountains, forests, rivers, lakes, villages, towns, and cities of the world until he reached Kashi. He became delighted at the site of that holy place full of palaces, ponds, and lakes. Everywhere, he was surprised to see sages, in their huts, who had conquered the fear of death. He saw Pashupata followers, limbs smeared with ash, heads covered with matted hair, garbed only in loin cloth, meditating on Shiva. The *hudutkara*—the bellowing sound like 'Hud'—produced by the big bottle gourds tucked under their armpits was as loud as thunder. He saw the Tridandi sannyasins with their three staffs, freed of fear as they had sought refuge with Vishveshvara. He saw celibates conversant with the Vedas. He saw Brahmanas whose hair had turned tawny from bathing daily in the Ganga.

Durvasa remarked to himself, 'In Kashi, there is a unique sense of satisfaction in domesticated animals, a special lustre in the forest animals, and a deep sense of joy in birds and other creatures not seen anywhere else.'

Durvasa performed austerities for a long time. But he became angry when he saw that his penance was not bearing fruit and was about to pronounce a curse that no one should find salvation there, castigating Kashi as a site that deceives all.

Shiva laughed loudly. A linga appeared there and became well known as Prahasiteshvara, the lord of the boisterous laugh. One will attain delight at every step upon visiting this linga.

Durvasa's anger was unquenched, and the fire of his rage began to pervade the sky. The sky turned blue from the columns of smoke arising from his anger. The ganas gathered their weapons and congregated around Kashi. They built a rampart touching the sky and stopped even the movement of the wind in Kashi. As the ganas agitated, all the three worlds shook. The sun and the moon lost their radiance. Out of compassion, the ganas permitted them to enter Kashi.

Finally, Shiva stopped the army of the ganas, telling them that Durvasa was a part of him. Shiva then came out of the linga of Durvasa, saving the city from the curse of the sage.

He said, 'Let not the curse of the sage be an obstacle to people's enlightenment at Kashi.'

Shiva then became visible to Durvasa and offered him a boon.

The sage, who had raised his hand to curse the city, became ashamed of himself.

He said, 'Blind with anger, I have committed a serious crime. Fie upon me for being overcome by anger! Fie upon me who attempted to curse the Kashi that bestows freedom for fear on all the three worlds! If anyone curses Kashi, he will get cursed; but Kashi will never become cursed.'

Shiva was delighted by his praise of Kashi. He said that one who utters the name of Kashi in the morning conquers both worlds and attains the position beyond all the worlds. He said that through the praise of Kashi, Shiva derives a pleasure that he does not receive even through religious gifts, sacrifices, or penance. If Kashi is sincerely eulogized, it is equivalent to Shiva being perfectly eulogized with all the Vedic hymns. He promised Durvasa that all of his desires would be fulfilled, and he would have the greatest knowledge that destroys the ties of samsara. He asked Durvasa to pick one more boon.

Durvasa requested that the linga be called Kamada and that his pond be called Kamakunda. Shiva consented and further provided that this linga named Durvaseshvara would thereafter be known as Kameshvara. By propitiating that linga, all of Durvasa's desires were attained. Therefore, those who have great desires should always worship Kameshvara and bathe in Kamakunda to remediate great sins.

Vishvakarmesha

Parvati asked Shiva to narrate to her the origin of the well-known Vishvakarmeshvara Linga. Shiva told her about Vishvakarma, the architect of the Devas, who was the son of Tvastr. He was clever in all the arts and crafts.

After his upanayanam, Vishvakarma stayed with his guru for training. His guru commanded him to make him a hut that would not allow in rain or ever collapse or become dilapidated. His guru's wife asked him to make a bodice that was neither too tight nor too loose, made of bark, that would always remain bright. His guru's son told him to make a pair of sandals that would never be contaminated with mud and that would be comfortable to run in, that would be usable in water and on dry ground. The guru's daughter asked him to make her a pair of gold earrings and toys made of ivory, as well as an unbreakable mortar and pestle and pots and pans. She asked him to also teach her how to cook so that her fingers never got burned. She also wanted a single-pillared house, constructed out of a single piece of wood, that she could hold like an umbrella whenever she wished.

Vishvakarma promised that he would do all of this and then fled to the forest out of fear. He did not know how to make any of these items. In the midst of his despair, as he was wondering what to do, he saw a sage in the middle of the forest. Rushing to touch the feet of that sage, Vishvakarma asked him if he was Shiva himself who had come to help him, and if he could instruct him on how to carry out the commands of his guru's family.

The sage responded that it was due to the blessings of Vishveshvara that even Brahma became competent at creation. He told the son of Tvastr that if he propitiated Shiva at Kashi, his name as Vishvakarma—the one who performs all tasks—would become true.

The boy, Vishvakarma, was delighted by these words and eagerly asked the sage how he could reach Kashi. He asked, in all innocence, who would take him to the city of Shiva.

The sage kindly offered to take him to Kashi. After reaching the city, the sage suddenly disappeared. Vishvakarma realized that the sage had been an embodiment of Shiva himself. Vishvakarma marvelled at the kindness of Shiva. He had never before worshiped Shiva, so he wondered at the cause of Shiva's grace. He realized that his guru bhakti could be the cause of Shiva's compassion, but then as he thought about it further, he realized that the grace of Shiva does not depend upon a specific cause; he blesses even those who do not propitiate him. His compassion is inherent and all-pervasive and causeless.

With a pure heart, Vishvakarma installed a Shivalinga that he worshiped every day after bathing and bringing from the forest plenty of different types of flowers. He subsisted on roots and fruits alone. He spent three years like this.

Shiva was very pleased and came out of the linga to address Vishvakarma.

'O, son of Tvastr, choose a boon, O boy who decided to work for the sake of your guru. I am pleased with your steady devotion. You will have the capacity to make the items requested by your guru and his family. I shall grant you other boons, too. Like another Brahma, you will know how to make things out of gold and other metals, wood, stones, gems, jewels, flowers, clothes, camphor and other scented things, water, roots, fruits, skins and peels of things. Whatever people may be interested in—houses, temples—you will be able to complete the task according to their preferences. You will know how to fashion dresses of all kinds, make varieties of dishes, all the fine arts, different kinds of machines and musical instruments, different types of weapons, and the arrangement of artificial ponds, reservoirs, and forts, etc. You will master all the tricks of jugglery and magical arts. You will be clever in all tasks. You will understand the mental predilections of everyone. Whether in Swarga or Patala or here, you will know everything supernatural and superb. Your name shall be Vishvakarma because you will be the knower of the activities of all the worlds and of everyone.'

He then urged Vishvakarma to choose an additional boon.

Vishvakarma requested that, although he had been the one to install that linga, others should also be the recipients of excellent knowledge by worshiping it. He also requested that he be allowed to construct a palace for Shiva.

Shiva agreed. He promised that those who worshiped the Vishvakarmesha Linga would attain excellent knowledge. He also promised that when Divodasa became a king, he would have Vishvakarma build his palace.

After granting these boons, Shiva vanished. Vishvakarma went back to his guru's place and carried out his instructions. He returned home and fulfilled the desires of his parents. Then he returned to Kashi and stays there even today. He is very much attached to worshiping the linga he had installed. There, he continues the activities that are pleasing to all of the Devas.

Daksheshvara

After the tragedy of the Daksha yajna, Daksha had gone to Kashi to perform expiation at the suggestion of Brahma. Brahma had told him that if he desired to remove the demerit of censuring Shiva, his only recourse was to go to Kashi.

Daksha performed a great penance in Kashi and installed a linga. Day and night, he worshiped Shiva and became absorbed in him for twelve thousand years. In the meantime, Sati had taken the form of Parvati and reunited with Shiva. Daksha continued his worship of Shiva and his steady penance.

When Shiva and Parvati came to Kashi, Parvati saw Daksha and took pity upon him. She asked Shiva to bless him. Shiva addressed Daksha and told him to request a boon.

Daksha requested that he have unruffled fixed devotion to Shiva's feet and that Shiva reside forever in the linga that he had installed. Finally, he requested that his sin be forgiven.

Shiva consented and further provided that the linga he had installed would be known as Daksheshvara. Shiva promised to forgive a thousand offenses committed by one who worshiped this Linga. He promised that at the end of two parardhas, Daksha would attain mukti.

Parvatisha

Once, Mena, the wife of Himavan and the mother of Parvati, asked Parvati where Shiva's native place was, where did he come from, and who his relatives were. She said dismissively that probably her son-in-law had no home or family anywhere.

Soon after, Parvati said playfully to Shiva, 'Today, I have decided to go to my mother-in-law's house. Take me to your home.'

Shiva, of course, understood everything. He brought Parvati from the Himalayas to Anandavana. On seeing the forest of bliss, Devi forgot about the Himalayan abode of her father. Parvati marvelled at the site.

Shiva explained, 'Devi, in this holy site, the abode of mukti, extending over pancha krosha, there is not a single spot even the size of a sesame seed that does not have a linga. Around each of these lingas, the ground extending one krosha around bestows bliss. In all the fourteen worlds, the contented and blessed people have attained the highest bliss by establishing lingas here that carry their name. That is why this holy spot is the cause of great bliss.'

Parvati then requested to establish a linga, too. With Shiva's consent, she installed the Parvatisha Linga. Shiva granted the special boon in honour of the linga lovingly established by his wife that anyone who worships Parvatisha Linga will himself or herself become a Kashi Linga after death and, after becoming a Kashi Linga, they will enter Shiva.

Gangeshvara

The Gangeshvara Linga was installed by Ganga Devi. It is rare to have darshana of this linga, particularly during Kali Yuga. But if one just hears about the greatness of Gangeshvara, he will never descend into hell.

Narmadeshvara

At the beginning of the Varaha Kalpa, the other rishis asked Markandeya which was the greatest river. Markandeya Rishi explained that there are hundreds of rivers that remove sin and bestow merit. Among those, the rivers that fall into the seas are the most excellent. Among those rivers, Ganga, Yamuna, Narmada, and Sarasvati are the most excellent. Ganga embodies the *Rg Veda*, Yamuna the *Yajur Veda*, Narmada the *Sama Veda*, and Sarasvati the *Atharva Veda*.

Ganga is the origin of all the rivers and no other river is on par with the Ganga.

Once, though, Narmada performed penance for a long time and requested from Brahma the boon to become equal to Ganga.

Brahma smiled.

He replied, 'If equality with Trilochana can be attained by anyone else, then equality with the Ganga can be attained. If at any place, another man can be equal to Puroshottama, then another river can become equal to the Ganga. If a woman can be on par with Parvati, then certainly another river shall attain equality with the celestial Ganga. If another city can become the peer of Kashi, then another river can become equal to the Ganga.'

Narmada refused to accept a boon from Brahma and came instead to Kashi. She then installed a Shivalinga in the Pilipila Tirtha near Trivishtapa.

Shiva offered her a boon.

Narmada simply asked for unswerving devotion to his feet.

Pleased, Shiva granted that boon. He also promised that all the stones on her banks would be in the form of lingas. He further granted her the boon that while the Ganga removes sins instantly, Yamuna in seven days, and Sarasvati in three days, she would remove sins at first sight. He also said that while there are many lingas in Kashi, the greatness of Narmadesha is something miraculous.

Satishvara

Once, Brahma requested from Shiva the boon that Devi would be born as the daughter of Daksha Prajapati and Shiva would be born as Brahma's son. Shiva consented and emerged from his forehead, crying out.

Brahma asked the child why he kept crying again and again. The child said he was crying for a name. Brahma then named him Rudra, the one who cries.

As Shiva assumed the form of Rudra, Devi grew in the form of Sati. She was desirous of a husband and performed fierce penance in Kashi. Shiva manifested himself in the form of a linga and said to her, 'O, great Devi, enough of your penance.'

He told her that the linga would be named Satishvara after her, and that just as her desire had been fulfilled there by attaining him as her husband, so also would the desire of anyone else be fulfilled by worshiping the Satishvara Linga. Specifically, a maiden would attain a husband beyond expectations and a young man an excellent wife. Whatever one wants, one would attain it by worshiping the Satishvara Linga. This linga is established to the east of Ratneshvara.

Amrtesha and Other Lingas

Once, there was a holy man named Sanaru in Kashi. He led the life of a householder. He taught the study of the Vedas and treated guests as Devas. He always worshiped a linga and never took monetary gifts from pilgrims. He had a son named Upajanghani.

Once, Upajanghani was bitten by a serpent in a forest outside of Kashi. His friends brought his body back to his father's hermitage. Sighing deeply, Sanaru took his son's body to the cremation ground near Swargadwara. A Shivalinga was concealed there in the shape of a bilva fruit.

Distraught at the thought of having to cremate his own son, Sanaru watched in wonder as Upajanghani suddenly revived and regained his health. Even as he was in shock, he saw an ant bring another dead ant. That dead ant also regained life and crawled away.

The sage dug the ground with his soft hands, unearthing the Amrteshvara Linga. One attains immortality by touching this linga. If one just hears about this great linga, he or she will never have cause to fear the influence of malignant planets.

In the vicinity of Mokshadvara is another great linga named Karuneshvara. On Mondays, a devotee shall observe the vow of eating just once during the day and then worshipping the Karuneshvara Linga with karunamalli flowers.

There is also the Jyotirupeshvara Linga on the banks of the Chakrapushkarini, which shines in Kashi. Worshiping this linga, one attains brilliance in the body. This linga manifested when Vishnu was performing penance there in ancient times. Simply by meditating upon Jyotirupeshvara, even at a long distance, one will attain siddhi.

Skanda concluded by explaining that among these fourteen Lingas, eight are of great power. The thirty-six lingas are conducive to the greatness of Kashi: the fourteen lingas beginning with Omkareshvara, the eight lingas beginning with Daksheshvara, and the fourteen lingas beginning with Shailesha. Shiva in the form of the thirty-six tattvas is embodied in these lingas and imparts the knowledge of Taraka from there.

CHAPTER 14

The Greatness of Vishveshvara

Shiva entered the palace built by Vishvakarma. He narrated to Parvati the significance of the various lingas and tirthas in Kashi, concluding with the glories of Vishveshvara, or Vishvanatha.

He said that Vishveshvara is the Lord of the Universe in the form of a stationary being. He brings about siddhis to his devotees. Sometimes he is manifest, sometimes he is unmanifest. He stays in Anandakana as he pleases and blesses all his devotees there forever. He will continue to stay in the form of the Vishveshvara Linga, bestowing all objects of thought. All lingas everywhere, whether svayambhu or not, will always come to see this Vishveshvara Linga.

Shiva said, 'While I dwell in all lingas, this one is my supreme form. It is the king of lingas. Seeing it with unwavering faith and pure vision is akin to beholding me directly.

'The mere touch of the swayambhu Vishveshvara Linga confers the merit of a thousand Rajasuya sacrifices. Offering flowers and a palmful of water with devotion equals giving one hundred gold coins. Worshiping the Vishveshvara Linga with panchamrta yields the Purushartha: dharma, artha, kama, and moksha. Bathing the linga with purified water through a cloth bestows the merit of one hundred thousand Ashvamedha yajnas. By offering fragrant incense, the devotee will become the receptacle of divine scent. By lighting ghee lamps, he will move about in an aerial chariot of radiant splendour. By offering a camphor lamp once to Vishveshvara, one will attain white splendour of the body and become three-eyed. By offering naivedyam to Vishveshvara, a devotee will reside on Kailasha for one yuga for each grain of cooked rice.

'By bowing to Vishveshvara once, a wise man becomes the lord of the earth and all the three worlds bow down to him. If a devotee visits Vishveshvara once but dies elsewhere, he will undoubtedly become liberated in his next life. How can there be rebirth if the name of Vishveshvara is at the tip of the tongue, the story of Vishvanatha in the ear, and the regular meditation of Vishveshvara in the mind? If one rejoices after seeing Vishvanatha Linga, he will become one of my ganas.'

Shiva continued. 'If one repeats during the three sandhyas "Vishvesha, Vishvesha, and Vishvanatha," I, too, shall utter the name of that meritorious devotee. O, Devas, this great linga is worthy of being worshiped even by me forever. Hence, it should be meticulously worshiped by the Devas, the sages, and the human beings.

'May all the groups of Devas, rishis, and ganas listen. I shall speak the truth for the sake of helping others. Nowhere in the worlds of Bhuh, Bhuvah, Svarga, Mahah, and Jana is there a linga equal to Vishvanatha. Not in Satyaloka, not in Tapoloka, not in Vaikuntha, Kailasha or Rasatala is there a tirtha on par with Manikarnika or a linga like Vishveshvara. There is no penance grove elsewhere on par with Anandavana. In this Anandakanana of mine, this linga which is the abode of nectar of moksha and from which the radiance of the Self originates has come out from the bottom of the seven nether worlds out of compassion for devotees. Whatever is beneficial should be offered to this linga by my devotees. Nowhere else do the sins committed by mortals perish as they do here.

'O, Vishnu, listen. O, Brahma, listen. May all the Devas, sages, and the ganas listen. This linga gives the greatest siddhi unto the good. Lifting up my hand, I tell you again and again that, in this world having the three Vedas, only three things are essential: the

Vishvanatha Linga, the waters of Manikarnika, and the city of Kashi. This is the truth, the three-fold truth.'

Then, Shiva arose with Shakti and merged into the Vishvanatha Linga.

Conclusion of the Kashi Khanda

Skanda's narration to Agastya Muni concluded. He told the rishi that he had shared all of these stories of Kashi because the sage was distraught upon being separated from Kashi. He promised him that he would soon once again reach Kashi. Looking at the setting sun, Skanda noted that the time for sandhya had come, and it was now the time for silence for both of them.

Agastya Muni and Lopamudra prostrated to Skanda and then set out for sandhya worship.

Phalashruti: The Fruit of Hearing the Kashi Khanda of the *Skanda Purana*

The recitation of a sacred text is incomplete without the *phalashruti*. It is like the *prasadam* that is to be consumed at the end of a puja. The phalashruti for the Kashi Khanda is provided by Veda Vyasa and summarized in part below.

By listening to Kashi Khanda, one attains the merit of bathing in all the tirthas. It bestows the profound merit usually acquired through rigorous penance and mastery over the four Vedas along with their ancillary branches of study. Hearing the Kashi Khanda equates to having heard all the Puranas. Reciting the entire Kashi Khanda is the worship of Shiva. Listening to a single story of Kashi Khanda is akin to hearing all the Dharmashastras. It leads to *kaivalya*. All the pitrs become pleased. All the immortal beings, beginning with Brahma, Vishnu, and Shiva, become pleased. The sages rejoice. All the four types of living beings become pleased by listening to this greatness of Kashi. If a learned man expounds this excellent narrative entirely, or even half, or even a quarter or half of that, or one excellent episode, he should be assiduously bowed to and made offerings to. If he is satisfied, Vishveshvara, too, is undoubtedly satisfied.

If anyone copies this and offers this beautiful book to anyone else, it is as though all the Puranas have been given by him. A giver of the manuscript is honoured in heaven for as many thousands of yugas as there are episodes in this, as there are verses in this, as there are words, as there are syllables, as many rows of words are here, as there are threads in the string, as many threads in the cloth, as many pictures as there are in the beautiful book.

Veda Vyasa concluded, 'Of what avail is speaking much, O Suta? Whatever may be one's wish, one shall be blessed by listening to this and obtain the same. Even if a man listens to this excellent Kashi Khanda from a faraway land, he will have the merit of residing in Kashi at the behest of Shiva. By listening to this, a man will be victorious everywhere; he will be of pure heart and he will enjoy bliss everywhere.

'One shall have interest in listening to this only if Vishveshvara is pleased with him. This book is the most excellent one of great auspiciousness among all auspicious things. It must be copied in writing and should be worshipped for the attainment of all auspiciousness.'

CHAPTER 15

The Pilgrimage Paths of Kashi

The conclusion of the Kashi Khanda portion of the *Skanda Purana* outlines various *yatra parikrama*, meaning pilgrimage paths, of Kashi, as narrated by Veda Vyasa to Lomaharshana. He explained that these yatras should be performed with great faith by those staying in Kashi, particularly during the festival days. Two yatras should be performed daily.

Certainly, one should bathe in the Ganga at Manikarnika and then visit Vishvanatha. Neglecting this leads to a wasted day and disappoints the pitrs, stated Veda Vyasa.

The Panchatirthika Yatra commences with a bath in the waters of the Chakrapushkarini, followed by the worship of Devas and the pitrs. The devotee should then prostrate before Aditya, Draupadi, Vishnu, Dandapani, and Maheshvara. Afterwards, Dhundhi Ganesha is visited, followed by a dip in the waters of the Gyaanavapi and adoration of Nandikeshvara. Tarakesha and Mahakaleshvara are worshiped before concluding with a final homage to Dandapani.

Next is the Vaishveshvari Yatra, granting fulfilment of all objectives. One should visit Omkareshvara after performing rites in the waters of Matsyodari. The pilgrimage continues through Trivishtapa, Mahadeva, then Krttivasas, Ratneshvara, Chandresha, Kedara, then Dharmeshvara, Viresha, and Kameshvara, followed by Vishvakarmeshvara, then Manikarnishvara. After seeing Avimukteshvara, one should worship Vishveshvara.

The Ashtayatana Yatra is a pilgrimage to eight lingas, particularly to be done on Ashtami. These sites are Daksheshvara, Parvatishvara, Pashupatishvara, Ganesha, Narmadesha, Gabhastisha, Satishvara, and Tarakesha.

The next yatra encompasses the bath in front of and darshana of the fourteen great lingas. After taking a holy bath in Varana, one should first visit Shailesha, then bathe in the Sangama and have darshana of Sangameshvara. Then, he should bathe in Svaleena Tirtha and visit the Svaleena Linga. After bathing in the Mandakini Tirtha, he should visit Madhyameshvara. After bathing and performing the water rituals in Hiranygarbhesha Tirtha, he should visit Hiranyagarbhesha. Then, he should bathe in Manikarnika and visit Ishaana. Then, he should again perform the water rituals in Goprekshakupa and visit Gopreksha. After bathing in Kapileyahrada, he should visit Vrshabhadhvaja. Next, he should visit Upashanta Shiva. After bathing in Panchachudahrada, he should worship Jyeshthasthana. After bathing in Chatuhsamudra Kupa, he should worship the linga there. He should visit Shukreshvara and perform the water rituals in the well there. After bathing in Dandakhata, he should worship Vyagresha. After bathing in Shaunakeshvara Kunda, he should worship the Jambukesha Linga. This pilgrimage should be performed in this order, beginning with the first lunar day in the dark half of the month and ending on Chaturdashi. After performing this pilgrimage, one is never reborn.

Next is the Ekadashayatani Yatra. Having bathed in Agnidhra Kunda, one should have darshana of Agnidhra. Then, he should proceed to Urvashisha and then to Nakulishvara. After visiting Ashadheesha and Bharabhuteshvara, then Langalisha and Tripurantaka, then Manahprakameshvara, he should proceed to Preetikesha. Then, he should visit Madalaseshvara and then Tilaparneshvara. One performing this pilgrimage will attain the status of Rudra.

Next comes the Gauri Yatra, which should be performed on the third lunar day of the bright half of the month. After bathing in

Gopreksha, a devotee should go to Mukhanirmalika. After bathing in the Jyesthavapi tank, he should worship Jyesthagauri. After performing the water rituals in Gyaanavapi, he should worship Saubhagyagauri. Then, he should worship Shrngaragauri. After bathing in Vishalaganga, he should proceed to Vishalakshi. After bathing in the Lalita Tirtha, the devotee should worship Lalita. After bathing in the Bhavani Tirtha, he should worship Bhavani. After performing the water rituals in the Bindu Tirtha, he should worship Mangala. Then, he should go to Mahalakshmi.

The Vighnaraja Yatra should be performed every Chaturthi. Modakas should be offered. On Tuesdays, Bhairava Yatra should be performed. Pilgrimage to Ravi, or Surya Deva, should be performed on the sixth lunar day when it coincides with a Sunday, and also on Ravi Saptami day, to vanquish obstacles. The Chandi Yatra is auspicious when performed on the eighth or ninth lunar day.

Every day, the Antargrha Yatra should be performed. An early morning bath is to be taken. Then the five Vinayakas are bowed down to. Obeisance is made to Vishveshvara. Then, the devotee makes a sankalpa to perform the Antargrha Yatra. Then, he proceeds to Manikarnika. After bathing, he will return silently and worship Manikarnikishvara. Then, he will bow to Kambala, Ashvatara, and Vasukisha. Then, he will visit Parvatesha, Gangakeshava, Lalita, and Jarasandheshvara in that order. After seeing Somanatha, he will go to Varaha, then bow to Brahmeshvara and Agastishvara. He should worship Kashyapesha and Harikeshavana. After visiting Vaidyanatha, he should visit Dhruvesha.

One must visit, worship, and prostrate before the following: Gokarneshvara, Hatakeshvara, Keekaseshvara in the Ashtikshepa lake where bones are cast, Bharabhuta, Chitragupteshvara, Chitraghanta, Pashupatishvara, Pitamaheshvara, Kalasheshvara, Chandresha, Viresha, Vidyesha, Agnisha, Nageshvara, Harishchandra, Chintamanivinayaka, and Senavinayaka, and visit the deities Vashishtha and Vamadeva. One must continue by visiting Seemavinayaka, Karunesha, Trisandhyesha, Vishlakshi, Dharmesha,

Vishvabahuka, Ashavinayaka, Vrddhaditya, Chaturvaktreshvara, Brahmisha, Manahprakamesha, Ishanesha, Chandi and Chandishvara, Bhavani and Shankara, Dhundhi, and Rajarajesha, then Langalisha, Nakulishvara, Paranesha, Paradravyeshvara, Pratigraheshvara, Markandeyesha, Apsaraseshvara, and Gangesha.

Then he should bathe at Gyaanavapi and bow to Nandikesha, Tarakesha, Mahakaleshvara, Dandapani, Mahesha, and Mokshesha. After bowing to Virabhadreshvara and Avimukteshvara, and the five Vinayakas, he should finally go to Vishvanatha. Then he should break his silence with this mantra: 'May Shambhu be pleased with this pilgrimage of the Antargrha (the inner sanctum), which has been duly performed by me, even if it be deficient or superfluous in any respect.' Then he should return home.

On Ekadasi, the pilgrimage to all of the Vishnu Tirthas should be undertaken. On the fifteenth day of Bhadrapada, one should worship Kulastambha.

CHAPTER 16

The Sacred Geography of Kashi

Sacred Geography

Flower-like are the heels of the wanderer
Thus his body grows and is fruitful
All his sins disappear
Slain by the toil of his journeying.
There is no happiness for him who does not travel!
Thus we have heard. Living in the society of men, the best of men becomes a sinner.
Therefore, wander!
The feet of the wanderer are like the flower, his soul is growing and reaping the fruit; and all his sins are destroyed by his fatigues in wandering.
Therefore, wander!
The fortune of him who is sitting, sits; it rises when he rises; it sleeps when he sleeps; it moves when he moves.
Therefore, wander!

    Aitareya Brahmana of the *Rg Veda*, VII.15–18 (Singh 2013)

This Vedic exhortation to wander is connected to the ancient tradition of tirtha yatra (journeying to the crossover places) or pilgrimage innate and essential to the chthonic (indigenous, or more precisely, earth-born, that which grows organically from the literal and metaphorical soil of the land) religions of the world, including

Hinduism. We have lost connection with the metaphysical reality of sacred geography that guided societies since time immemorial, when sites of sacred power based on the features and inherent spiritual energies of the land or its position with respect to the sun or the stars, places of power due to mythological associations with birth places and sites of leela—the divine play—of the gods, dominated the landscape through the maps of sacred geography.

Nor was the significance of these sites limited to the religious dimension alone. Sites like the Acropolis, Delphi, and Delos—among the most important spiritual sites of ancient Greece—grew into important centres of trade, travel, and commerce, bustling towns of great civilizational import to the ancient world.

In recent decades, there has been a significant body of research into understanding space through these intangible dimensions of sacred geography and associated other concepts. Core to this idea is that space is not just about the physical; it is about the cultural, the mental, and the psychic. 'Before it can ever be a repose for the senses, landscape is the work of the mind. Its scenery is built up as much from the strata of memory as from layers of rock' (quoting Schama in Eck 2012, 26). As Brereton puts it, quoted by Singh, a sacred space 'includes spaces that can be entered physically, as the outer geography of a holy land, imaginatively as the inner geography of the body in Tantric yoga, or visually, as the space of mandala' (Singh 2002).

In other words, when we reduce discussions of space to legalese about property deeds, archaeological evidence, and individual or organizational ownership as a technical matter of law, we miss the bigger picture about the importance of a place or a site to a culture, society, people, or civilization based on maps drawn not by the contours of legal ownership but by the topography of cultural memory and meaning. This chapter explores the concept of sacred geography as it applies to Bharat and specifically Kashi.

Sacred Geography of Bharat

Professor Rana P.B. Singh, professor of cultural geography and heritage studies at Banaras Hindu University, has published extensively on geographical thought, sacred geography, pilgrimage studies, and heritage planning in India. He has done meticulous research in this area, and his books are a treasure trove on sacred geography in both the abstract and granularity, specifically as applied to Kashi and more generally to Bharat.

Tirthas

As Singh notes, sacred geography engenders 'faithscapes' that encompass sacred places, sacred time, sacred meanings, and sacred rituals. Within Hinduism, the focal points for pilgrimage are tirthas. The word 'tirtha' means a 'ford' or river-crossing and, by extension, these are places that allow passage between the mundane and spiritual realms (citing Bhardwaj and Lochtefeld in Mittal and Thursby 2004, Singh 2013, 8–9). Each Hindu pilgrimage is a tirtha yatra and the geographical manifestation of each such journey evokes a new kind of landscape that, for the devotee, overlays sacred and symbolic meaning upon a physical and material base. Hindu pilgrims often conceive of their sacred journeys as an earthly adventure that combines spiritual seeking and physical tests (citing Sax 1991, Singh 2013, 8–9). As Singh notes, the number of Hindu pilgrimage sites is so vast and the practice of pilgrimage so ubiquitous that the whole of Bharat can be regarded as a continuous single sacred space organized into a system of pilgrimage centres and their hinterlands (citing Bhardwaj 1973, Singh 2013, 8–9).

This is not just theoretical. According to a study performed twenty years ago, of all domestic travels in India, over one-third is for the purpose of performing pilgrimage (quoting Rana 2003, Singh 2013, 52).

What makes a site sacred according to Hinduism? According to the Mahabharata (13.111.18), pilgrimage places are auspicious for Hindus because of the extraordinary power of their soil, the efficacy of their water, and because they were made holy by visits by rishis. The *Rg Veda* expands on this, categorizing tirthas into four categories: (i) a route or a place where one can receive power (*Rg Veda*, 1.169.6, 1.173.11) (ii) a place of purification where people can dip in sacred waters as a rite of purification (*Rg Veda* 8.47.11, 1.46.8) (iii) a sacred site where Ishvara is immanent through possessing the power of manifestation (*Rg Veda* 10.31.3) and (iv) places associated with the religious territory (kshetra) that are sacralized based upon divine happenings and work of the Gods that took place there (Shatapatha Brahmana 18.9) (Singh 2013, 56).

The Mahabharata captures the art of establishing a tirtha poetically and profoundly through the speech of Yudhishthira to Vidura after the latter had returned from a long tirtha yatra: 'Devotees like you, who have become tirthas themselves, are the ones who make the tirthas into tirthas by embodying the presence of [the Divine] there' (Goswami 1971, 1.13.10).

Diana L. Eck in her seminal book, *India: A Sacred Geography*, delves into the notion of 'tirtha' more deeply. She says, 'More than any other term, it is the term tirtha that signals the linkage of place and space' (Eck 2012, 660). 'At a spiritual crossing place, one's prayers are amplified, one's rites are more efficacious, one's vows more readily fulfilled. Tirtha, with its many associations, is a word of passage and, in some ways, a word of transcendence' (Eck 2012, 20). Eck also notes that the word 'tirtha' belongs to a set of Indo-European linguistic cognates that encompass concepts of passage and pilgrimage, terms that we find in the West even today. For example, there are 'through', 'durch', and 'trans' with all their related words, which include in English 'thoroughfare', 'transition', 'transformation', 'transport', and 'transcend' (Eck 2012, 19).

Over time, the concept of tirtha expanded to include divine sites constructed by humans as temples. As Eck notes,

> Among the most important developments over the thousand years during which the mahatmyas of the tirthas came to prominence

was the emergence of the constructed tirtha—the temple, built with the durability of stone. In most tirthas, the temple itself is not what is important; it is the place, the power, the manifestation of the divine. The great tirthas were there long before elaborate temples were constructed, and we will come across many instances where it serves us well to remember this. A tirtha does not need to have a temple, and when temples are destroyed or fall into ruin, the tirtha remains. (Eck 2012, 118–119)

This is particularly important to remember in the context of the surge of temple destruction suffered throughout Bharat during the periods of Islamic attacks. Even where the edifices of temples have been destroyed, the underlying sanctity of the site remains intact.

Bharat: Unity through Sacred Geography

While the focus of this book is on Kashi, Kashi is just one node in an 'extensive network of pilgrimage places stretching throughout the length and breadth of India' (Eck 2012, 11). As Eck explains,

> It became increasingly clear to me that anywhere one goes in India, one finds a living landscape in which mountains, rivers, forests, and villages are elaborately linked to the stories of the gods and heroes. The land bears the traces of the gods and the footprints of the heroes. Every place has its story, and conversely, every story in the vast storehouse of myth and legend has its place. (Eck 2012, 15–16)

This network of tirthas provided the foundation for the civilizational and proto-national unity of Bharat since ancient times. In his introduction to the Sanskrit text of the *Tirthavivecana Kanda of Lakshmidhara*, a twelfth-century digest of pilgrimage places, K.V. Rangaswami Aiyangar states, 'Long before wise statesmanship attempted or accomplished Indian unification, Akhand Hindusthan [One Hindusthan] had sprung from the wanderings of pilgrims' (quoting Aiyangar 1942, Eck 2012, 31).

Modern notions of the nation-state look to linguistic, racial, or ethnic ties while the more intangible ties and bonds from shared sacred geography are not respected or are dismissed as fanciful or revisionist. This bias is emblematic of a Eurocentric or Westernized mindset that tries to project onto all of human history the experience of a small corner of the world over the course of a century or two. It dismisses worldviews and cultures that find identity in sources deeper than the colour of one's skin or the language they speak. The Western approach is one steeped in historicity, grounded in dates and human figures, which is antithetical to the broader strokes with which sacred geography paints based on cultural and civilizational memory and belief and shaped by lore transmitted through the oral tradition, more than dogma or doctrines masquerading as historical fact. As Eck pithily notes, 'The resistance to ideas of India's unity is embedded in colonial thought and often in postcolonial thinking as well' (Eck 2012, 76).

The inspiration behind Eck's book was this very exploration of the idea of India:

> [T]hat is shaped not by the modern notion of a nation-state, but by the extensive and intricate interrelation of geography and mythology that has produced this vast landscape of tirthas. [...] This idea of India had its genesis long before the Mughal Empire stretched its network of alliances across much of the subcontinent in the sixteenth century, long before the British Empire formalized a nation-wide civil service and linked the land by rail. (Eck 2012, 73)

Evolution of Bharat's Sacred Geography

While the notion of pilgrimage and the importance of tirtha yatra dates back to the early Vedic texts, the sacred geography of Bharat flowered fully over the course of fifteen centuries with the composition of the Puranas and associated Sthala Purana and other texts and oral traditions that mapped across the territory of India various circuits of holy sites.

The Puranas are replete with rich descriptions of the various mountains, rivers, and sacred sites of Bharat. The lore of Hindu tradition is inextricably intertwined with the geography of Bharat. As

Eck describes it, 'There is arguably no other major culture that has sustained over so many centuries, and across such diverse regions, a fundamentally locative or place-oriented worldview' (Eck 2012, 87).

For example, the *Skanda Purana*, the largest of the Puranas, is structured entirely around the description and glorification of various tirthas. Eck describes it as 'the mother lode of sacred geography' (Eck 2012, 115). The first of the seven sections of the *Skanda Purana* describes and glorifies three prominent sites devoted to Shiva: Kedarnath, Mahisagara Sangama, and Arunachala. The second, devoted to Vishnu, covers Tirupathi, Jagannatha Puri, and Badrinath as well as descriptions of the glories of Mathura and Ayodhya. The Kashi Khanda is its own section of the *Skanda Purana*, summarized earlier in this book.

With the proliferation of the composition of Sthala Purana in southern India, Tamil translations of the Sanskrit Puranas were added to the corpus of this flowering literary tradition. In other words, tirthas did not function just as local sites of pilgrimage but rather came together in a network that was greater than the sum of its parts, a network of sites of sacred geography that became the foundation for the civilizational identity of Bharat and Hinduism.

In the twelfth century AD, a new genre of sacred literature emerged—the composition of *nibandhas*, or digests, of information about sacred sites from the Puranas and other sacred texts. One such digest, the *Krityakalpataru*, was composed by Lakshmidhara, who was in the court of the Gahadavalas and served as chief minister to Govindachandra. In addition to the *Krityakalpataru*, Lakshmidhara also composed books on subjects such as *rajadharma* (the duties of kings), *dana* (ritual gift-giving), *samskara* (sacraments of the life cycle), *vrata* (vows), *tirtha yatra* (pilgrimage), and *shraddha* (death rites). This important text details over three hundred temples and tirthas within Avimukta or Kashi (Eck 2012, 150–152).

There are multiple aspects to this notion of sacred geography that is core to Hinduism and the history of Bharat. First, the underlying sanctity of the place. Second, the Sthala Purana or the lore that describes the glories and leela of the site; this is related to but distinct from 'history' as we understand it in the modern sense. It is not so much about what happened where but whether a place for various reasons—its inherent spiritual energies; the result of being sanctified by the footsteps of sages and countless other pilgrims or the play of the divine; the significance of the site in cultural memory—can evoke within a traveller or devotee the experience of the divine, a transcendence of physical place into an exalted space of metaphysical transformation. Third, the actual experience of pilgrimage that sustains and reenergizes the sites to keep them continually powerful and effective and therefore able to transform the individual pilgrim.

In other words, a mountain is never just a mountain and a river never just a river. This mountain has been sanctified with the footsteps of Shiva and Devi; that river is the embodiment of a goddess cast away from the heavens; here is where Kunti and the Pandavas slept for a night during their long exile and built a temple. This lore, this deeper meaning encoded into the cultural memory of Hindus, is what gives colour and meaning to the landscape; this is what transforms physical space into the lived reality of a place.

Lived Reality of Sacred Geography

The Mahabharata contains descriptions of two pilgrimage circuits by Pulastya and Dhaumya. As Eck notes, '[T]he fact that the journey is described as circumambulatory, including within its mental frame the whole land, is very significant in our exploration of this idea of India' (Eck 2012, 113).

In fact, as the Puranas and the associated Sthala Puranas developed, there was inherently already a sense of unity and cohesion across the entire subcontinent of Bharat. The Mahabharata, for example, contains descriptions of southern India. While it may lack the detailed descriptions of other sites in the northern regions of India, the fact that such attempts were made shows that a sense of civilizational unity already existed, based on ties of religion and shared sites of pilgrimage—the tirthas. Similarly, the Tamil epic *Shilappadikaram* describes the journey of the king to the Ganga then to the Himalayas on a quest to take a stone from the mountains, bathe it in the holy waters of the Ganga, and bring it back home. The very fact of the hero's journey in this instance shows the reality of the sacred geography of Bharat being recognized and lived by the people of Bharat in ancient times (Eck 2012, 125).

In other words, sacred geography did not exist in the abstract, relegated to the theoretical realm of texts. Rather, the people of Bharat identified themselves as belonging to a territory bounded by the contours of sacred geography and cemented these notions through their acts of pilgrimage that often took months if not years to consummate. Organically from this grew a superstructure that even today governs the sacred geography of Bharat. For example, the Char Dham—the four sacred sites of Puri, Badrinath, Dwaraka, and Rameswaram—marked by the *mathas* established by Adi Shankaracharya, is one of the most, if not the most, preeminent and important of pilgrimage circuits within Hinduism. Purohitas from south India officiate at Badrinath, while those from the north officiate at Rameswaram under the traditions established by Adi Shankaracharya. You may recall the story of Shivasharman and his journey to the Saptapuri—because he lived in Ayodhya, his voyage across the seven sacred cities added Prayaga. The whole idea of tirtha yatra is to go to other places within Bharat that are sacred—that is the antithesis of being insular or fragmented.

An interesting parallel is found in the practices of the *ashta mathas* of Udupi, established by the great Dvaita preceptor, Madhavacharya, that is still followed today. As each pontiff prepares to take the leadership of the Udupi Krishna Temple on a rotational basis, he travels on a yatra through the tirthas of Bharat from Kanyakumari to Badrinath in order to obtain blessings from across the land. This again shows how the sacred geography of Bharat operates in real and practical ways from ancient times until today.

To put it bluntly, the concept of Indian nationhood did not come with the British or the Mughals or the Western discovery of the nation-state. It was already embedded in the consciousness of the people and culture of Bharat since time immemorial, traced through the contours of the sacred geography of Hinduism and Bharat. So palpable was this that even foreigners understood this fundamental unity and cohesion. As Eck points out, 'And it is remarkable that even in a time when the subcontinent had no political unity whatsoever, those who described this territory to Alexander's company thought of it and described it as a single land' (Eck 2012, 108).

Threats to Sacred Geography

While this book deals mainly with the attacks that came upon the sacred geography of Kashi externally, it would be remiss to not take note of the internal threats to the living reality of sacred geography. Rather like a garden, sites of sacred import require constant tending and nurture. After all, today, even the great sites of spirituality from antiquity—like the Acropolis, Delos, Delphi, and the great temples of Egypt—lay in ruins. Even if the physical site remains intact, without the continuous, constant watering of the soil with worship and sacrifice, without the tending of the earth by the tread of the feet of pilgrims, sites will be sapped of their powers and sanctity.

Today, much of the threat to the holy sites of Hinduism in Bharat comes from within. Overdevelopment without regard for the impact on the physical and psychic environment, promoting tourism at the expense of preserving the sanctity and sattva of the site, and prioritizing Instagrammable moments over the rites of pilgrimage—if unchecked, all of this will wreak havoc on our holy lands as much as any invader ever could.

These are very real challenges. As Singh notes, the pressure to develop this kind of tourism in old cities like Kashi is immense. Since heritage zones naturally attract tourists, there is increasing pressure to commercialize heritage sites. This becomes particularly problematic when these structures are inside densely populated heritage zones of the city, like the ghats, where they are in disharmony with the spiritual and religious atmosphere of the place and where they also overburden the carrying capacity of the urban and cultural environment, such as water resources and sewage systems (Singh 2008, 173).

Singh makes an eloquent and compelling plea for us to rethink how we treat our sacred sites within Bharat:

> The disappearing presence of Hindu thinking about the man-nature-cosmos relationship is one of the basic causes for the present environmental crisis that is facing India today. Ethical and moral pollution by materialism and consumerism is replacing the old value system which supported sustainability. [...] During the past seven hundred years of foreign cultural domination—beginning with Islam and followed by British Christianity—the ancient Hindu value system has lost many of its facets. Nevertheless, the seeds of this ancient system of spiritual wisdom are still preserved in religious ethics found in writings and rituals. A mass awakening of awareness in the context of old cultural values would promote a new spirit of sustainability. (Singh 2013, 187)

Along these lines, Singh (2013, 339) also offers up a ten-point plan for developing sustainable religious tourism—a set of guidelines that are well worth sharing here:

1. Site building and other construction should avoid significant cutting of trees and should minimize disruption to heritage ruins.
2. Maintenance of the eco-system and the serenity of nature should be given priority.
3. In the hilly regions, trail systems should respect travel patterns and the sacredness of wildlife and nature.
4. Buildings should be spaced out so as to allow the maintenance of wildlife travel patterns and forest growth while also preserving the pristine serenity of nature.
5. The use of automobiles and other vehicles (e.g., boats in holy rivers, like the Ganga) should be strictly limited and not allowed at all within a certain distance from pilgrimage routes.

6. Provide ecologically sound restroom and trash disposal facilities and raise consciousness among stakeholders of key religious and spiritual insights.
7. Designate a clear area for medical emergency and aids and spiritual healings based on nature therapy.
8. Site lighting should be limited and controlled to avoid wildlife diurnal cycles and the local religious traditions.
9. Architecture should be based on local construction techniques, materials available and befitting cultural images and keeping the archetypal symbolism and religious notions intact (e.g., spacing the deities at proper places).
10. Involvement of local people and their religious traditions at different levels and in various activities should be prioritized. Policy and strategy should always be guided by the local environmental and religious perspectives.

The Sacred Geography of Kashi

The Sacred City of Kashi

> There is hardly any city in the world, that can claim greater antiquity, greater continuity and greater popular veneration than Banaras. Banaras has been a holy city for at least thirty centuries. No city in India arouses the religious emotions of Hindus as much as Kasi does. (Kane 1953, 618)
>
> Benares is to the Hindoos what Mecca is to the Mohammedans, and what Jerusalem was to the Jews of old. It is the 'holy' city of Hindostan. I have never seen anything approaching to it as a visible embodiment of religion; nor does anything like it exist on earth. (Norman Macleod in Eck 2012, 10)

As Sri Ramakrishna Paramahamsa once said, 'One may as well try to draw a map of the universe as attempt to describe Varanasi in words' (Singh 2013, 173). And yet attempt we must.

To begin with, the significance of Kashi to Hindus, to India, to the story of humanity, cannot be overstated. A single, continuous thread of civilizational and religious cohesion stretches across the vast expanse of time from the hoary past to today. The record of artistic and archaeological remains is virtually unbroken since Mauryan times in the fourth century BC (Eck 1982, 11–12).

The previous section discussed the work of Lakshmidhara and other authors of *nibandhas* about tirthas and pilgrimage more generally. Lakshmidhara's *Tirthavivechana Kanda* begins with a discussion of Kashi, a precedent followed by later digests, and nearly half the book is devoted to Kashi alone. In this section, he compiled scriptural references to over 350 sacred sites in Kashi and also select verses, enhanced by his own commentaries, about the Hindu tradition of pilgrimage. He emphasized the internal journey of transformation that must accompany the external voyage (Eck 1982, 127–128).

Mapping Kashi through Sacred Geography: The Sacred City

Building on Eliade's ideas about sacred space and Wheatley's 1971 studies on the origin of Asian cities, Jeffrey Meyer (1991) laid out the characteristics of what may be considered a 'cosmocized sacred city' of which Beijing was the last of a long line in China in his analysis (Singh 2013, 290). Singh notes that such examples are rare in India but in the few instances that exist, such as Kashi, there generally appear to be four reference routes delimiting the sacred space: (i) the *antargrha* (the core, the inner sanctum) (ii) the *parikshetra* (the next surrounding layer) (iii) the *kshetra* (sacred territory) and (iv) the *kshetra mandala* (the outer boundary).

Kashi can be understood through this framework. Kashi itself is the largest unit—a symbolic circle with a radius of five kroshas (the pancha krosha, discussed in more detail in the subsequent section), which is roughly the equivalent of sixteen kilometres (ten miles). This sacred zone extends far beyond the city itself into the countryside to the west and is circumambulated on the Panchakroshi Yatra. Varanasi today encompasses the urban area from the Varana to the Asi rivers. Avimukta is a smaller unit, and the antargrha is smaller still, including only the dense centre of the city surrounding the Vishvanatha Mandir. Thus, the structure of the sacred city, in this view, is a series of concentric sacred zones like the symbolic structure of a mandala (Eck 1982, 69).

Originally, the circular bounds of the pancha krosha territory demarcating Kashi stretched from Madhyameshvara to Dehali-Vinayaka, but as a result of political conquests in the northern and eastern parts of the city, it has now become a conch-shaped unit stretching 5 kroshas wide from east to west and about 2.5 kroshas north to south. According to the *Matsya Purana*, the area of Varanasi is located between the Varana and Asi rivers from north to south and between Pashapani Ganesha to the Ganga from west to east, narrowing to a mile-long stretch near the Rajghat Plateau. While the *Linga Purana* and the *Skanda Purana* define the boundaries of Avimukta to be extending one krosha in length from all sides of Krittivaseshvara or Madhyameshvara, the *Padma Purana* defines it as an area extending four hundred yards in length from all sides of Vishveshvara. This detail is shared not to highlight inconsistencies across texts, but rather to show the level of precision and detail to which our ancient rishis and acharyas went to carefully identify the contours of sacred geography all across Bharat, including Kashi.

The antargrha of Vishveshvara stretches between Manikarnikeshvara in the east to Gokarneshvara in the west and between Bharabuteshvara in the north and Brahmeshvara in the south. There is also the Trikantaka, which represents the triangular area between Madhyameshvara, Swarlineshvara, and Avimukteshvara.

There are also two other antargrhas: one of Kedareshvara and one of Omkareshvara. The former of these runs south of Vishveshvara and the latter to the north of it. The southern limit of the former is Lolarka and the northern boundary of the latter is the Varana river (Sukul 1974, 163–164).

The most iconic image of Kashi is that of the ghats lining the riverfront of the Ganga, ranged between the Asi to the south and the Varana to the north—eighty-four of them lined across an arc spanning a little over six kilometres. Cosmologically, each ghat represents one hundred thousand of the total of 8.4 million species that exist. Another perspective is that there are twelve zodiacal signs and seven layers of atmosphere—multiplied together, this comes out to eighty-four. Thus, the annual cycle of the cosmic journey is fulfilled by bathing at all of the eighty-four ghats. Furthermore, ninety-six sacred sites have been identified on the waterfront, which can be taken to indicate the twelve months or zodiacal signs and the eight directions of space, again multiplying to ninety-six (Singh 2013, 175).

Sukul notes that in the past the tirthas along the Ganga also carried temples on top of the ghats, often sharing the same name. Most of these temples were destroyed in AD 1194. Several of these temples were reconsecrated elsewhere and carried the name of the original ghats with them to their new location; in the course of time, the old sites were forgotten (Sukul 1974, 271–272).

It should also be noted that although the worship of Surya Deva is no long as prominent as it once was in Kashi, the temples and tirthas dedicated to Surya Deva are still regularly visited and worshipped. Historical evidence documents that during the Gupta period, in AD 4–5 centuries, sun worship was common and by the turn of twelfth century it was well established in the region. However, near the end of that century, all the temples and shrines devoted to Surya Deva, along with most of the other temples in the city, were demolished by Mughal invaders.

Fragments of the temples and images of Surya Deva exist and are still today visited by pilgrims, so great has been the power of Surya Deva in Kashi. The Kashi Khanda lists fourteen sites devoted to Surya Deva. All of them exist at present and are part of the ritual landscape of Kashi (Singh 2013, 249–251).

Singh notes that the location of Madhyameshvara close to the centre of the triangle of Aditya temples is significant. Prior to the Muslim occupation of the city, Madhyameshvara was the site of the oldest and greatest temple of the city:

[I]t was the original centre of Kashi, and as such it would have been surrounded and symbolically protected by the various forms of the sun as represented by the Aditya temples. Today's centre of Varanasi is at a different location, i.e., Jnanavapi, a holy well associated with Vishvanatha temple. (Singh 2013, 249–251)

Also serving a protective function in Kashi are the circles of eight Ganeshas standing guard on the threshold of the city and removing obstacles for the devotees of Shiva. There is a circle of eight Ganeshas around the centre of the old city. Beyond the centre are seven concentric circles of eight Ganeshas each, creating an entire grid of protective Ganeshas around the holy city. These fifty-six Ganeshas are said to be situated at the cardinal and intermediary directions (Eck 2012, 57–58). This array of Vinayakas was also documented in the *Skanda Purana*.

Swami Medhasananda in his seminal two-volume book on Kashi recounts that in the late 1700s, a Bengali pandit, Ramachandra Vidyalankar, and his son, Umashankar Tarkalankar, meticulously scoured nearly every nook and cranny of Kashi, pored over many old texts, and over time identified and located many tirthas that had been lost or long forgotten. They also wrote a pilgrimage guide, entitled *Kashiyatrapaddhati*, in which they recorded the locations and other details of the holy sites.

Almost one hundred years later, Gorji Dikshit, a Gujarati pandit, carried on the work of restoring holy sites in Varanasi. Reverend Sherring gave the following testimony:

Gorji is a remarkable man, and has done more to revive Hinduism, in the city of late years, than perhaps any other person. Having diligently read the Kashi Khandam, he has searched about for the temples and idols referred to in that book, and wherever he has found old temples in decay and abandoned, or has discovered sacred sites now neglected and generally unknown, he has endeavoured to restore them to honour and popularity. (Medhasananda 2002, 171)

Again, we see the painstaking efforts undertaken to preserve, maintain, and restore the sacred sites of Kashi. There were the composers of the digests from the time of the twelfth century, who followed in the footsteps of the great seers of the Puranas and the Sthala Puranas, and then there were those who, in the face of widespread destruction and desecration of all the temples in Kashi, nevertheless persevered to restore those sites and maintain the sacred geography of Kashi to the best of their abilities.

City of Shiva

In addition to the Kashi Khanda, which we have covered extensively, there are other Puranic accounts of the association between Shiva and Kashi. In the earliest versions of the lore, such as that of the *Vayu Purana*, Kashi was already the most beautiful place in the world and Shiva was attracted to it. After his marriage to Parvati, he could not immediately bring her to Kashi as King Divodasa was already ruling over it. He had to first remove the king (Eck 1982, 147).

Shiva summoned his attendant, Nikumbha, and commanded him to go to Kashi and empty out the city. Nikumbha entered the dream of a barber and told him to establish and worship the image of the Nikumbha Gana at the edge of the city. The barber did this, and Nikumbha was worshipped as the Lord of Ganas, Ganesha, at the city gate. He became popular and granted all the desires of his followers.

King Divodasa's childless wife repeatedly worshipped Nikumbha in order to get a son, but Nikumbha did not answer her prayers. King Divodasa was angered and eventually ordered the shrine of Nikumbha Ganesha to be destroyed. Then Nikumbha cursed the king and the city, proclaiming, 'Because my sacred place has been destroyed, this city shall be empty of all its inhabitants.'

Then Shiva arrived and established his abode there. In place of Divodasa, Shiva and his entourage took over the rule of Kashi. Shiva told Parvati, 'I will not leave my home, for my home is Never-Forsaken, Avimukta' (*Vayu Purana*, 92.56–9, cited in Eck 1982, 147–148).

Panchakroshi Yatra and Other Kashi Yatras

Within the framework of Hindu sacred geography, each kshetra, or holy territory, must be approached and entered into in a certain sequence that progressively purifies and prepares the pilgrim for the full experience of the divine site. Here we cover some of the many different types of yatras prescribed for Kashi.

The importance of Kashi yatras

To attain the full fruits of pilgrimage to Kashi, various yatras are prescribed. The *Kashi Tattva Bhaskara* and the *Kashi Yatra Prakasha* are two guidebooks for observing yatra in Kashi. The former begins with a glorification of Kashi with Sanskrit verses and explanations in Hindi. Then follows a description of the rites and pilgrimages to be performed on special occasions and those to be performed on a daily, weekly, and yearly basis. The latter describes various pilgrimage circuits, such as the Antargrha Yatra, the yatra for the nine Gauris, the fifty-six Ganeshas, the twelve Adityas, and more (Eck 1993, 19).

Generally, people formed large groups and travelled together either by boat or on foot to visit Kashi. To take one example, pilgrims, particularly from Bengal, Maharashtra, and south India, would visit the city in large groups consisting of hundreds of people. From various references to visits by pilgrims from different quarters and also from the number of resident Brahmana priests attending the pilgrims, Swami Medhasananda estimated the number of pilgrims visiting Kashi. Records show that, at one point in time, some 11,311 Maharashtrian Brahmanas attended to pilgrims from Maharashtra while 3,000 Bengali Brahmanas attended to pilgrims from Bengal (Medhasananda 2002, 107). As far as the total number of pilgrims is concerned, Swami Medhasananda cites Valentia, who wrote in the early nineteenth century that the average number of pilgrims might be taken at ten thousand, but that at the time of certain Hindu festivals, the number of visitors defied all calculations (Medhasananda 2002, 107). On the occasion of an eclipse in May 1826, Prinsep determined that the number of new arrivals on that occasion was around 55,000 but commented that the eclipse on this occasion was a rather partial one and that it was not unreasonable to conclude that the number of visitors during a total eclipse or some such occasion could surpass 100,000 (Medhasananda 2002, 107).

The five most important yatras

While there are many yatras and kshetras identified in Kashi, five pilgrimage circuits have traditionally been considered the most important: the Chaurashikroshi, Panchakroshi, Nagara Pradakshina, Avimukta, and Antargrha. The four inner circuits meet at Gyaanavapi, the axis mundi. The temple of Madhyameshvara serves as the centre for the covering circle in the Chaurashikroshi Yatra and the yatra was first described in the *Padma Purana* (Srishthi Khanda, 65.14–20) (cited by Singh 2013, 247). This yatra is now rarely performed (Singh 2013, 247).

The Chaurashikroshi Yatra is also referred to as the Brhat Panchakroshi Kshetra. The centre lies at Madhyameshvara and the radial point at Dehali Vinayaka. The shrine of Dehali Vinayaka—Ganesha at the Gate—identifies the entrance to the cosmic mandala (Singh 1988, 8). Pilgrimage along this route symbolizes the circumambulation of the entire cosmos. Over time, the Chaurashikroshi Yatra has shrunk to the present path of the Panchakroshi Yatra (Singh 2002, 26).

The circuit of the Chaurashikroshi Yatra is divided into eight directions and protected by the guardians of the directions. Each such dikpalaka is under the direction of twelve forms of Devi. It is said that these ninety-six forms of Shakti had helped Durga slay Mahishasura's army. After the war, Durga recited their names. These Shaktis are under the supervision of the Kshetra Devi, a manifestation of Durga. This combination represents the cosmic merger of time (twelve months) and space (eight directions) being controlled and maintained by the Shaktis (Singh 2002, 28).

There is also a Panchatirtha Yatra that encompasses Dashashvamedha, Lolarka, Keshava, Bindu Madhava, and Manikarnika.

Panchakroshi Yatra

Of all these yatras, the Panchakroshi is the most famous. In the *Kashi Rahasya*, a sixteenth-century text, the sacred path and the rules of the Panchakroshi Yatra are described. The text tells the story of a wicked young man, Mandapa, who becomes purified and transformed through the performance of the Panchakroshi Yatra. Along the path covering a distance of approximately twenty-five kroshas, or 55.2 kilometres (88.5 miles), one comes across 108 shrines and sacred sites (Singh 2002, 65).

The Vishveshvara Antargrha journey is prescribed as an essential introductory or closing rite before or after performing the Panchakroshi Yatra. This journey has been considered so important that James Prinsep in his 1822 map of Kashi had fully outlined it (Singh 2002, 164).

The Panchakroshi Yatra is completed by finally requesting and praying to Vishveshvara. After reaching home, the pilgrims are to perform a yajna during which the names of all the 108 shrines and images visited are recalled.

Describing the Panchakroshi Yatra in the late nineteenth century, Sherring remarked, 'It is necessary that every good Hindu residing in the city of Benares [Varanasi] should twice a year accomplish this pilgrimage, in order that the impurity which the soul and body have contracted during the year may be obliterated' (Singh 2002, 129–130).

The Panchakroshi Yatra starts with the worship of the Vishveshvara Linga. Gyaanavapi, together with Vishveshvara, serves as the 'centre', the axis mundi, of the yatra. From here, the pilgrimage starts with *sankalpa lena* (the rite of taking a vow) and ends with *sankalpa chodana* (being released from the vow). According to Singh, the Panchakroshi Yatra kshetra symbolizes the intermediate realm of integration between the macrocosm (here, the Chaurashikroshi kshetra) and the microcosm (here, the area surrounding the Vishveshvara Temple compound) (Singh 2002, 51).

By the sixteenth century, the Panchakroshi Yatra had become highly popular. A Marathi treatise, the *Guru Charitra* (41.265–317), dated AD 1538, described the details of the pilgrimage (cited by Singh 2002, 31). Tulsidas (1497–1623) also glorified and eulogized the Panchakroshi Yatra. During the period of Mughal rule, many of the important images and shrines along the Panchakroshi Yatra were destroyed. The identification of the path itself may have become lost in places. According to lore, there are many lingams and images buried in the earth.

At the end of the eighteenth century, during a period of strong Hindu revival, many such images and lingams were recovered and many new replicas have been established. By the end of the nineteenth century, the Panchakroshi Yatra path had returned as a popular pilgrimage circuit—five stopping places for the night were established, and forty-four dharmashalas were built (Singh 2002, 31).

Due to the resilience and perseverance on the part of Hindus to rebuild and reconsecrate, the Panchakroshi Yatra was revived from the late 1700s onward. Rani Bhavani of Natore, Bengal, renovated and reconstructed the water pools at the halting stations of the Durgakunda, Kandava, and Bhimachandi villages in the 1750s. In 1835, the pandits of Kashi held discourses to properly identify and correct the route, which took an accepted shape in 1853. This is reported in the proceedings of a set of discourses—titled *Thoughts on the Panchakroshi Marga* and published in Hindi in 1872—under the supervision of Bharatendu Harishchandra, known as the pioneer of modern Hindi (cited by Singh 2002, 36–37).

In that report, it is mentioned that during the period of the destruction of temples by the Muslim rulers between the seventeenth and eighteenth centuries, perhaps the Panchakroshi Yatra had become defunct, and the route and associated shrines may have been neglected during that time. In the early 1800s, Mahadeva

Bhatta took strides to revive the tradition of the Panchakroshi Yatra by clearing the path, building bridges over streams, and bringing awareness to people about the need for active participation in the pilgrimage (Singh 2002, 36–37).

Adaptation and Evolution

It is worth noting that while meticulous care has been taken over the centuries to identify and preserve the sacred shrines and temples of Kashi in their original sites, there is a dynamic process of evolution and adaptation that keeps Kashi from becoming ossified. Part of it is borne out of necessity and the fact that certain mosques were constructed on the original sites of important temples and to date Hindus have not taken over those mosques and re-established their temples there. This dislocation requires creativity and adaptation to rebuild elsewhere and softly redraw the maps of sacred geography while never sacrificing the memory of the destruction and violence done to the original sites. Part of it is also natural evolution and change through the shifting sands of time and circumstance.

But even within those shifts, there is an underlying continuity that remains unbroken. Singh makes an important and profound point in this regard. He notes that first it was Madhyameshvara that was viewed as the navel point or centre of Kashi, and later it was Gyaanavapi. While this may seem like a change, there is a consistency and continuity in that Madhyameshvara can be viewed as defining the centre of the outer territory while Gyaanavapi is the centre of the innermost segment. Singh explains this beautifully:

> By this one finds a state of non-equilibrium, however it is dynamic and functioning, what Cambel (1993:4) has expressed, 'Complex systems are dynamic and not in equilibrium; they are like a journey, not a destination, and they may pursue a moving target.' (Singh 2002, 35)

Dangers of Historiography: Counting and Dating Temples

It is worth taking a moment to touch upon various debates that have arisen over the dating of texts and temples related to the sacred geography of Kashi. Exercises of counting and dating have been used to allege that certain texts or temples came about or became prominent as a result of or in response to Mughal rule. The sly implication of these arguments is that therefore these sites or texts lack the authentic imprimatur of original sacrality.

It is an incontrovertible fact that the number of temples for Shiva and other deities in Kashi has varied from time to time. Hieun Tsang enumerated approximately one hundred popular and sacred temples during the time of his visit in AD 635. Qutub-uddin Aibak is reported to have destroyed a thousand temples in the late twelfth century. Lakshmidhara, in the twelfth century, referred to the existence of 340 temples. Allauddin Khilji (1296–1316) boasted of destroying a thousand temples during his reign from AD 1296 to 1316. Prinsep counted 1,000 temples and 333 mosques as of 1828. Finally, M.A. Sherring estimated 1,454 temples and 272 mosques to have existed in Kashi as of the early twentieth century (Chandramouli 2018, 73).

Singh has set forth an exhaustive alphabetical index of the 524 Shivalingas referenced in the Kashi Khanda of the *Skanda Purana* and their present location in Varanasi. He notes that out of 524 Shivalingas listed in the Kashi Khanda, 200 are not known or may be lost (Singh 2008, 421–442).

Sukul also makes a detailed count. He notes that the Kashi Khanda enumerates 1,099 temples and tirthas with 383 delineated as being the most important, while the *Linga Purana* as quoted in the *Kritya Kalpataru* of Lakshmidhara enumerates 462 as being the most important. He further notes that the Kashi Khanda provides the names and descriptions of 513 temples dedicated to Shiva, 49 to Vishnu, 75 to Devi, 71 to Vinayaka, 3 to Skanda, 13 to Surya Deva, 11 to Bhairava, 1 to Vetala, 64 to the yoginis, 8 to the Shiva ganas, and 3 to the nagas (Sukul 1974, 164–165).

While the count may vary, there is a remarkable consistency and continuity from the hoary past to today. As Sukul notes, the earliest details about the sacred geography emerge from the *Linga*

Purana and other Puranas, which were authoritative by the time of AD 1110. He observes that different shrines were then in the same location as they are now. For example, Adi Keshava was and is near the confluence of the Varana and Ganga rivers; Shaileshar was and is in the northern parts of the banks of the Varana river; Lolarka was and is near the southern-most point of the confluence of the Asi and Ganga rivers with Durgakund to its west. Gokarna and Dhruveshvara marked back then and still mark the western limit. The earliest site of the Vishveshvara Temple was clearly mentioned to be on the site where Razia's Mosque was deliberately built over the ruins (citing Bhatta, Sukul 1974, 7–8).

Sukul makes an impassioned and compelling rebuttal to those who have claimed, like Reverend M.A. Sherring, that it was only simultaneously with the later development of these texts that new temples were constructed to which ancient importance was fraudulently attached. Sherring, to back his claim, quoted that there were 1,654 temples in his day while there were only 1,000 during Prinsep's time (Sukul 1974, 165).

Sukul's wit here is so biting that it is worth quoting him in full:

> I am sure if a census were taken today there will be found over three thousand temples in Varanasi, but no one has ever said that all of them are ancient and sacred temples. It is considered a very pious deed to build a temple in Varanasi and everyone who can afford it does build one. Thus the number of temples increases all the time but it is wrong to suggest that the number of sacred temples is on the increase and that new temples have been added and given old names as has been suggested. It is actually libellous when it accuses Bhatta Narayan (writer of *Tristhali Setu*) and Mittra Misra (writer of *Vira-Mitrodaya*) of giving names of temples built in the fourteenth, fifteenth and sixteenth centuries as ancient and sacred ones because they have done absolutely nothing of the kind. They have not mentioned even one temple which was not mentioned in the Kashi-Khanda or Kritya Kalpataru. These historians forget that Padmeshvara or even Karnameru—two of the most splendid

temples of their time—have found no mention in Puranic records and even in religious essays like Tristhali Setu and Vira-Mitrodaya. When temples built by kings did not find a place in the sacred list it is preposterous to suggest that people deliberately set about building new temples and spuriously passing them on as old and mythological ones. (Sukul 1974, 167–168)

In other words, the acharyas and the pandits and the religious leaders of their times did not adopt a laissez-faire attitude and haphazardly conflate the newest or wealthiest or biggest temple of their times with the temples hallowed by their sanctity and antiquity through the time-tested tradition of the Puranas and their accompanying oral traditions. A distinction was made between the important sites based on sacred geography and those that were prominent due to royal patronage or other reasons.

Sacred geography, while it is subtle, is not vague and nebulous to be manipulated at will. Why did our ancestors spend so much time and energy to preserve and reconsecrate and carry forth the memory of the most sacred sites with the deepest roots into the kshetra of Kashi? They could have adopted the flip attitude espoused by many posturing intellectuals today that if a temple can be built in our home or in our heart there is no need to cast our eyes on the destruction and violence done to our sacred geography, that there is no justification for the desire to repair the tears and breaks that have been wrought onto our sacred geography.

Instead, they painstakingly set out to identify the precise sites lauded by the ancient texts and to preserve them the best they could, physically as well as by emblazoning them onto the individual and collective memories of Hindus so that all Hindus would honour, make pilgrimage to, and support these sacred temples and sites.

Along the lines of the charges levelled by Sherring and others, discussed above, some scholars, such as Motichand, have also opined that the Panchakroshi Yatra is likely of recent origin, not older than the twelfth century AD. Evidence proffered to back this charge points to the fact that Laksmidhara has not mentioned the

Panchakroshi Yatra in the *Krtyakalpataru*. Sukul again rebuts this charge by citing many verses from different Puranas. Moreover, many ancient dilapidated divine images have been found at various places along the Panchakroshi Yatra route, such as those of deities like yakshas, nagas, kuber and gandharvas at Kardameshvara; images of Navagrahas, Varaha, and folk goddesses at Moksheshvara in the village of Abare; Lakshminarayana in the Radhakrishna temple in Harsons; Surya and Ganesha images in the Kameshvara Temple, Chaukhand; the ten-headed Kali in Bhimachandi, and several other ruined deities along the route (Sukul 1977, 241). These discoveries certainly establish the ancient historicity of the Panchakroshi Yatra.

Dangers of Historiography: The Dating of the Puranas

Did the composition of the *Skanda Purana* as we know it today fructify after the Muslim invasions? This is yet another charge levelled against the validity of Hindu sacred geography in Kashi. Eck provides a befitting reply:

> [I]t seems to this writer unlikely that the literary care and attention lavished upon the many shrines of [Kashi] would have arisen from the era of ruin and debilitation that followed the attack of Mahmud of Ghur's general Qutb-ud-din-Aibak in 1194. The [Kashi Khanda] makes no mention of Muslim invaders or the destruction of holy sies [sic]. It seems plausible, therefore, that much of the [Kashi Khanda] came into existence during the brilliant era of the revivalist Hindu empire of the [Gahadavalas], even though its final compilation may have been later. In [Lakshmidhara's] time the work would have been in process of formulation and, thus, too new to have been included in his digest. The heyday of the [Gahadavala] empire, however, would have been the natural climate for the growth of such an extensive eulogy to [Kashi], even if its completed form came later. (Eck 1993, 10)

Moreover, this revisionist distortion of Hindu sacred geography flies in the face of the fact that the religious origins of Kashi and its association with Shiva had already been established in earlier Puranas whose antiquity are widely accepted. For example, the *Brahma Purana*, *Brahmanda Purana*, and *Vayu Purana* all contain accounts of the rivalry between the Kashis and the Haihayas with a thousand-year occupation of the city by rakshasas. In the *Brahmanda* and *Vayu Puranas*, they are referred to as ganas or Ganeshas. Moreover, the *Brahmanda* and *Vayu Puranas* describe how the ganas or Ganeshas were deliberately sent by Shiva to expel Divodasa, a king of the Kashi lineage, as Shiva had chosen it to be his capital on earth. Both the *Brahmanda* and *Vayu* are said to be among the earliest Puranas (Eck 1993, 12). It is also worth noting that the *Matsya Purana* describes Manikarnika as the holiest tirtha of Varanasi, and *Kashi Ka Itihas* accepts the *Matsya Purana* as dating back to the fifth century AD (Sukul 1974, 172).

III

Resistance and Resilience in the Hindu Holy City

CHAPTER 17

Timeline and Overview

This chapter provides a chronology and timeline of Kashi, adapted from the timeline published by Professor P.B. Rana Singh (Singh 1993a, 309). This provides an overview of the history of Kashi, aspects of which we will delve into in more detail in subsequent chapters.

Ancient Period

BCE

Date unknown: Suparshvanatha, the seventh-century Jaina Tirthankara, was born in Kashi.

Ninth century: Date of the last layer of the excavation at Rajghat. Until the ninth century, Kashi was an independent and vast state.

Eighth century: Parshvanatha, the twenty-third Jaina Tirthankara, was born in Kashi.

Seventh century: Ashrama of Kapila Muni established at Shivalaya Ghat.

Sixth–fourth centuries: Annexation of Kashi to Koshala, Magadha, and Kaushamabi. The rule of Nanda.

*c.***528:** First sermon of the Buddha at Sarnath. The turning of the Dharma Chakra.

Fifth century: Panini composed the *Ashtadhayayi* in Kashi.

*c.***240:** King Ashoka visited Kashi.

CE

First–Second centuries: Rule of Kushana, later replaced by the naga dynasty, the chief of whom, Bharashiva, performed the ten-horse sacrifice at Dashashvamedha Ghat.

Third century: Creation of a new Buddhist township at Sarnath.

Fourth century: Kashi and Koshala fall to the rule of Chandra Gupta Maurya I. The beginning of the Gupta rule.

c.405: Fa-Hein, the Chinese pilgrim, visited the city.

c.490: Construction of Vishveshvara Temple, perhaps for the first time, during the reign of Vainya Gupta, the Shaiva king.

c.635: Hiuen-Tsang, another famous Chinese pilgrim, visited the city.

Seventh century: Rule of Harsha (c.607–647).

Eighth century: Adi Shankaracharya stayed in Kashi, first came in c.716, composed the *Brahmasutra Bhashya*, and built the Tila Bhandeshvara Temple. The rule of the Yashovarman of Kannauja, which was later replaced by the Palas of Bengal.

Mid-ninth century: Rule of the Chedis.

Tenth century: Rule of the Gurjara-Pratiharas.

Medieval Period (CE 1000–1750)

Early eleventh century: Rule of Gangeya Deva Kalachuri

c.1021–1025: Al-Biruni, who came with Mahmud of Ghazni, visited the city and learned Sanskrit.

1033: Anmad Nialtagin, treasurer of Sultan Mahmud Ghaznavi, plundered the city and demolished many Hindu temples.

1042–1080: Karnadeva/Lakshmidhara Chedi ruled the city.

1090–1100: The rule of Chandradeva, the foundation of the Gahadavala dynasty.

Twelfth century: Up to 1193, the rule of Gahadavala kings. Visit of Ramanujacharya. Completion of the Kashi Khanda of *Skanda Purana*, containing 100 chapters and 11,624 verses.

1194: Qutb-ud-din Aibak demolished the Vishveshvara and its associated Vishnu Temples, converting them into the Dhai Kangura Mosque; he also demolished the Avimukteshvara Temple.

1197: Second invasion by Qutb-ud-din Aibak.

1248: Invasion by Muhammad Ghori, Shihab-ud-din.

1294: Sant Jnaneshvara visited the city.

Thirteenth–fourteenth centuries: Turko-Afghan domination.

1353: Brahmanas protested against Firoz Shah Tughlaq for Jazia-tax but later paid it.

1375: Firoz Shah Tughlaq demolished many Hindu temples.

Fourteenth–fifteenth centuries: Ramananda (1299–1411) settled in Varanasi, lived and taught at the Panchaganga Ghat, and founded a subdivision of Vaishnavism. Ravidasa, a cobbler-saint, became a disciple of Ramananda.

1440–1518: The life period of Kabir.

***c*.1447–1448:** Demolition of Padmeshvara Temple by Mahmud Shah Sharqi and also the Vishveshvara Temple upon which he built the Razia Mosque.

1460: Vachaspati Mishra composed the *Tirtha Chintamani*.

1469–1539: Guru Nanak visited the city and stayed at Gurubag in *c*.1473 and later had religious dialogue with the pandits of the city.

1479–1531: Vallabhacharya settled in Kashi during the latter part of his life and died here.

1485–1533: Chaitanya Mahaprabhu lived for many years in Kashi, having close friendship with Swami Prakashananda.

1494: Sikandar Lodi invaded the city and demolished almost all of the Hindu temples.

1529: After defeating Ibrahim Lodi, Babar invaded the city.

1535: Shershah Suri subjugated the city together with Chunara Garh.

1540–1623: Madhusudana Sarasvati lived in Kashi at Chaushatthi Ghat.

1558–1623: Tulsidas Maharaj (1547–1632) composed the *Ramacharitamanas* in *c*.1582–1584 and died here in 1623.

1545–1550: Narayana Bhatta composed the *Tristhali Setu*.

1567: Akbar defeated Jayachandra, the king of Kashi, partly plundered the city and established a mint.

1584–1585: Restoration and repair of Vishveshvara Mandir by Todaramala (Raghunatha Pandit), the famous minister of Akbar, under the guidance of Narayana Bhatta.

Sixteenth century: Composition of *Kashi Rahasya* and *Kashi Kedara Mahatmya.*

1600: Construction of Mana Mandira Ghat and many temples nearby by Raja Mana Singh of Jaipur.

1623: Plague in the city; Tulsidas Maharaj and Madhusdana Sarasvati died.

1627: Kina Rama, the founder of the Aghora sect of Tantra and Shaktism, lived and died here.

1628: Renovation of Gyaanavapi by Baija Bale, the queen of Gwalior.

1630: Renovation and reconstruction of Pishacamochana Kunda by Gopala Shahu.

1632: Demolition of newly constructed or under construction temples, about 76 in number, by Haider Begh under the order of Mughal emperor, Shahjahan.

1642: Restoration and reconstruction of the temple of Bindu Madhava by Jai Singh, king of Jaipur.

***c*.1650:** Visit of Jean-Baptiste Tavernier, a French jeweller and traveller.

1656–1657: Dara Shikoh translated the Upanishads into Persian with the help of 150 pandits from Kashi.

1658–1659: City came under the rule of Aurangzeb, and he demolished the Krttivaseshvara Temple.

1664: Battle of Gyaanavapi between the Dashanami naga sannyasis and the army of Aurangzeb.

1666: Shivaji found refuge with the Brahmanas of the city, near Panchaganga Ghat, during his flight from the imperial court of Aurangzeb.

1669–1673: By the order of Aurangzeb, the temples of Vishveshvara (in 1669) and Bindu Madhava (in 1673) were demolished and mosques erected on those sites.

Seventh century: Guru Tegh Bahadur, the ninth Sikh guru, visited the city.

1719: The beginning of the rule of the Nawab of Awadh.

1725: Baji Rao Peshava I of Pune reconstructed the Annapurana Mandir. Establishment of Kashi Raja.

Modern Period (1750–1947)

1755: Second Bindu Madhava Temple built by a Maharashtrian king.

1756: Rani Bhavani constructed the Gandharva Sagara Kunda at Bhimachandi.

1764: The East India Company gained control over the city.

1775: Cremation site at Manikarnika Ghat constructed.

1777: Ahilyabai Holkar, the Queen of Indore, constructed the present Vishveshvara Temple.

1785: Ahilyabai Holkar constructed and extended the Dashashvamedha Ghat and renovated many temples of Varanasi, including Vishveshvara.

1791–1794: Construction of Manikarnika Ghat.

18th century: Construction of Durga Temple by Rani Bhavani of Natore, Bengal.

1807: Amrit Rao Vinayaka Peshava built Agnishvara Ghat, now known as Raja Ghat.

1809–1810: The great Hindu-Muslim riot for possession of the land between the Gyanvapi Mosque and the Vishvanatha Temple, and conflict at Gai Ghat Mahalla.

1815: Renovation of Trilochana Temple by Nathua Bala of Pune.

1818: Birth of Maharani Lakshmibai of Peshava in Peshava Bhavan.

1825: Construction of Kaala Bhairava Temple by Baji Rao Peshava II.

1828: Queen Baija Baie of Gwalior built the Gyaanavapi Kupa.

1839: The Vishveshvara mandir was gilded by Maharaja Ranjit Singh of Punjab.

1850–1885: Bhartendu Harishchandra, the founder of modern Hindi and the great writer, lived in Kashi.

1868: Sri Ramakrishna Paramahamsa visited the city.

1869: Swami Dayananda Saraswati, founder of the Arya Samaj, visited the city and took part in religious dialogue.

1891: On 8 April, the demolition of the Rama Temple in Bhadaini to establish a water pump led to the Ramalalla protest movement. On 15 April, the demolished temple was reconstructed overnight by the residents of Varanasi.

1895: Visit of Mark Twain.

1897: Hindu College was founded by Annie Besant.

1909: Foundation Bill for the Banaras Hindu University enacted.

1915: Construction of the Darbhanga Ghat and Nilakantha Mahadeva Mandir in Brahmanal, by Rameshwar Singh, the king of Darbhanga state (Bihar).

1916: Foundation of the Banaras Hindu University.

1920: Foundation of Kashi Vidyapith by Gandhi.

1936: Bharata Mata Mandir opened by Gandhi, built by Shivprasad Gupta.

1841: Establishment of Dharma Sangha by Swami Karpatriji.

1944: Kothi Maharudhra Yajna performed by Karpatriji near Asi Ghat.

CHAPTER 18

The Classical Age of Kashi

The following chapters are less focused on chronology than they are on qualitative aspects of Kashi's character and trends and themes that recurred and repeated themselves over the centuries and millennia of this great city's history. So, for example, this chapter on the classical age of Kashi is less about a particular time period than it is capturing the quintessential traits that have defined Kashi as the zenith of Hindu civilization, from the Vedic period until today. Nor are these chapters comprehensive; these few pages are insufficient to do justice to the full breadth and depth of Kashi's history. Rather, these are snippets that provide us glimpses into the unique characteristics of this Hindu holy city.

Dr Hobert Fael Waxy in his book *History of Hinduism* wrote,

> As a Historian I am in a position to assert that the citizens of Varanasi are privileged to be placed in a divine atmosphere by having taken birth in the lap of Indian civilization, the greatness of which cannot be compared with the history of any other place in the world. (Sukul 1974, 27)

As Sukul notes, even though for the last several centuries the two names Kashi and Varanasi have interchangeably been used for the city, in the ancient past they represented different entities. Then Kashi was the name of the kingdom and Varanasi the name of the capital (Sukul 1974, 1). The ancient town of Varanasi from the third century BC to seventh century AD, as has been laid bare in the Rajghat excavations, consisted of houses big and small built along narrow streets with temples interspersed here and there, and this pattern continued to be the norm even afterwards right up until the seventeenth and eighteenth centuries (Sukul 1974, 6).

The approximate date for the establishment of a kingdom in Kashi appears to have taken place before 1800 BC, almost in 2000 BC. According to Sukul, this date is corroborated by a quotation from the 'Maha Govind Sutta' of *Diggha Nikaya*, a Buddhist text stating that Varanasi was founded long before Buddha by Mahagovinda, the Brahmana minister of King Renu, who in turn was the first overlord with Dhritarashthra taking the role of the first sovereign. Renu was the son of Vishvamitra according to the *Aiterya Brahmana* (7.17.7) and the *Sankhyayana Shrauta Suta* (15.26.1) (cited in Sukul 1974, 18–19).

After the founding of the kingdom, the rulers of Kashi specialized in scholarship, and as time progressed, many acclaimed philosophers came to live in Kashi. This earned for the kingdom the appellation of Brahma Vardhana, and one of its kings, Ajatashatru, was a noted philosopher in his day (Sukul 1974, 19).

After the Mahabharata war, the kingdom of Kashi was attacked by Vasudeva Krishna's army and the town of Varanasi was burnt down. Ultimately, the kingdom fell to Magadha and the Koshala Janapadas by turns and became annexed thereto. With reference to this period of history, the term 'Kashi-Koshala' appears frequently. According to the Buddhist Jatakas, it was Kansa, the king of Koshala, who conquered the Kashi Janapada and united it with his own kingdom (Sukul 1974, 21).

Later, by the time of the present version of the Mahabharata, which has been differently placed by scholars between 500 and 800 BC, per Sukul, Varanasi had already attained the status of a dharma kshetra. Valmiki had already written a verse in praise of Varanasi, proclaiming that it is preferable to be born and die and suffer troubles in Varanasi rather than be born elsewhere and rule as a king with elaborate fanning by the damsels (Sukul 1974, 149).

As Sukul concludes,

> It is obvious, therefore, that Varanasi had been recognised as a holy place long before the fifth or even sixth century before Christ. In fact, Buddha's choosing Varanasi as the appropriate place to preach his first sermon, known as the Dharmachakra-Pravartana, indicates that Varanasi was already being considered a stronghold of Brahmanical religion, and this takes us quite a couple of centuries earlier, if not a little more. (Sukul 1974, 21)

A verse in the Shatapatha Brahmana (SBR XIII.5.4.21), as translated by Kane, carries reference to Kashi, stating that '[A] Gatha … states that Satanika, son of Satrajit, carried away the sacred horse of the Kashis' (cited in Jayaswal 2019, 13). It is also mentioned that after King Dhritarashthra of Kashi was defeated by Satanika, the Brahmanas of Kashi gave up the kindling of the sacred fire.

Two inferences may be drawn from this, as noted by Jayaswal. One, that Vedic rituals were very much prevalent in Kashi. And, two, that the region was politically not very strong. The later assumption also gets support from *Gopatha Brahmana*, which mentions Kashi in combination with the Koshala kingdom (citing Kane, Jayaswal 2019, 13). The other important development during this time is that as people were migrating from the Sarasvati valley, Vedic influence came to Kashi, which was on the pathway during the eastward movement of the Vedic people.

The Anushasana Parva of the Mahabharata mentions Divodasa and his family ruling Kashi. The legendary Divodasa also figures in the *Rg Veda*. The same king is said to ascend the throne of Kashi in the epic. The seventeenth shloka of the Anushusana Parva of the Mahabharata describes the composition of the city. The settlement had rich collections of articles and produce, and its markets and shops were affluent. The other aspects that find mention in the Mahabharata are the prevalence of Shiva worship, mentioned in the Tirthayatra Parva in Vana Parva, and the name of the river

Varanasi, mentioned in the long list of rivers of India (Jayaswal 2019, 15).

Eck quotes Jayaswal in describing an intriguing fragment of sculpture in the Bharat Kala Bhavan that shows a man balancing a linga on his head with his hand. It is dated back to the third century AD:

> We can only imagine that the man is going somewhere with this load, perhaps to Varanasi to establish this emblem of Shiva in a shrine or temple. Some clues to the meaning of this piece may be found in the records of a local dynasty, the Bhara Shivas, who ruled in the vicinity of Varanasi and were the first of the Hindu revivalist empires, which included the Vakatakas and then the Guptas. These were Shaiva kings. They are said to have performed ten ashvamedhas on the banks of the Ganga.
>
> Inscription: 'Of [the Dynasty of] the Bhara Shivas whose royal line owed its origin to the great satisfaction of Shiva on account of their carrying the load of the symbol of Shiva on their shoulders—the Bhara Shivas who were anointed to sovereignty with the holy water of the Bhagirathi which had been obtained by their valour—the Bhara Shivas who performed their sacred bath on the completion of their Ten Ashvamedhas.' (Jayaswal in Eck 1982, 105–106)

In the seventh century AD, during the reign of King Harsha in Kanauj, Hiuen-Tsiang visited Varanasi and described the city as thickly populated, prosperous, and an important seat of learning. Tsiang described the city as a conglomerate of congested houses separated by narrow lanes, gardens and groves, and water pools with lotus flowers. He noticed a predominance of Shiva temples and shrines with beautifully carved stone and wooden pillars and roots. He also described the nearby Buddhist township of Sarnath, with its many stupas, commemorative pillars, temples and shrines, eight divisions of residential quarters for the monks, surrounding wall, three water pools and numerous wells, a deer park, and a forest tract (Singh 2008, 81).

Adi Shankaracharya is said to have come to Varanasi for the first time around AD 805. It is likely that he might have come to Varanasi again on a couple of occasions. He is said to have stayed in many places like Manikarnika Ghat, Ganesha Mahal, and Kedara Ghat. His encounter with a chandala in a narrow lane leading possibly to Manikarnika Ghat is one of the most famous and inspiring incidents from his life story. He is said to have composed in Kashi many famous and popular Sanskrit verses like Kashi Panchakam, Shiva Stotra, Annapurna and Kaala Bhairava Ashtaka, Moha Mudgara or Bhaja Govindam, and others (Chandramouli 2018, 101–102).

In the early medieval period, Kashi had passed from one ruler to another—from the Maukharis of Kannauj to the Gurjara Pratiharas in the ninth century. In the mid-tenth century, Kashi was under the rule of the Pratihara Dynasty and had expanded southwards. At the turn of the eleventh century, the city came under the sway of the Kalachuris, a period that is generally acknowledged as the golden era of the city's history. In the early part of the same century, Kashi went under the reign of Gangeyadeva, the king of Kannauj and a descendant of the Kalachuris.

The Gahadavalas provided strong Hindu leadership and saw themselves as the protectors of the tirthas, especially four of the great tirthas of their realm, the most important of which were Kashi and, further west along the Ganga, ancient Kannauj. Now Kashi and Kannauj became not only the recipients of the religious patronage of the Gahadavalas but the administrative centres of their empire as well. With the Gahadavala kingdom, the city of Kashi came into political prominence for the first time in nearly two thousand years—not since the days when Kashi vied with other north Indian kingdoms for prestige in the sixth and seventh centuries BC had this been an imperial capital.

The Gahadavalas were liberal and eclectic in their religious patronage. In their inscriptions, the kings described themselves as 'great worshipers of Shiva', the Lord of Kashi. Shiva is referred to as Krttivasa in some inscriptions, indicating that the great temple of Krittivasa was at its height of prominence during this period. Nonetheless, the most famous of these kings, Govindachandra, had two queens who espoused and patronized Buddhism. For the most part, however, the Gahadavalas were worshippers of Vishnu, and in one inscription, Govindachandra (1114–1154), the greatest ruler in the history of this dynasty, is praised as an incarnation of Vishnu, commissioned to protect Vishnu's favourite abode, the city of Varanasi.

Govindachandra defeated Muslim invaders twice between 1114 and 1118. Queen Kumar Devi, his wife, came from a Vajrayani Buddhist family. She restored several buildings at Sarnath and built a new vihara there.

In the days of Govindachandra, the city was known as an important centre for learning the Vedas, Sanskrit grammar, philosophy, and medicine. It may have been perhaps later in this period that the Kashi Khanda became attached to the *Skanda Purana* as a major section thereof.

Govindachandra was a great patron of scholars, and in this regard, one of the most important accomplishments of his entire reign was the appointment of Lakshmidhara as the chief minister. Almost single-handedly, Lakshmidhara inaugurated a new era in Hindu religious literature by compiling one of the earliest, most reputable, and most extensive digests of literature on dharma, composed in fourteen volumes, known as the *Krityakalpataru*. In one of the volumes, he mentions the scriptural references to over 350 shrines in Kashi and also points out the close connections between the scholars of Banaras and Kashmir. He had also carried forward the theory and philosophy of Hindu tirtha.

As Singh notes, citing Diana Eck:

> This period records some notable writings, e.g., the Matsya Purana (ca. the early 11th century), the Linga Purana (CE 1110), Lakshmidhara's Krityakalpataru (1125), Hemachandra's Kumara Charita (1184), and Damodara's Ukti-Vyakti Prakarana (ca. 1190), which describe the contemporary condition and glory of the city

of Banaras. The descriptions tell us that the Gahadavalas were worshippers of Shiva, but also of Vishnu [...] Shiva was called Krttivasa, and the temple of Krttivaseshvara was at the height of its glory in the 11th–12th century. (Singh 2004, 71)

The three sacred zones of Kashi, surrounding the present Omkareshvara, Vishveshvara, and Kedareshvara Temples were fully developed and inhabited by traders and migrants from different parts of the country. A chain of shrines linked by pilgrimage routes delineated these three sections. Various occupational groups with artisans, craftsmen, and other service providers settled in Kashi to contribute to its development. Most of the ponds and lakes were converted into *jala tirthas*, or sacred water sites, associated with Puranic and other deities. Govindachandra is credited with the development of proper ghats along the Ganga as well as the construction of several sacred wells, gardens, groves, and pools.

The rule of the Gahadavalas lasted until the end of the twelfth century. During this period, Buddhist and Hindu ascetics and scholars in both Sarnath and Varanasi lived in harmony discussing, debating, and explaining their respective doctrines.

With the spread of Shaivism across northern India, the religious prestige of Kashi continued to increase. Shiva, the principal divinity of Kashi, was recognized as Mahadeva. Thus, there spread hundreds of temples and shrines with the suffix 'ishvara', such as Tarakeshvara (built in 1792 by Ahilyabai Holkar), Ratneshvara (built in 1828 by Baijabai), and Samrajeshvara (built in 1843 by Rajendra Vikram Shah, king of Nepal)—all being dedicated to a particular manifestation of Shiva.

The growth of the city's population, including migrants from different parts of Bharat, led to the development of a cosmopolitan character in the city. It was during this period that the Avimukteshvara Linga came to be replaced in provenance by that of Vishveshvara, which will be discussed later in the book. Nevertheless, the Adi Keshava Mandir seems to have served as the favoured temple for the royal family (Singh 2008, 83–85).

The *Varanasimhatmya* provides us with a snapshot of what Varanasi may have looked like in the twelfth century, a time when the holy town was ruled by the powerful Gahadavalas, the last major Hindu dynasty of north India. It is also one of the first *mahatmyas* that gives extensive praise to the linga that would become the sacred centre of Varanasi for centuries to come, until the present day: Vishveshvara, or Vishvanatha, the 'Lord of All'. The *Varanasimahatmya* of the Bhairavapradurbhava is the first in a compendium of mahatmyas of Varanasi, which survives in an old palm-leaf manuscript now in the Kaiser Library in Kathmandu. The manuscript may be dated on palaeographical grounds to the end of the twelfth century or the early thirteenth century at the latest. It was most probably penned in Varanasi itself, as suggested by a comparison of the old Nagari script with that of other manuscripts written in twelfth-century Varanasi but now likewise surviving in the collections of Nepal. It is an extensive but incomplete manuscript: 145 folios survive but the text breaks off in the middle of a long quotation from the *Skanda Purana* (Bisschop 2021, 4–5).

Alas, this period of grandeur and rapid growth of the prestige and flowering of the city of Kashi is today only a matter of remembered history. As Swami Medhasananda notes,

> [A]ll manifestations of its pomp and grandeur in the form of magnificent temples, mansions and statutes were demolished later by Muslim invaders. Had the Muslim invasions been less devastating, it would probably have been possible for at least some of these masterpieces of architecture and sculpture to withstand the ravages of time—as they have in South India. (Medhasananda 2002, 14)

Cultural Aspects of Kashi: The Land of Sants and Savants

How did the people of Kashi live? According to Swami Medhasananda, it appears from the study of contemporary sources—mainly histories of the city's old and venerable families as recorded or told by their descendants—that the prevalent structure was the institution of the joint family, which was patriarchal in nature, with the senior-most male member being its head. As Swami Medhasananda wryly notes, 'Relations among family members were quite cordial and unlike their counterparts in Calcutta, people with Western educations rarely challenged traditional values or indulged in confrontation with their families and society at large' (Medhasananda 2002, 129).

Over time, Kashi, being the city of Shiva, naturally developed as a unique centre for the practice and study of both Yoga and Tantra. The presence of spiritual giants like Trailanga Swami, who was both a yogi and Tantric, and Baba Kinaram, a Tantric, was highly conducive to the practice of both.

The quintessential snapshot of Kashi can be captured from the following passages of James Prinsep's diary from the nineteenth century:

> Indeed there are few objects more lively and exhilarating than the scene from the edge of the opposite sands, on a fine afternoon, under the clear sky of January. The music and bells of a hundred temples strike the ear with magic melody from the distance, amidst the buzz of human voices; and every now and then the flapping of the pigeons' wings is heard as they rise from their crates on the house tops, or whirl in close phalanx round the minarets, or alight with prisoners from a neighbour's flock. At the same time the eye rests on the vivid colours of the different groups of male and female bathers, with their sparkling brass water-vessels, or follows the bulls as they wander in the crowds in proud exercise of the rights of citizenship, munching the chaplets of flowers liberally presented to them.
>
> Then as night steals on, the scene changes, and the twinkling of lamps along the water's edge, and the funeral fires, and white curling smoke, and the stone buildings lit up by the moon, present features of variety and blended images of animation, which it is out

of the artist's power to embody. [...] Let it be borne in mind that upon the ghats are passed the busiest and happiest hours of every Hindoo's day: Bathing, dressing, praying, preaching, lounging, gossiping, or sleeping, there will he be found. (Medhasananda 2002, 330–331)

As Kashi had become the most important religious centre over the last two thousand years or so, most of the acharyas and religious leaders who founded new *sampradayas* or *paramparas* or attained the status of revered gurus came to Kashi at one time or another. For example, Guru Nanak came to Kashi and stayed near Kamachcha while his disciples built the Guru Bagh. Guru Gobind Singh also visited Kashi. Chaitanya Mahaprabhu stayed at Kashi for some time while on his way to Mathura from Puri. He met with Vallabhacharya, the founding acharya of the Pushti Marg, during his stay in the city. Sri Ramakrishna Paramahamsa also visited Kashi, where he encountered Trailanga Swami, whom he revered as his *paramaguru*—teacher's teacher. Swami Vivekananda also visited Kashi (Sukul 1974, 226).

Vallabhacharya's doctrine of Vishuddhadvaita was propagated while he lived at Varanasi; he accumulated many followers during that period. His commentaries on the Bhagavad Gita and Badarayana's *Brahma Sutras* were composed during his stay in Kashi (Sukul 1974, 150).

In this list, it is impossible to leave out Tulsidas Maharaj. He lived through the reigns of two Mughal kings: Akbar (r.1556–1605) and Jahangir (r.1605–1627) (Singh 2004, 114). He penned the *Ramcharitmanas* while in Kashi. Writing in the folk languages of Avadhi and Braj was controversial and many scholars in Kashi opposed him. However, the recommendation and support of the then greatest Sanskrit scholar of Kashi, Sri Madhusudana Sarasvati (1540–1623)—more will be described about him later—garnered acceptance for Tulsidas Maharaj (Singh 2004, 115).

According to one report, there were as many as 1,400 maths in Kashi by the 1770s (Medhasananda 2002, 213). As Kashi grew in prominence, Brahmanas from different parts of the country came and settled around the important Hindu temples. The priests of the Vishvanatha Mandir and also of the major temples of the Omkareshvara Khanda (in the northern part) were Sarayuparina Brahmanas. The priesthood of the southern segment, Kedara Khanda, was controlled by the Gauda Brahmanas from south India; however, the Bhadaini and Asi areas were mostly under the priesthood of Sarayuparina Brahmanas. South Indians were mostly concentrated in the Kedara Khanda, but many Tamils were clustered around the Vishalakshi Mandir and the Hanuman Ghat. Maharashtrians were settled in Duraghat, Chowkhambha and the Brahmanal area, and Gujaratis were concentrated in Hatakeshvara, Bhaironath, and near Kath-ki-Havel and Soot Tola (Singh 2008, 50).

It would take many books to cover the life stories of all of the important religious and spiritual personages who have graced the landscape of Kashi. For the sake of brevity, I will share just one story that somehow perfectly encapsulates the special power and magic of Kashi.

Swami Vishuddhanand Sarasvati was born near Unnao and served as a soldier in the army when he was posted to southern India. One evening, he visited a prostitute. She did not understand Hindi, and he did not understand Telugu. So, she started talking in Sanskrit, which he also did not know. The prostitute scolded him for being a Brahmana and not knowing Sanskrit, while she, a humble prostitute, was able to converse in it. Shaken, the young man quit the army and came to Kashi to learn Sanskrit.

When he approached a famous Sanskrit pandit to learn from him, the pandit laughed at him, dismissing him as being too old to try to learn Sanskrit now. The young man persevered. He crossed the street and sat on the platform of the public well there and listened to the classes. He did this every day for three years and in that time mastered not only Sanskrit grammar but also Vedanta.

One day, he challenged the best student of the pandit to a *shastrartha*—debate on the Shastras. The debate continued for hours. The pandit offered to take his student's place and engage in the shastrartha with him directly, but the young man fell at his feet and said he would never dare do that as it would be a sign of disrespect to the pandit whom he revered as his guru. The pandit was highly pleased and from then on taught him directly, regarding him as his best disciple.

In time, Swami Vishuddhanand Sarasvati became a master of masters; he took sannyasa and became a great yogi, too (Sukul 1974, 222–224).

Just as these great personalities enhanced the prestige and power of Kashi, Kashi also had a powerful and transformative impact on them. For example, Sri Ramakrishna described in his own words his experience at Manikarnika Ghat:

> I saw a tall white person with tawny matted hair walking with solemn steps to each pyre in the burning ghat, raising carefully every jiva (soul) and imparting into his ear the Mantra of Supreme Brahman. While sitting on the pyre, on the other side of the jiva, the all-powerful universal Mother, Mahakali, was untying all knots of bondage—gross, subtle, and causal—of these jivas produced by past impressions and sending them to the indivisible sphere by opening, with Her own hands, the door to liberation. Thus did Vishwanatha, the divine Lord of the Universe, endow the jiva in an instant with the infinite Bliss of experiencing Non-duality, which ordinarily results from the practice of Yoga and Tapas for many cycles. Thus did he fulfil the perfection of the jiva's life. (Saradananda in Medhasananda 2002, 228–229)

City of Gyaana

In addition to being the abode of Shiva and one of the Saptapuri that bestows mukti, the quality most associated with Kashi is as a city of knowledge and scriptural study. To learn about the shastras, to learn about metaphysics and philosophy, to learn about Dharma, one would go to Kashi and all of Bharat would greatly regard the pronouncements that came out of the panditas of Kashi.

The Samskaras

From time immemorial, Kashi has represented the city of knowledge and wisdom to all Hindus. In some parts of India, the initiation sacrament for twice-born boys, i.e., the *upanayana samskara*, includes a ritualistic journey to Kashi. After receiving the sacred thread and the initiation into the mantra that he will recite daily for the rest of his life, the boy takes seven steps in the direction of Kashi. This act of taking the seven steps allegorizes the journey towards *gyaana*, which itself is a term for liberation from the cycle of apparent birth and death, or moksha. This samskara instils in the young boy a reverence for Kashi and that which it symbolizes—wisdom and liberation (Eck 1982, 88).

This rite is echoed and repeated in Hindu marriage customs in certain parts of India. As part of the marriage ceremony, the bridegroom sets out on a pilgrimage to Kashi. Yet, as he passes the outskirts of the village and turns to the north, his future father-in-law awaits and persuades him to turn back with the proposal to give his daughter to him in wedlock. The bridegroom accepts this proposal and returns to the village. This custom, which was observed by a French traveller named J.A. Dubois at the time of his stay in India between 1792 and 1832, continues to this day in many places (Medhasananda 2002, 7).

Again, this ritual is full of philosophical import and can have a profound impact on the couple to be married if understood properly and undertaken with sincerity. The upanayana samskara occurs during the first ashrama when one enters *brahmacharya*; while the *vivaha samskara* occurs in the initiation into the second *grhasthashrama* stage of life. In this transition, this rite is reminding the groom and the bride that the ultimate aim of their lives, individually and as a couple, is to journey towards Kashi, which again represents wisdom and liberation. It is just that now they will travel this path as a couple and as a family but with a timely reminder to not become diverted from the ultimate goal.

Such is the exalted status Kashi enjoys in the Hindu mind even today.

Vedic Education

In his seminal book on Kashi, *Varanasi Down the Ages*, Sukul provides an important overview of the Vedic education system, linking it to the practice of teaching and scholarship that later grew in Kashi. As he describes it, the earliest sphere of Vedic culture was the Sapta-Saindhava region with its centre around Kurukshetra. It was here that the Vedic education system developed. Every *dvija* child had to learn the Vedas and the Vedangas. Accordingly, arrangements needed to be made for this teaching.

In the Vedic education system, every Brahmana had to teach the Vedas and Vedangas to students who approached him for this purpose. Thus, a Brahmana's home would often become a school. Some of the more prominent or learned Brahmanas would then form larger centres. They would live in forests or gardens, usually away from the cities, conducive to yogic practices and austerities.

As Sukul describes it, the disciples who lived with their guru at the home of the guru were considered to be members of the family. Accordingly, they shared in the duties of the household while also learning from their guru. According to Sukul, the society was well-knit and usually the standards of educational achievement were very high (Sukul 1974, 82).

There was definite specialization. Thus, for example, a Yajurvedin would know the basics of all the Vedas but would be focused on the *Yajur Veda*. Elaborate rules for learning how to recite a particular Veda had to be meticulously learned and practised.

This education was lifelong. A student would generally join his guru's ashrama by the time he was eight years old and would stay there for perhaps sixteen years or more, until he had fully mastered his subject area. During this time, it was incumbent upon the guru to provide for his physical needs. At the end of his discipleship, the student would make an offering of guru dakshina and return home. After reuniting with his family and relatives, he would be initiated into the life of a *grhastha* after marriage (Sukul 1974, 83).

When leaving the ashrama, the student would be given the following parting advice:

> Speak the truth. Practise virtue. Do not neglect the study of the Vedas. Having paid the honorarium to your preceptor (i.e., having returned home at the close of your studies) do not cut off the line of children (i.e., marry and bring up a family). Do not swerve from the truth. Do not swerve from virtue. Do not swerve from the good. Do not be indifferent to the attainment of greatness. Do not neglect your duties to the gods and to your parents. Honour your mother as a deity. Honour your father as a deity. Honour your guest as a deity. Do those deeds which are commendable, and not those that are otherwise. Imitate our good deeds and not those that are otherwise [...] Give alms with a willing heart. Do not give with an unwilling heart. Give wisely. Give with modesty. Give with fear. Give with a sympathetic heart. (Sukul 1974, 84)

Quoting the above, E.B. Havell remarked, 'The ethical standpoint of the Aryan race, as put forward in the Upanishads some three thousand years ago can hardly be surpassed in the present day' (Havell 1905, 11–12).

Even learned men and thinkers would visit these ashramas either to get their own doubts removed or with a desire to get some sort of a recognition for their learning and even of their spiritual prowess. Discussions and debates were often held not only in the ashramas but also sometimes in the courts of kings, who were themselves often scholarly as in almost all cases they had passed their boyhood and early youth in some gurukula or the other steeped in the same traditions of learning.

Writing about these discussions, Havell observes,

The greatest freedom of thought was allowed and the rules, which regulated the debates were only those which were approved of as likely to lead to sound conclusions. The rewards for debaters who showed profound thought and argument were not less liberal than those which were given to successful composers and sacrificers, but the penalties for those who infringed the rules of logic or spoke foolishly were heavy. (Sukul 1974, 85)

Sukul describes the workings of the ashrama at Naimisharanya. Citing the book *Ancient Indian Education* by Radha Kumud Mukerji, Sukul notes that it was a full-fledged ashrama with the following eight departments: (i) Agnisthan (department of worship and prayers) (ii) Brahmasthan (department of the Vedas) (iii) Vishnusthan (department for teaching rajaniti, arthaniti, and vartta) (iv) Mahendrasthana (military section) (v) Vivasvatsthana (department of astronomy) (vi) Somasthana (department of botany) (vii) Garudasthana (section dealing with transport and conveyances) and (viii) Kartikeyasthana (department teaching military organization, how to form patrols, battalions, and the army) (Sukul 1974, 86). There was also the ashrama of Rishi Kanva, situated on the Malini river. It was a large settlement surrounded by other hermitages. As Sukul pithily puts it,

In modern phraseology it was a University-colony in the midst of a forest, where the whole forest resounded with the chanting and recitation of the Vedas by the families of a large number of teachers and their pupils. There were specialists in all branches of learning in that colony: specialists in each of the four Vedas, in sacrificial literature and art, Kalpa Sutras, in the art of reciting the Samhitas according to the Pada and Kramapatha, and in orthoepy generally, and in Shiksha (Phonetics), Chhandas (Metrics), Sabda (Vyakarana), and Nirukta. There were also philosophers well-versed in Atma-Vijnana (Science of the Absolute), in Brahmopasana (worship of Brahma), in Mokshadharma, and in Lokayata (Vaisheshika). There were also logicians knowing the principles of Nyaya and of Dialectics. There were also specialists in physical sciences and arts, e.g., experts in the art of constructing sacrificial alters of various dimensions (solid geometry), dravya-gyana (chemistry and medicine), physical processes and their results, causes and their effects, and zoologists having special knowledge of monkeys and birds. (Sukul 1974, 87)

The ashramas of Vyaasa, Vasishtha, Vishvamitra, and several others near Kurukshetra and on the banks of Sarasvati were also famous for producing eminent rishis, who carried forth the torch of Vedic learning (Sukul 1974, 87).

As time advanced, the Vedic religion continued to grow and develop through the periods of the composition of the Sutras and the Itihaasa / Puranas. Eventually, three important centres of education were conceived at Takshila, Kashi, and Mithila. The Upanishads describe Mithila under the reign of the famous king Janaka, and make references to King Ajatashatru, who reigned in Kashi. Gradually, Mithila fell from prominence and learned scholars thronged at Takshila and Kashi in greater numbers.

During the Buddhist period, Vedic education continued to prosper. Even in Buddhist sources, Kashi finds respectful acknowledgement along with Sarnath. For example, the *Koshiya* and *Titter Jatakas* clearly mention that the teachers at Varanasi taught the three Vedas and eighteen crafts (Sukul 1974, 88).

Educational Institutions

By the time of the Mahabharata war, Kashi had already become renowned as a centre for learning due to the reign of Ajatashatru, its great philosopher king, and even later it was considered as a great centre of philosophical disciplines. Sukul demonstrates that the system of education then practised in Kashi was the same as the Vedic system described in the previous section. Seals of Charanas and Chhandas, educational institutions of the earliest Vedic type, have been found during the Rajghat excavations at Varanasi dating right up until the Gupta period in AD 500 (Sukul 1974, 90).

Furthermore, schools of medicine, law, and military science were established in Kashi. According to the Buddhist Jatakas, Kashi as a city was so renowned for education and scholarship that it had garnered the title of Brahma-Vardhana. Moreover, Kashi was described as one of the six most important educational centres in India. It is said that there was free exchange of teachers and pupils between Varanasi and Takshila; teachers from Varanasi were often graduates from Takshila. There is also an anecdote of a king of Kashi who, at his own expense, sent a Brahmana boy to Takshila to be schooled in archery (Sukul 1974, 25, 88–89).

Sukul observes that, despite the proliferation of these institutions, teaching was still transmitted individually and perhaps there were no formal schools where large numbers of students studied. Even in the Gupta period, when Nalanda and Vikramashila had come up as organized centres of education, Kashi did not establish such an institution. It was perhaps satisfied with the individual teachers carrying on their sacred duty of teaching by themselves.

As Sukul puts it, 'There was to be no mass production of Pandits so far as Kashi was concerned; they were to stand on the sounder principle of personal contact and individual attention' (Sukul 1974, 91).

The Educational System in Kashi

By the time of the eleventh and twelfth centuries AD, Sanskrit education had split into two approaches. On the one hand there were the traditional Vedic *pathashalas*, which specialized in the transmission of the shastras and where students received expert and specialist instruction in the Vedas, *sahitya* (literature), grammar, different systems of philosophy like Nyaya, Mimamsa, Sankhya, Yoga, Vedanta, and Vaisheshika, astronomy and astrology, and Ayurveda.

These institutions were often connected with famous temples and monasteries. They were the lifeblood of Sanskrit education, and they produced renowned experts over the ages. One example is that of Bhatta Lakshmidhara, the chief minister of Maharaja Govindachandra of Varanasi and Kannauj and the author of *Krityakalpataru*, an encyclopaedic book running into several thousand pages. Not only was he a great scholar but he was also a reputed soldier and a talented administrator (Sukul 1974, 92).

The other variety of pathashala was that which gave the pupils an elementary knowledge of Sanskrit for daily use (Sukul 1974, 92–93). Describing the system of Sanskrit education at Varanasi in AD 1660, Bernier writes,

> Varanasi actually is a sort of University but unlike the European Universities there are no colleges and no organized classes. Teachers are spread all over the city and teaching goes on at their residences. Some teachers have four, others six pupils, the most famous teacher may have twelve to fourteen students but never more. These pupils first learnt Sanskrit with the help of grammar. Puranas came next and ultimately they specialised in philosophy, medicine, astronomy, etc. (Sukul 1974, 98)

The Shenbai Matha, a leading Vedic pathashala of the time, was an example of how the Vedic education system operated. The students were required to reach the school by six in the morning after partaking of a light meal of rice, ghee, and salt. If a child came without this morning meal, the teacher arranged for it in his own house. No one was allowed to sit for class on an empty stomach. The teacher would proceed with instruction until eleven in the morning. The school was again to meet at two in the afternoon to continue until six. There were no holidays; the days off were devoted to reviewing old lessons (Sukul 1974, 101).

The pandits and gurus who taught in this way depended on the patronage of others to be able to teach and provide for their students. The Gahadavala rulers often granted villages to such pandits. The royalty of Bharat in general employed learned pandits in their courts and also bestowed land and housing upon them in Kashi. They also established *chaatras* where students could avail of free food. It was by using these resources that pandits and gurus were able to support their disciples and their families (Sukul 1974, 93, 99).

Within this tradition of great scholarship, Kashi produced several renowned scholars in the area of medicine. It is said that Dhanvantari was born as Kashiraja and taught Sushruta in the city of Kashi itself. Sushruta specialized not only in *rasa-prakriya*, which is the use of metals and their salts as medicines, but also in surgery; plastic surgery of today is said to be born directly from his writings as acknowledged by Western surgeons (Sukul 1974, 93–94).

The Role of the Kashi Pandits

The pandits of Varanasi have traditionally been the upholders of Sanskrit learning and also served an important role in the social, religious, and cultural life of the country. They facilitated the study of the shastras by opening private seminaries, popularly known as *pathashalas, chatushpathis,* or *tols,* maintaining students, writing works, copying manuscripts, and holding and participating in shastrarthas. They would also issue *vyavasthas,* or verdicts, on socio-religious issues, give popular talks on the scriptures and conduct rituals. Unlike the unfortunate situation today, traditional pandits were highly respected and it was a societal obligation, particularly on the part of the affluent, to maintain the pandits so they could freely devote themselves to scholarship and the spread of knowledge.

Swami Medhasananda describes a book by Pandit Baladeo Upadhyaya, *Panditya Parampara,* which he had written after many years of research on the history of Kashi pandits and their works. That research found that in Kashi, local pandits had certain common characteristics, including deep religious faith in Vishvanatha, Annapurna, and the Ganga, imparting free education, efficiency in disputation, dedication to the study of the scriptures, perfection in pronunciation, and above all, leading a life of plain living and high thinking, Swami Medhasananda notes that Mahamahopadhyay Pandit Gopinath Kaviraj also wrote a short monograph on the same subject under the title *Kashi ki Saraswat Sadhana*. (Medhasananda 2002, 482–483).

As Swami Medhasananda describes, pandits were generally expert in a particular branch of Sanskrit or the Vedas and would teach only that one; yet there was no shortage of pandits proficient in the various branches of Sanskrit. In addition to local students, students from different parts of the country would flock to Varanasi to study Sanskrit. They would find hostels and other guesthouses to stay at and receive a plentiful supply of food from various almshouses. Although vocations for pandits were not always easy to secure, they always enjoyed a certain prestige throughout Bharat for having studied in Varanasi (Medhasananda 2002, 484).

By the time of the sixteenth century, widespread scholarship was produced on religious and philosophical discourse. Digests on various matters of dharma were compiled. Manuals on everything from temple rites to cremation rites appeared.

This activity was stimulated in no small part by six families of pandits from Maharashtra—Brahmanas who after their migration to Banaras, became the most prominent intellectual leaders of the city. One of them, Narayana Bhatta, earned the title of Jagadguru and composed texts, including *Prayaga-ratna* and *Tristhali setu*. He was also responsible in AD 1585 for the resurrection by Todar Mal of Vishveshvara Temple, which had lain in ruins since AD 1496 when it was demolished by Sikandar Lodi (Sukul 1974, 97). The Kashi Khanda gained popularity and importance in this period, in part because it evoked the vivid memory of Kashi in its time of glory. Other great mahatmyas were also written, such as the *Kashi Rahasya* and the *Kashi Kedara*. During the Mughal period, the poet Jagannatha composed *Ganga Lahari*.

During the heyday of Kashi's greatness as a centre of scholarship, the city was graced with the presence of great masters of philosophy, especially of the schools of Nyaya and Advaita, as well as Sanskrit grammar. The great scholar Bhattoji Dikshit penned the *Siddhanta Kaumudi* in Kashi, whereby he rearranged Panini's Sanskrit grammar, a text that even today is considered to be the last word in modern Sanskrit grammar.

The Impact of Muslim Rule

While the rule of the Muslims resulted in the wholesale destruction of the physical edifice of the Kashi landscape, it was tougher to destroy the intangible networks of scholarship, religious life, and philosophical discourse that underpinned Kashi society. As Eck notes, the traditions of learning for which the city was famous could not easily be broken, for they were independent of the rise and fall of temples. During the latter part of this period, the French scholar and medical doctor, Francois Bernier, visited Kashi, which he called the Athens of India. Bernier observed in a letter:

> The town contains no colleges or regular classes, as in our universities, but resembles rather the schools of the ancients; the masters being dispersed over different parts of the town in private houses, and principally in the gardens of the suburbs, which the rich merchants permit them to occupy. Some of these masters have four disciples, others six or seven, and the most eminent may have twelve or fifteen; but this is the largest number. It is usual for the pupils to remain ten or twelve years under their respective preceptors. (Eck 1982, 131–132)

The lack of centralization and formal organization is exactly what kept the traditions of learning and teaching intact in Kashi for all these years. Sukul remarks that, after AD 1194, when Varanasi was conquered by Qutubuddin Aibak, Sanskrit education was undoubtedly dealt a blow but still it survived:

> The Vedas were perhaps recited in the seclusion of rooms in a lower voice. The narrow winding lanes of the old town helped because the Muslims were not always going into the interior. [...] We find that in the reign of Mohammad Tughlaq (AD 1325–1351) Varanasi was once again flourishing as a centre of Sanskrit learning. According to Jina Prabha Suri, a Jain savant,

who had received respectful attention in the court of that sovereign, there were quite a number of speicalists [sic] not only in Shabdanushasana (grammar and linguistics, dramatics, and figures of speech), astronomy and astrology, Churamani, Nimitta Shastra and literature, but also experts in Dhaturvada (metallurgy), Rasavada (chemistry including medicine), Khanyavad (geology and mining), and Yantravidya (mechanics). We may remember here that soon after this period in the reign of Firoz Tughlak (1351–1388) considerable anti-Hindu activities continued in Varanasi. Not only Jazia was imposed on the Brahmanas for the first time but also quite a number of mosques were constructed in place of Hindu temples, and the tone of Vedic Education must have been, therefore, rather subdued. It is on record that during the fourteenth and fifteenth centuries quite an exodus of learned Pandits took place towards south India. It is, however, averred that Kullabha Bhatta wrote his commentary on the Manusmriti at Varanasi during this period. (Sukul 1974, 94–95)

Development of the medical sciences continued even after AD 1194 but surgery suffered a huge decline and was practically given up. In later centuries, however, an influx of scholars from Maharashtra and Karnataka would revive scholarship in all branches of learning, including medicine (Sukul 1974, 95).

Soon after Sikander Lodi came to power, another wave of iconoclastic violence attacked Kashi. As Sukul says, we do not know what the actual condition of education in Varanasi was back then, but we can imagine its grim fate. Practically all of the temples in Kashi were destroyed once more and along with them the associated educational institutions. Individual teachers were thus the only source of education left, and they, too, faced persecution and hardship (Sukul 1974, 95–96). That Sanskrit learning was in doldrums for three centuries and more since AD 1194 is proved by the fact that practically no books of learning were written during this period (Sukul 1974, 97).

Writing in the eleventh century AD, Firdosi observed that learned men had already left the places of Muslim influence and had fled to

Kashmir or Varanasi (cited in Sukul 1974, 97). In the meantime, as Muslim power reached the southern parts of India, the exodus of scholars from Kashi to the south also dried up. In fact, soon a reverse migration started with pandits from Maharashtra and Karnataka now moving to the north, eventually arriving at Kashi to resurrect Sanskrit education. Dharmadhikaris, Sesas, Bhattas, and Maunis were the chief among these, and as Dr Altekar noted, 'Members of these families and their disciples dominated Benares scholarship for more than three centuries' (quoted in Sukul 1974, 97).

The hard times were not over, though. In the earlier years of his reign, Akbar took a hard line against Kashi, and in AD 1567, when he conquered the city for the second time, he ordered it to be plundered (Sukul 1974, 96). It was only after AD 1584 when the fort at Allahabad had been completed and the headquarters of the Suba had been transferred there that Kashi escaped the scrutiny and notice of the Mughals, and in this twilight of political neglect, a reconstruction of intellectual Varanasi took place (Sukul 1974, 96).

As Dr Altekar remarked in *History of Benares*, '[The] [c]ontribution of Benares to Sanskrit scholarship and literature during the period AD 1500–1800 is undoubtedly much greater than that of any other three contemporary centres of Sanskrit learning put together' (quoted in Sukul 1974, 98).

Buddhism and Other Dharmic Traditions

In the long course of its history, Kashi has been a place of significance not just for Hindus but also other Dharmic traditions.

Development of the Buddhist Tradition in Sarnath

As the historian Moti Chandra once wrote, 'Varanasi at this time was so celebrated that it was only suitable for the Buddha to teach a new way and turn the wheel of the law there' (quoted in Eck 1982, 90). In other words, it is a testament to Kashi's prominence that Shakyamuni Buddha chose to turn the wheel of dharma and deliver his first sermon there.

Over time, a township developed in Sarnath inhabited by Buddhist monks and others, and populated with a large number of ashramas, viharas, and temples. The queen of Maharaja Govindachandra also built a vihara there in the twelfth century. Sarnath soon became a centre of the Mahayana sect of Buddhism.

For 1,500 years, Sarnath continued to be an active monastic centre of Buddhism. In the fourth century BC, the Buddhist Emperor Ashoka had a great stupa constructed there. In the Gupta period of the fourth to sixth centuries AD, Sarnath became one of the great centres of Buddhist art, producing exquisite sandstone images of the Buddha. When Hiuen-Tsang visited Varanasi in the seventh century, he reported that there were some thirty monasteries and three thousand monks.

Towards the end of the twelfth century, Sarnath was a stronghold of the Vajrayana School of Buddhism, when the sword of Islam fell on it and the township was sacked and burned (Sukul 1974, 13).

Decline of Buddhism

Buddhism travelled to Ceylon, China, Tibet, and Japan, but as soon as it lost royal patronage in Bharat with the rise of the Shungas as emperors, it went into a decline in the subcontinent. The Shungas were themselves tolerant and did not do anything to actively suppress Buddhism, but over time, the number of the followers of Buddha's religion started diminishing. Buddhism revived briefly under Kushan rule, but subsequently, even though the Gupta emperors and Harshavardhan were sympathetic towards it, Buddhism languished in the land of its birth while flourishing in countries where it had been exported (Sukul 1974, 141).

Of course, a strong contributing factor to the decline of Buddhism was the fierce debate between Vedic scholars and the Buddhists that took place in Bharat. The churning of this debate between the two sides continued for over a thousand years until the eighth century AD when the advocacy of Adi Shankaracharya and

Kumarila Bhatta revived the supremacy of Vedic thought across the land.

However, Buddhist institutions and monasteries continued to exist, and Buddhists were left in peace as is evident from the accounts given by Fa-Hian, Hiuen-Tsang and I-tsing from the fifth to seventh centuries AD (Sukul 1974, 142-143). It must be emphasized in this context that the religious conflict that carried on for a millennium was, for the most part, entirely intellectual. There was no place for any kind of physical force or compulsion on any significant basis.

Writing about these disputations, Havell says,

> [T]he methods of the Inquisition, and the argument of the sword and stake never became popular with Hindu religious teachers. Whatever may be urged against the Hindu system, it must be admitted that it has always stood for absolute liberty of conscience. One religious movement after another has swept over Indian soil, but until the Mohammadan conquest it was never considered justifiable, and necessary to suppress the voice of the preacher and the arguments of the philosopher with torture, bloodshed, or judicial murder. (Sukul 1974, 143)

While Varanasi grew increasingly famous as a Hindu place of pilgrimage, it continued to have a significant Buddhist monastic presence until the twelfth century AD, when Qutb-ud-din Aibak's armies demolished Sarnath as well as Varanasi's great Hindu temples. While the Hindus recovered from the blow, the Buddhist tradition, dependent entirely upon its monks, monasteries, and centres of learning, was virtually eradicated.

Jainism

In addition to the Buddha and his followers, Kashi also attracted seekers of Jainism. According to the Jain tradition, the seventh *jina*, Suparshvanatha, was born in Kashi and his mother was the earth herself. The twenty-third jina, Parshvanatha, is the first to be dated historically. He lived in the eighth century BC and was also said to have been born in Kashi. Parshvanatha was followed in the sixth century by the jina Mahavira, a younger contemporary of the Buddha, who also visited Kashi during his forty-two years of itinerant teaching (Eck 1982, 90–91).

Jainism appeared on the scene as a reform movement. Parshvanatha, the son of Kashiraja Ashvasena, focused on Kashi as the main stage of his religious reform efforts. At the time of Mahavira, Kashi had grown in prominence such that it could not be ignored and he, too, focused his efforts on Kashi. While some people, particularly among the Vaishyas of Kashi, adopted Jainism, the majority did not (Sukul 1974, 138).

From the time of Parshvanatha to the present, Jains have continued to have a presence in Varanasi and to count it among their own sacred tirthas (Eck 1982, 92).

Trade and Commerce

Another, more practical, factor that contributed to Kashi's greatness has been its key geographic location for travel both by road and river. Throughout history, Kashi has served as a central market for articles from all over India, and horses from Sindh and elephants from Himalayan forests were available here at regular well-organized fairs. There is evidence to show there were well-organized guilds, known as *shrenis* or *senis*, for the development of handicrafts (Sukul 1974, 29).

Many merchants would have stopped by Kashi on their eastward journeys across India. Roads also directly connected Kashi with all of the other important centres of the time. Kashi enjoyed the same privileged status when it came to river transport, too.

Moreover, the merchants of Kashi also traded overseas. As noted by Sukul, they carried their merchandise from Kashi to Suvarna Bhumi (south Burma) by boat via Tamralipti (Sankha Jataka). Some of these voyages lasted up to six months at a time. According to Sukul, Balahassa Jataka mentions a group of five hundred Kashi merchants going to Ceylon by river and sea and Milind-panho mentions merchants voyaging to China in connection with business transactions. Journeys to Malaysia, Indonesia, and Indochina were also not uncommon (Sukul 1974, 31).

Commerce within India encompassed agricultural products and animals, including horses from Kamboja, elephants from northern Bihar, pedigreed dogs from Kekaya, and peacocks and other birds from different places. Cows and bullocks were bought and sold in large numbers. International commerce, however, dealt chiefly with textiles, particularly fine silk, and the trademark cotton and semi-woollen cloth of Kashi, shawls from Shivi and blankets from Gandhara, and swords and daggers of Dasarna. Sandalwood preparations for the body and articles of ivory were also exported from Varanasi, as were golden ornaments and jewels. Silk cloth embellished with gold and studded with gems, head-dresses for kings made of *kanchana patta*, silk interwoven with gold thread and embedded with gems, were also supplied by Varanasi (Sukul 1974, 33–34).

Centuries after Mughal invasion and rule, the arts declined but commerce of Kashi continued to flourish, and it was considered a rich city all through the Middle Ages and even afterwards. Sukul provides a few examples of fine artwork to illustrate the depth of Kashi's artistic expertise and tradition. He recounts the beautiful figure of Skanda discovered near the Mahatha Ghat, which was perhaps worshipped in the Skandeshvara Temple of Pishangila Tirtha, from where it was removed during the iconoclastic attacks on Kashi in AD 1194. Then there is what Sukul describes as the superb figure of Govardhandhari Krishna, retrieved from inside the Bakaria Kund Lake, where it had been thrown after mutilation perhaps in the same year. Sukul surmises that it must have been installed there in one of the important temples of that locality, many of which had been appropriated into mosques or mausoleums (Sukul 1974, 53).

Sukul observes that while some artistic works of the tenth century also exhibit beauty, a decline soon followed in the artistic traditions of Kashi:

As a result of the conquest of Varanasi by Kutubuddin Aibak artistic life of this great city suffered a serious setback and images constructed during the thirteenth and fourteenth centuries show a further decline. […] The form is there but the soul is lost. […] This was true not only of Varanasi but of art as such all over northern India. It seems as if the creative originality and spiritual outlook perished with the country's independence. (Sukul 1974, 54)

CHAPTER 19

Destruction and Devastation: Mughal Invasion and Desecration

General Themes and Trends

When discussing the wholesale destruction wrought by the Mughals on Kashi in particular and Bharat in general, it is easy to miss the forest for the trees in listing this and that temple. It is worth stepping back to see the big picture. Eck eloquently captures the tragic loss and trauma resulting from the waves of successive invasion and iconoclastic fervour to destroy and desecrate the native sacred sites and temples:

> There is no major religious sanctuary in all Banaras that pre-dates the time of Aurangzeb in the seventeenth century. The sacred geography of the city changed considerably in these centuries. The city of the Puranic mahatmyas was no more. Its greatest temples—Krittivasa, Omkara, Mahadeva, Madhyameshvara, Vishveshvara, Bindu Madhava, and Kala Bhairava—were in ruins. Some never recovered, like the Shiva temple of Krittivasa, the site of which is today occupied by a run-down mosque. Others went into hiding, like the guardian deity Kala Bhairava, who was housed in humble quarters for hundreds of years and did not appear in a fitting temple until the eighteenth century. Likewise, the Vishnu image of Bindu Madhava, whose site was usurped by a huge mosque, was moved to a nearby house. And some temples were continually resurgent, like Vishveshvara, Kashi's supreme sanctum of Shiva,

which was destroyed and rebuilt at least three times during these centuries. The memory of Kashi as the brilliant capital of Lord Shiva, set amidst the Forest of Bliss, faded into a time almost as distant as the time before the Ganges fell from heaven to earth. (Eck 1982, 131)

The scholar Andre Wink offers his own interpretation of the motivations behind the actions of the Muslim rulers:

> From the eleventh to the thirteenth century, temples were destroyed, to be sure. [...] In some cases, images of the gods were broken or smashed. Some were hauled away to be used as doorsteps in mosques and 'trodden underfoot by believers'. [...] Comprehensive destruction, clearly, was not always the aim. It was essential to render the images powerless, to remove them from their consecrated contexts. Selective dilapidation could be sufficient to that purpose. (Wink in Eck 2012, 136)

In other words, to extract the maximum humiliation from the subjugated Hindus, the Islamic invaders deliberately left remnants of temples and other sacred sites so that the wounds of the populace would fester. Nor was the damage limited to the number of temples destroyed. As Wink observes,

> If the temples were not destroyed, patronage dried up, and few great temples were built in North India after the thirteenth century. Even without conversion, India's sacred geography was uprooted by the Islamic conquest, and the newly evolving Indo-Islamic policy transcended it in the name of the new universal religion. (Wink in Eck 2012, 136)

In the face of these attacks, Hindus did not back down; they instead resisted bravely. They preserved and protected their traditions of temple worship and pilgrimage. As Eck notes,

> The imposition of a tax upon Hindu pilgrims became a persistent issue in the centuries that followed, but we know, of course, that Hindu pilgrimage did not cease. The sense of sacred geography

could not really be uprooted. After all, the tirthas were only secondarily temples that could be destroyed. (Eck 2012, 137)

In other words, even if the temples had been destroyed, the underlying land and the site on which the temple had been built were themselves inherently sacred, sanctified by the religious history and spiritual past of the place.

During the dark period of these Middle Ages, which stretched for hundreds of years, there were waves of iconoclastic attacks followed by brief periods of seeming respite and rebuilding, followed again by an even fiercer attack, over and over again. That in the midst of this Hindu society somehow maintained its morale and was able to hold onto its traditions and rebuild again and again, adapting their practices to accommodate the stark new reality Hindus now lived in—hiding deities, housing them in new temples or underground in their own homes, at risk to their own lives—is a testament to the strength and depth of the shraddha, reverence, nishtha, and conviction of our ancestors.

Centuries-long Attack against the Sacred Geography of Kashi

During the eleventh and twelfth centuries AD, the entire region surrounding Kashi began suffering from Mughal invasions and internal conflicts within kingdoms and territories. The area became so troubled that scholars and craftsmen left the area and settled in far-off lands like Kashmir (which were not to remain safe for much longer, sadly). This shattered the cultural prosperity of the region of Kashi.

Nialtagin was the first to overrun Kashi in AD 1034, but he came only for plunder and stayed for just a few hours. Mahmud of Ghazni, however, had already attacked several places in western India, where in addition to plunder, his main purpose was the destruction of Hindu temples and the establishment of Islam. He had proudly declared at Somnath that he was an idol-breaker, not an idol-seller. In the course of these attacks, there was the set pattern of general massacre of the Hindus—the only way to escape was to accept Islam and convert. This was an altogether new situation for India, as until then force had never been used in religious matters to a significant degree.

Mahmud's last invasion took place in AD 1024. In 1034 or 1035, his nephew, Syed Salar Masaud, started from Ghazni with an army and a body of his followers and proceeded towards Gonda and Bahraich in Uttar Pradesh via Ajmer, Multan, Delhi, Meerut, Garhmukteswara, Deoband, and Kannauj. Before reaching Bahraich, he was opposed by Raja Suhridhwaja, or Sohal Deva, and killed. The main purpose of this attack was religious conversion rather than conquest. While on his way to Bahraich, he dispatched a portion of his retinue and army under one of his commanders Malik Afzal Alavi towards Kashi.

The army of Alavi succeeded in reaching as far as the outskirts of the town, almost up to the boundary wall of the city. There was then a great fight in which the entire invading army was annihilated. The soldiers of the Muslim army had been killed, but consistent with the Hindu code of warfare, the civilians, including women and children, were not harassed but were permitted to settle down in the forest area towards the north of the town (Sukul 1974, 4). Later on, when another Muslim army under Qutubuddin Aibak conquered the city and Muslim rule was established, the locality where these Muslim citizens had been permitted to live was named Alvi-pura after Alvi, their erstwhile leader (Sukul 1974, 152–154). Those Muslims became loyal subjects of the Hindu rulers of Kashi. In the late eleventh and early twelfth centuries, they established two settlements in other parts of the city and named them Madanpura and Govindpura after Maharaja Madanpal and Maharaja Govind Chandra Deva, respectively (Sukul 1974, 4).

Jayachandra, the grandson of Govindachandra Gahadavala, was a rival of the Chahamana king Prithviraja. Both of them wanted to establish their hegemony over the whole of north

India; both wasted their efforts in this rivalry and the loss was their own and that of Bharat. Taking advantage of their internal conflict, Qutbuddin Aibak, a slave-general of Muhammad Ghori, after vanquishing Prithviraj, defeated Jayachandra in 1193–94 and beheaded him. His army sacked and looted the city of Kashi, destroying nearly one thousand temples in the city alone and raising mosques on their foundation using the debris of the temples.

Mosques like Dhai Kangure, Chaubisa Khambha, Bhadaon, and Ganje Shahida are representative of this period; they were built with the debris of the Hindu temples demolished in the recent past, mostly at the same sites. In addition to the massacre and conversions that had become par for the course, a thousand temples were demolished, the town was plundered, and 1,400 camel-loads of gold, silver, and jewels were delivered to Ghori at Delhi, as acknowledged by Muslim historians (Sukul 1974, 5; Singh 2002, 26–27). Subsequently, Ghori left India after placing Qutubuddin Aibak on the throne of Delhi as the first Muslim king of India, but Kashi once again shook off the Muslim yoke and had to be reconquered in AD 1197. Afterward, a Muslim governor was appointed who ruled over the city ruthlessly and tried his best to remove 'idolatry' from there.

Aibak issued an order for the destruction of temples. This was the period when the major Shiva temples in Kashi, like Vishvanatha, Krttivasheshvara, Avimuktheshvara, Kaala Bhairava, Adi Mahadeva, Siddheshvara, Kumbhishvara, Hiranyaksheshvara, Yajnavalkeshvara, Baneshvara, Balishvara, Kapaleshvara, Kapileshvara, and others, were demolished.

Sixteen years after the first wave of destruction wrought by Aibak, a revolt took place in the city which slowed down the speed of destroying the temples. It is said that in this period the temple of Vishveshvara was rebuilt. In the period of Allaudin Khilji (r.1292–1316), the process of destruction of Hindu temples continued (Singh 2008, 86–87)

This was a most difficult time for Hindus and Hinduism. All the temples of Kashi lay in ruins and remained so for many years. A large number of Hindus were converted to Islam on pain of death. Eventually, the situation apparently relaxed, and by AD 1297, temples were reconstructed. Alauddin Khilji was now on the throne of Delhi, and in the beginning of his reign he did not interfere with Kashi. According to Sukul, this is evidenced by the fact that two grand temples were built in AD 1302—Padmeshvara near the gate of Vishveshvara Temple and Manikarnikeshvara at the Manikarnika Ghat. Vincent Smith suggests that the Kashi temples earned Khilji's wrath later on, but it is not known when exactly this happened (cited in Sukul 1974, 154–155).

However, the process of coercive conversion continued unabated throughout these hundreds of years. After Khilji's death in AD 1316, temples were once again reconstructed but many of them had to be built at different locations.

According to Sukul, there is no clear evidence of the iconoclastic zeal of the Tughlaqs at Kashi, but in AD 1376, Firoz Shah started the construction of the Atala Mosque in Jaunpur after demolishing the temple of Atala Devi there. If a temple in Jaunpur was demolished, it is only reasonable to conclude, surmises Sukul, that those at Kashi were similarly targeted. Shah's representative at Kashi was vigorously constructing quite a large number of mosques at the sites of and with the material obtained from demolished Hindu temples. Obviously, these temples had first been destroyed. This marked the third general destruction of temples in Kashi (Sukul 1974, 155). Moreover, the Shirqi sultans imposed heavy taxes on Hindu pilgrims visiting Kashi.

In 1393, the Shirqi dynasty was established in Jaunpur. Not only did the Shirqis complete the Atala Mosque started by Firoz Tughlaq, but they also built several others—all with stones stolen from demolished temples. These appropriated stones came from temples constructed during periods ranging from the fifth to the fourteenth centuries AD, as evidenced by the Padmeshvara inscription in the Lal-Durwaza Mosque and on the basis of several stone pillars of the Gupta period that were then used as stools in the mosque gardens (Sukul 1974, 156). The presence of the Padmeshvara stone in Jaunpur proves that the stones of Varanasi temples already demolished by Firoz Tughlaq were carried to Jaunpur for the construction of these mosques.

With the end of the Shirqui rule in Jaunpur, Kashi had a brief respite, and its temples were built again but not to their full glory. Sukul describes the plight of the Hindus eloquently:

> The Hindus of Varanasi had by now realised that it was useless to build beautiful temples, for who knew when another iconoclastic storm would burst; and they were right, for in AD 1496 the first thing that Sikandar Lodi did on ascending the throne was to order a wholesale demolition of all Hindu temples at Varanasi. The Hindus of Varanasi now gave up the attempt of rebuilding their shrines and they remained in ruins for eighty-nine years. There was no Vishveshvara temple or that of any other deity at Varanasi during this period and the people had to be content with paying their homage to the ruins. (Sukul 1974, 156)

During the sultanate period from *c.*1200 until the reign of Akbar (r.1556–1605), the history of the city cannot be easily reconstructed per Sukul. The fact that few temples of this or earlier periods have survived is significant. Not until Akbar ascended the throne did Hindu patrons again begin to build religious edifices. Man Singh and Raja Todar Mal, the two senior Rajput ministers in the court of Akbar, participated actively in repairing the temples and ghats of Kashi. During the reign of Shajahan, however, an order was issued that new temples under construction at Kashi should be pulled down without delay. The subedar of Allahabad reported to the court about the destruction of seventy-six temples in Kashi in 1632 (Elliot 2013, 36).

In his book *Kashi ka Itihas*, Moti Chandra succinctly summarizes the situation during the period of these intervening centuries:

> In short, although the history of Banaras during these centuries was not an unmitigated tale of woe, the scenes of destruction were repeated and frequent enough in the drama of those years that the city must have seemed constantly to be regaining its footing only to stagger again. (Moti Chandra in Eck 1982, 130)

Sukul movingly laments about the short-lived existence of the Vishveshvara and Bindu Madhava Temples constructed in 1585:

> Who knew at that time that these beautiful temples were not destined to last even a hundred years! In AD 1658 Aurangzeb ascended the throne and in AD 1659 he ordered the demolition of the famous temple of Krittivaseshvara [...] in the heart of the city and the construction of a mosque at its site. This was a solitary case of iconoclasm in the first ten years of that Emperor's rule, but in AD 1669 orders came forth to the king's officers at Varanasi to demolish the temple of Vishveshvara and that of Bindu Madhava—and of course all other important ones—and to build mosques on the sites thereof. (Sukul 1974, 157)

Thus, three mosques were erected: (i) the present Gyanvapi Mosque on the earlier site of the Vishveshvara Temple (ii) the present Alamgir Mosque at Panchaganga Ghat in place of the Bindu Madhava Temple and (iii) the mosque at Daranagar in place of the Krittivaseshvara Temple (Sukul 1974, 157).

A Note on Aurangzeb

Before turning to Aurangzeb's blaze of destruction across Kashi, it is useful to step back and consider Aurangzeb's rule overall and how he treated Hindus and Hindu holy sites throughout his reign. Sir Jadunath Sarkar provides the perfect introduction to this tyrannical ruler who created terror and destruction in his wake:

> Aurangzib began his attack on Hinduism in an insidious way. In the first year of his reign, in a charter granted to a priest of Benares, he avowed that his religion forbade him to allow the building of new temples, but did not enjoin the destruction of old ones. During his

viceroyalty of Gujrat, 1644, he had desecrated the recently built Hindu temple of Chintaman in Ahmadabad by killing a cow in it and then turned the building into a mosque. He had at that time also demolished many other Hindu temples in the province. An order was issued early in his reign in which the local officers in every town and village of Orissa from Katak to Medinipur were called upon to pull down all temples, including even clay huts, built during the last 10 or 12 years, and to allow no old temple to be repaired.

Next, on 9 April 1669, he issued a general order 'to demolish all the schools and temples of the infidels and to put down their religious teaching and practices.' His destroying hand now fell on the great shrines that commanded the veneration of the Hindus all over India, such as the second temple of Somnath, the Vishwanath temple of Benares, and the Keshav Rai temple of Mathura. (Sarkar 2019, 155–156)

There is no major religious sanctuary in the city of Banaras that predates the time of Aurangzeb in the seventeenth century. The only temple complex that was saved from destruction is at Kandwa (i.e., Kardameshvara), because of its location in the countryside making it nearly inaccessible during that period. The city of Puranic glory and beauty as it was known in the twelfth century had completely disappeared by the end of the seventeenth century.

The situation had worsened materially for Hindus by AD 1700. After murdering his two elder brothers, Dara Shikoh and Murad Bakhshi, and younger brother Shah Shuja, and imprisoning his father Shahjahan, Aurangzeb ascended the throne. He was even more fundamentalist than other preceding Mughal emperors in his disdain for the temples and shrines of the Hindus (Singh 2008, 94–95).

Aurangzeb's reign—and to a lesser extent the reign of his predecessor Shah Jahan—witnessed an upsurge in Sharia legalism, renewed efforts at conversion, the demolition of key temples and the desecration of their deities, differential customs duties based on religio-ethnic identity, a renewed pilgrim tax, and the reimposition of the jizya, the poll tax on non-Muslims, abolished by Akbar a century earlier.

The violence against and persecution of Hindus by Aurangzeb was strategically targeted. Leaving aside temples destroyed in the process of military conquest, the particular targets of Aurangzeb's wrath were large, such as public structures recently built or embellished by members of the nobility. Some examples include the Vishvanatha and Bindu Madhava Temples in Kashi, the Somnath Temple in Gujarat, and the Keshav Rai Temple in Mathura. These structures were seen as challenges to Aurangzeb's revivalist Islam. In 1659, he issued the following order, probably in the context of disputes over the ancient temples of Kashi: 'It has been decided according to our canon law that long-standing temples should not be demolished but no new temples be allowed to be built.' A later order, probably issued in the early 1670s in response to the construction of a temple in Orissa, elaborated this principle into a policy: 'Every temple built during the last ten or twelve years [in Orissa] should be demolished without delay.' Officials were instructed, in addition, to 'not allow the Hindus and infidels to repair their old temples' (Pinch 2006, 220).

In the interim, Aurangzeb had learned to his dismay that 'in the provinces of Thatta, Multan, and Benares, but especially in the latter, foolish Brahmans were in the habit of expounding from frivolous books in their schools, and that students [...] Musulmans as well as Hindus, went there, even from long distances, led by a desire to become acquainted with the wicked sciences they taught'. This news was reported to Aurangzeb on 9 April 1669 and led to his general order to 'all the governors of provinces to destroy with a willing hand the schools and temples of the infidels' so as 'to put an entire stop to the teaching and practising of idolatrous forms of worship'. Soon thereafter, the Vishvanath Temple in Kashi and the Keshav Rai Temple of Mathura were 'levelled with the ground' (Pinch 2006, 220).

Aurangzeb even tried to rename the city as Muhammadabad and issued coins bearing that name (Singh 2008, 96). But it never took on.

Vishvanatha

The medieval temple of Vishvanatha stood near the bend of Chauk Road close to the mosque of Bibi Raziyya (r.1236–1240), but nothing of it now survives. Bibi Raziyya's mosque, occupying a central location in the ancient city, erected over the dismantled Vishvanatha Temple, shows an act that effectively 'Islamicized' a site particularly holy to the Hindus. This mosque was built from previous materials, in particular pillars of an older Hindu temple, and consists of two chambers connected by a three-arched opening. At the next site, occupied by the present Aurangzeb Mosque, only traces of Raja Todar Mal's temple, rebuilt around 1585 in Chunar sandstone less than hundred metres to the south of old Vishvanatha Temple, can be seen. The *qibla* wall rises above the plainly visible remains of the temple, which was not completely demolished. (Singh 2008, 104).

The map reproduced here shows the changing sites of the Vishvanatha Mandir over time.

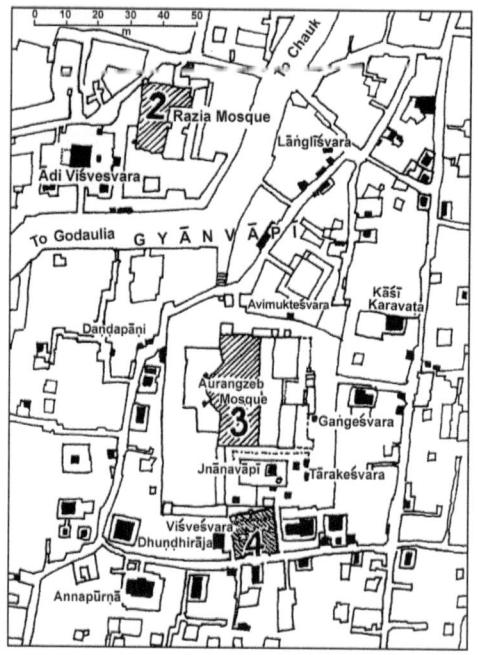

Source: Singh 2008, 106

Key: (1) Unknown, before *c.*7th century AD
(2) *c.* 7th century to 1194
(3) From 1594 to 1669
(4) Since 25 August 1777 to the present

During her reign, Razia Sultana had built a mosque on the deserted site of Vishvanatha Temple, which had been earlier demolished by Aibak *c.*1194. By the end of the thirteenth century, the Vishvanatha Temple was rebuilt in the compound of Avimukteshvara and there it remained until the next wave of destruction under the rule of the Sharqi kings of Jaunpur (r.1436–1458). In 1490, Sikandar Lodi completely demolished the temple.

In *c.*1585 with the support of Todar Mal, one of the senior courtiers of Akbar, the great scholar and writer Narayana Bhatta (1514–1595) had rebuilt the temple again, most likely on the structural plan of the previous temple of the thirteenth century. In 1669, even this temple was demolished by the order of Aurangzeb, and today the Gyanvapi Mosque stands on its site.

As it would have been only a little additional trouble for Aurangzeb to order the demolition of the entire temple, one can only assume that the back portion was consciously spared as a warning and insult to the feelings of the city's Hindu population (Singh 2008, 108). This echoes Wink's commentary discussed earlier that selective destruction was often an intentional strategy to salt the wounds of Hindus.

It was one century later, on 25 August 1777, under the patronage of Queen Ahilyabai Holkar of Indore, that the present Vishvanatha Mandir would be completed (Singh 2008, 108).

In the hoary past, the only icon of Vishnu installed was the one consecrated in the *muktimandap* of the Vishveshvara Mandir. Not only was this deity of Vishnu given a place of honour, but it was also incumbent on every person to worship that deity of Vishnu first, before worshipping Vishveshvara. Up to 1669, the importance of this image was extraordinarily high but with the destruction of the muktimandap, its worship practically ceased although tradition maintains that the image of Vishnu installed there was removed and placed in the current Vishvanatha Mandir (Sukul 1974, 187).

Gyaanavapi

As described earlier, according to the Kashi Khanda of the *Skanda Purana*, Ishaana dug a well to get water from the earth so that he could worship Avimukteshvara. This well of liquid wisdom came to be known as Gyaanavapi. Over bouts of successive attempts at destruction, all that remained of the Gyaanavapi area was confined just to a masjid, a temple, and a well. The beautiful steps of Gyaanavapi and its surroundings were entirely disfigured in subsequent onslaughts. A columned arcade was built to house the well in 1828 (Chandramouli 2018, 406).

Bindu Madhava

As Eck notes, citing Moti Chandra's book, *Kashi ka Itihas*, the Bindu Madhava Mandir was probably destroyed several times between the twelfth and the sixteenth centuries AD before being rebuilt for the last time by the Rajasthani Maharaja Man Singh of Amber in the late sixteenth century (Eck 1982, 348). It was this grand temple that Tavernier saw on his trip to Banaras shortly thereafter and described as the 'great pagoda of Banaras' (quoted in Tavernier in Eck 1982, 348). Tavernier describes the 'idol' in this temple as five to six feet high, garlanded with a chain of riches, such as gold, rubies, pearls, and emeralds (Eck 1982, 348).

The Bindu Madhava Mandir was the most important Vishnu temple in Varanasi since the fifth century AD. The *Matsya Purana* enumerates it along with Adi Keshava as being among the five most important tirthas in Varanasi. Every wave of destruction resulted in the temple's destruction, again and again, and every time it was rebuilt. In AD 1585, at the same time that Raja Todar Mal built the Vishveshvara Mandir, a new grand temple was constructed for Bindu Madhava by the Maharaja of Jaipur.

Tavernier visited this temple and has left a detailed description of it. It was a grand building with four lofty towers at the four corners, with stairs running inside them for people going to the top stories of the temple. A temple dedicated to Sri Rama and a Vedic pathshala were also built next door, and the temple of Mangalagauri was also inside its wall enclosure (Sukul 1974, 186). In 1669, the temple was demolished and a mosque with two tall minarets built in its place under the orders of Aurangzeb. The minarets of the mosque, however, never received recognition as minarets of the mosque by the Hindus. They were always called 'Madhavarao ka Dharahara' in memory of the temple towers they had once displaced. They have, however, ceased to exist now as one of them fell down and the other was taken down as a safety hazard (Sukul 1974, 187).

The mosque now completely dominates the riverfront skyline of the Hindu holy city.

Kaala Bhairava

The temple for Kaala Bhairava was originally near the Omkareshvara Mandir in Pathani Tola. In the Kashi Khanda, after all, it is said that Bhairava stands right there, facing the Kapalamochana Tirtha and devouring all the sins of his devotees. The deity was later reconsecrated at the present site sometime in the beginning of the thirteenth century, when the temples of Omkareshvara were destroyed. He was housed in a thatched hut, which later on was tiled. There was no temple, no ostentation or display, and this inconspicuousness saved him from defilement in subsequent iconoclastic waves of destruction. Thus, Kaala Bhairava remained very well-known to the Hindus but of no consequence to the Muslims for about six hundred years. The present temple housing the deity was constructed by Sardar Vinchurkar, Commander-in-Chief of the Peshawas, somewhere around AD 1825 (Sukul 1974, 191).

Annapurna

The temples of Bhavani Gauri and Bhuvaneshvari were demolished in 1496. A new temple for Annapurana, also known as Bhuvaneshvari, was built at the site of the demolished Bhuvaneshvari Temple in 1781. An idol of Bhavani Gauri was reconstructed in a small temple of Sri Rama attached to the present Annapurna Mandir. Annapurna became very popular in due course and was worshipped in the way prescribed for Bhavani Gauri. This temple was also destroyed by the Muslim rulers.

It is said that one Vishnupanth Gaide, a Maharashtrian Brahmana, found a Sri Yantra near a tree close to Annapurna Mandir. He persuaded Bajirao Peshava II to consecrate this yantra and that is how probably Annapurna Mandir was built in 1825–1828. Since one hand of the deity was broken, a new deity sculpted in stone was brought from Guntur and the reconsecration took place in the presence of the Shankaracharya from Sringeri, Mahasannidhanam Sri Sri Abhinava Vidya Tirtha Mahaswamiji in 1976 (Chandramouli 2018, 46–47).

Omkareshvara

The Omkara Mandir was once the central temple of Omkara Khanda. The entire sector of the city was circumambulated in a pilgrimage that began and ended at Omkara. Pilgrims who followed that route in the twelfth century would have stopped at many of the greatest and oldest temples of the city: Mahadeva, Trilochana, Krittivaseshvara, Kaleshvara, Madhyameshvara, and others. This was clearly the heart of the sacred city until the twelfth century, and it was this part of the city that was dealt the hardest blows during the Muslim centuries. Even though certain temples in the northern sector are flourishing today, such as Mrityunjaya and Trilochana, the area as a whole has never really recovered (Eck 1982, 182).

Other Temples

The most important Shiva temple on Manikarnika Ghat is the one containing the Tarakeshvara Linga, the form of Shiva that imparts the Taraka mantra. This linga was formerly located in the compound of Vishveshvara in the heart of the city. The Tarakeshvara pavilion was one of the eight-sided pavilions of the great sixteenth-century temple of Vishveshvara. It was destroyed along with the rest of the temple and is remembered at its old site today by a mere fragment of stone located underneath the small shrine of Gauri Shankar by the Gyaanavapi pavilion (Eck 1982, 363).

The Krittivaseshvara Mandir was the first to receive the attention of Aurangzeb. It was not only destroyed but also replaced by a mosque on the site of the ancient important temple in 1659. A small empty tank, which marks the first, second, and third reconstruction sites, is still worshipped by the Hindus on Mahashivaratri (Sukul 1974, 185).

In 1296, a saint named Padmasadhu built a grand temple of Padmeshvara facing Vishveshvara. However, during the reign of Sharqi Sultana, this temple was destroyed and the Lal Darwaza Mosque (Atala) was built in Jaunpur using the materials of this grand temple from 1447. The inscription on the wall of this mosque also refers to its having been constructed with the remains of the Padmeshvara Temple. Based on inscriptional information, it is demonstrated that during the period 1296–1447, Vishveshvara was the preeminent sacred landmark of the city.

As Eck notes, beyond Trilochana, the procession of ghats becomes much more rudimentary. Many of the ghats are still clay-baked, *kachcha* ghats. They front the river in an area of the city that is largely Muslim and lack the patronage that would produce finer ghats. A thousand years ago, however, this section of the river was surely one of the most popular, surmises Eck. On the bank and in the lanes above it were some of the city's most important temples, which were destroyed with the invasion of 1194. Many of these same temples, such as Vireshvara and Sankata Devi, were then re-established further south, where they are found today (Eck 1982, 344–345).

Buddhist Sites

Through excavations undertaken in Sarnath, archaeologists have 'found everywhere traces of the great catastrophe which destroyed in one holocaust the monks, monasteries, and temples of Sarnath. Charred bones and wood, lumps of melted brass, half-fused bricks, and calcined stone testified to the fury of the invaders' (Havell 1905, 49).

While by the eighth century AD, Buddhism as a separate religion had faded from mainstream Indian society, the Buddhist monasteries continued to exist in Sarnath and elsewhere in India, until they were finally destroyed by the Islamic invaders of the thirteenth century (Havell 1905, 64). Havell also notes that the Afghans, who in 1194 burned the Buddhist monasteries at Sarnath, probably laid waste to Benares, too (Havell 1905, 26).

CHAPTER 20

The Warrior Sadhus

The Battle of Gyaanavapi

This book started with the image of the Battle of Gyaanavapi—the force of sixty thousand naga sadhus arrayed against the army of the sultan, presumably Aurangzeb, in the year 1664 to defend the seat of Vishvanatha and defend the site Gyaanavapi. That day, the naga sadhus fought from sunrise to sunset and won. In so doing, they protected the great temple of Shiva until Aurangzeb finally had his revenge in 1669 and razed the temple to the ground.

What led to the battle that day? What kind of sadhus—renunciates who have given up their possessions, their family, their home, their very identity—would take up arms? What were they fighting for that day, and why is the tradition of these warrior sadhus so important and key to the development of Hinduism and Hindu civilization? These are the questions that this chapter will seek to answer.

Whether or not one chooses to believe as documented fact the battle of Gyaanavapi as outlined here, what is undeniable is that there has been a continuous and strong trend of warrior sadhus from the very beginnings of Hindu society, and these sadhus have played an important role in defending Hinduism and the organization of Hindu society.

To begin with, let us delve more deeply into the incident of the Battle of Gyaanavapi. Sir Jadunath Sarkar in his book, *A History of the Dasnami Naga Sannyasis*, recounts his discovery of a Hindi manuscript in the Nirvani Akhara. This manuscript purports to provide the dates of the foundation of the different *akharas* and describe some of the battles fought. Sarkar does not independently vouch for the contents of the manuscript that he proceeds to summarize; rather, he explains that he is transmitting the story as preserved by tradition from mouth to mouth among the family of bards who hold the oral history of the Nirvani Akhara. He surmised that the manuscript was not more than fifty years old (Sarkar 2018, 140). Here is his account:

> Subject to all of these caveats, the account provided in this archival manuscript from the Nirvani Akhara can be summarized as follows:
>
> 'At the Battle of Gyaanavapi in the Benares kshetra, near the Gyaanavapi Mandir, a number of Nagas fought and performed heroic deeds. Ghanashyam Puri planted a saffron flag. Dharam Puri Harihet-Jangsar (?) played the naubat music. Bishwambhar Bharati held the sword, Lalit Bhagwan Puri held the peacock fan. Jogindra received honour. Narayan Ban's family was holder of the mace. This victory increased the glory of Kashi.
>
> 'At the Kashi kshetra in Samvat 1721 (AD 1664) they won, the victory in a fight with the Sultan (? Aurangzib) and gained great glory. From sunrise to sunset the battle raged and the Dasnamis proved themselves heroes; they preserved the honour of Viswanath's seat. They defeated the Muslims ... Shiva gave help and thus saved the honour of the Dasnami.' (Sarkar 2018, 143)

The History of Dashanami Naga Sannyasi Sampradaya

Monastic orders of Hindu ascetics have existed in India since ancient times. The Greeks, when they came with Alexander, encountered the nagas, whom they referred to as naked philosophers, the gymnosophists. Most of the nagas belong to the Dashanami sampradaya organized by Adi Shankaracharya, the oldest, the biggest, and the most effective of Hindu monastic orders (K.M. Munshi's Foreword, Sarkar 2018, 91).

Upon initiation into the Dashanami sampradaya, one is given a name to be combined with one of ten words: Giri, Puri, Bharati, Van, Aranya, Parvat, Sagar, Tirth, Ashram, or Saraswati. The initiate has to make strict vows not to indulge in more than one meal a day; not to beg for food from more than seven houses; not to sleep anywhere but upon the ground; not to salute, not to praise, nor speak ill of anyone; not to bow to anyone but a sannyasi of a higher order; and not to cover himself with a cloth, unless it were of a *bhagwa* (saffron) colour.

The Dashanamis are divided into two sections: the Shastradharis, who specialize in sacred lore, and the Astradharis, who specialize in arms. The fighting wing is organized into akharas, and, in the past, played a historic role (K.M. Munshi's foreword, Sarkar 2018, 91–92).

The Dashanami order made Hindu monasticism serve the good of the vast body of Hindu society, of which the only parallel was supplied by Mahayana Buddhism in its best days, according to Sarkar. As Sarkar notes,

> The Dashanami monks have held the twofold ideal of astra and shastra [sword and scripture], i.e., the cultivation of theology for the spiritual education of the people and the pursuit of arms for the defence of their religion against the attacks of brute force. In this respect they have anticipated the fighting monks of Christianity, who originated as late as the twelfth century, while the Nagas or militant Sannyasis of India first appear in history several centuries earlier. (Sarkar 2018, 96–97)

The Dashanami monastic order was established, or rather, inspired, by Adi Shankaracharya. Sarkar puts the dating of the birth of Adi Shankaracharya to somewhere between AD 688 and 788 (Sarkar 2018, 109). He notes that this date is supported by the Jagadguru Paramparastotra, still read at the Sringeri Matha today, which proclaims that Adi Shankaracharya was born in Kaliyuga era 3889–710 Shalivahan Shaka, i.e., AD 788 (Sarkar 2018, 111).

While Adi Shankaracharya was the conceiver and inspirer of the monastic order, the actual work of organizing the order is attributed to Sureshvaracharya, the third in pontifical succession to Adi Shankaracharya in Sringeri (Sarkar 2018, 123).

Sarkar describes the significance of the ten names in the Dasanami sampradaya: Giri (hill), Puri (city), Bharti (learning), Ban (wood), Aranya (forest), Parbat (mountain), Sagar (ocean), Tirtha (temple), Ashram (hermitage), and Saraswati (perfect knowledge) (Sarkar 2018, 125). Puri, Bharti, and Saraswati are attached to Sringeri; Ban and Aranya to the Govardhan Matha in Jagannath Puri; the Giri, Parbat, and Sagar orders to the Joshi Math in Badrinath; and the Tirtha and Ashram branches to the Sharada Math in Dwaraka (Sarkar 2018, 125). Of the ten names, Tirthas, Ashramas, Saraswatis, and half of Bhartis are called Dandis, while the remaining six and a half groups are entitled to call themselves Gosains (Sarkar 2018, 127).

When a person has resolved to enter the monastic order, he expresses his request to the head of the order and after due examination he will be granted permission if he is deemed ready. As part of the rites of initiation, he must give away all of his earthly possessions except a loincloth, staff, and waterpot with ceremonies and mantras (Sarkar 2018, 131–132).

The chief work of the Mathadharis of the Dashanami order is to propagate dharma among the people, and properly educate the monks. The head or *mandaleshwar* must be a master of grammar, logic, astronomy, the Vedas, and Vedanta. When the mandaleshwar is out on tour, his best disciple conducts the teaching at the matha in his absence. It would be a mistake to suppose that the two sections of the Dashanamis, namely the fighters and the theologians, are strictly segregated. A good deal of valuable teaching in scriptures is also done by the akharas. For example, the Nirvani Akhara has established schools, such as in Allahabad and Haridwar (Sarkar 2018, 139).

Traditionally, there were six principal akharas, namely Juna, Mahanirvani, Niranjan, Atal, Avahan, and Agni. The Hindu term 'akhara' means a wrestling arena. In the past, there was a strong network of akharas throughout Bharat, particularly in the north, where men trained in wrestling and other methods of fighting. Akharas specialize in various techniques of fitness and combat, which include the use of weights, clubs, and maces. Various akharas came into existence in the pre-Mughal period in Jaipur, Jodhpur, and some other parts of Rajasthan, at Prayaga, and principally in Varanasi.

Visible characteristics of the naga sannyasins include worship of both Bhairava and Dattatreya, and an emphasis on maintaining the sacred fire, *dhuni*, and aspects of outward appearance such as earrings, ochre robes, ash-besmeared bodies, and the use of a ritual drinking vessel (Pinch 2006, 40–41).

The Incident of Sri Madhusudana Sarasvati and Akbar

It was earlier mentioned that Sri Madhusadana Sarasvati, the renowned Sanskrit scholar and spiritual luminary, had supported Tulsidas Maharaj when his writings in Awadhi and Braj were considered controversial. It is worth going into a bit more detail about the life and character of Sri Madhusudana Sarasvati. He was born into a Vaishnava family and originally studied Advaita in order to refute it; in the process, he became a staunch Advaitin and his *Advaita Siddhi*, a text countering the Dvaita point-of-view, is unparalleled and remains unequalled in its exposition of Advaita as a counter to Dvaita. He was as much a bhakta of Sri Krishna as he was a proponent of Advaita, and he syncretized bhakti and gyaana. Of him, it is said, 'Only the Devi of Learning, Sarasvati, knows the limits of the knowledge of Sri Madhusudana Sarasvati. And only Sri Madhusudana Sarasvati knows the limits of Devi Sarasvati [the embodiment of wisdom].'

J.N. Farquhar, a missionary and scholar, provides an account of the famous incident that, it is held, resulted in the organization of armed sannyasins in Kashi. He presents this account that he holds to be grounded in historical fact:

> In the sixteenth century there were in North India thousands of Muslim faquirs who went about armed, took part in the wars of the time, and when there was no regular war, fought for their own land. One of their practices, as good Muslims, was to attack and kill sannyasis as representatives of Hinduism. As ascetics, these faquirs held a privileged position, and were thus protected from mob violence and also from interference on the part of the government, which was then Muhammadan. Thus, when sannyasis were killed, no one was punished, while sannyasis themselves were prevented from taking violent measures against their enemies by their vow of ahimsa.
>
> Madhusudana Sarasvati, a well-known sannyasi scholar of the Sarasvati suborder, who lived in Benares in the middle of the century, at last went to Akbar to see whether anything could be done for the protection of the ancient order to which he belonged. Raja Birbal was present at the interview and suggested the way out of the difficulty. He advised Madhusudana to initiate large numbers of non-Brahmins into the sannyasi order and arm them for the protection of Brahman sannyasis. The Emperor agreed that armed sannyasis should be protected by their sacred character from government interference. Madhusudana therefore, went and initiated large numbers of Ksatriyas and Vaisyas into seven of the sub-orders, Bharati, Vana, Aranya, Parvata, Sagara, Giri and Puri. (Farquhar 1925b, 482–483)

Farquhar did not just take this account at face value. This account was shared with him by members of the Chaushatha monastery in Banaras and by members of a 'Giri monastery near Allahabad'. In addition, he attended the Allahabad Kumbha Mela in 1918 and had numerous discussions concerning the historical origins of the various ascetic orders there. Farquhar did not treat the story as fanciful legend but rather as 'a piece of history which has been faithfully preserved by tradition' (Farquhar 1925b, 483; Pinch 2006, 31–32).

Farquhar explains,

> Readers will not find this agreement between Akbar and Madhusudana Sarasvati mentioned in any historical work. So

far as I know, it has not been recorded anywhere. I picked up the information from the lips of sannyasis, who told it [to] me to explain how large numbers of their order came to be fighting men. But though it has come down to us by tradition, there can be no doubt about its truth. All sannyasis in North India hold the tradition; and we may also be certain that the Emperor who had given the Hindu an equal place with the Muslim in his empire would at once recognise the justice of Madhusudana's appeal and would respond to it. (Farquhar 1925a, 443)

We do not just have to take Farquhar's word for it. The oral tradition of the sannyasis also carry this account. This point is confirmed by two later recordings of the oral tradition, one in 1954 by a government official conducting an inquiry into a disaster that occurred earlier that year at the Allahabad Kumbha Mela and the other reported by two anthropologists collecting ethnographic data on the ascetic institutions of Banaras in the 1970s.

The head of the 1954 government inquiry reported, 'Madhusudan Saraswati Ji of Banaras, possibly with the assistance of Birbal and Abdul Rahim Khankhana, the well-known Ministers of Emperor Akbar, and with the approval of the Emperor, had put the organization of these Akharas on a proper footing' (quoting the report of the committee appointed by the Uttar Pradesh government to enquire into the mishap that occurred at the Kumbha Mela in Prayaga on 3 February 1954, Pinch 2006, 35-36).

This information was based on interviews with the head of the Mahanirvani Panchayati Akhara. Two decades later, a slightly different version was collected from the ascetics of the Juna Akhara, a related institution in Kashi. According to this version:

> From ancient times the Naga ascetics were peregrinating in the country in groups, called Jhundi. During the reign of Akbar, the Moslem Malanga faquirs were troubling the Hindu villagers, because the Hindus used to receive the Naga sannyasins respectfully while the Malanga faquirs were more feared than respected. This eventually exploded into an open clash between the Nagas and the Malangas.

The Malangas were already equipped with swords, they killed the Naga ascetics mercilessly. When the Hindus approached Akbar for justice, the latter said: two cows are fighting, which indicated his helplessness or non-interference in the religious matter. On this the princes of Rajputana sent some solders in the guise of ascetics to defend the Hindu sannyasis and villagers from the ravages of the Malanga faquirs. It was on this occasion that for the first time the Naga ascetics were supplied with arms by Hindu kings. These ascetics gradually trained themselves in fighting, and subsequently fought many battles and took part in many a skirmish. (Pinch 2006 35–36)

What can we take away from these accounts? Clearly, the Dashanami Naga Sannyasi sampradaya existed since soon after the time of Adi Shankaracharya. It is not that Sri Madhusudana Sarasvati necessarily created something new. He was a devout follower of Adi Shankaracharya, of course. But as the situation changed and the needs of Hindu society changed with the reality of Muslim rule, Sri Madhusudana Sarasvati was inspired to reorganize and revive the order in a dynamic new way to protect dharma. It is this situational approach to dharma, as opposed to ossification of the old ways, that has kept dharma alive against all the odds. It is the ability to see what is needed in the moment and to do it while honouring traditions and the old ways based on their underlying spirit. This is the lesson of the great service Sri Madhusudana Sarasvati provided to Hindu civilization and society by reorganizing and reviving the warrior sadhu tradition.

The History of Warrior Sadhus and Their Rise during Muslim Rule

Of course, the history of warrior sadhus or warrior yogis did not start in the middle of the sixteenth century. Vishvamitra and Vasishtha were great rishis who also took up arms when needed, for example. Pinch notes references to armed yogis occurring as early as in the seventh-century *Harsacharita* authored by Banabhatta (Pinch 2006, 59).

Bhattacharya, in his introduction to Sarkar's book, notes that the Dashanami sannyasis first entered into military service at the beginning of the Turko-Afghan period because they were good fighters. This was not only to protect themselves in those violent days but also to preserve their material possession, particularly, their mathas, akharas, and wealth (Sarkar 2018, 58–60).

He further attributes their brave, militant, and self-sacrificing nature in the battlefield to the guru-chela relationship and akhara-based organization that imparted a militant ideology and training.

The purpose of the akharas was to uphold the ideas of Hinduism as well as to defend the faith from Muslim inroads. Due to recurring conflicts with fakirs since the medieval period, sannyasis belonging to different orders ignored their theological differences and turned to their military leaders, who in the role of mahants of respective akharas could best provide effective protection. According to Surajit Sinha, the naga sannyasis gradually trained themselves as fighters and fought on behalf of such princely states as Kutch, Jodhpur, Indore, Gwalior, and several others in western India against the Islamic invasion (Sarkar 2018, 58–60). Similarly, the akharas situated in Jodhpur during the Mughal period helped the Jodhpur Rajputs to repel the attacks of Muslims from Baluchistan and Kabul. The akharas turned into warehouses of weapons, and the sannyasis became well-organized experts in the field of warfare (Sarkar 2018, 58–60).

The rise of militant sadhus or yogis is generally attributed to responding to the rise of militant Islam in Bharat. As Pinch notes, '[Farquhar's] explanation pointed to the rise of Islam in South Asia—and more particularly to the persecution (according to sectarian legend) of non-violent Hindu sanyasis by fanatical Sufi warriors intent on stamping out pagan religious practices' (Pinch 2006, 7). Lorenzon also suggests that the coming of Muslim rule in India—and with it broad legal, political, and cultural sanctions in Islam for the persecution of non-Muslims—probably acted as the catalyst that resulted in the formal militarization of Hindu ascetic orders (Lorenzen 1978).

More descriptions emerged of warrior sadhus after AD 1500 with the arrival of more European travellers in Bharat. These accounts '[make] clear that armed yogis were a regular feature of the early modern Indian landscape, but also suggest that the seventeenth century was a time of ascetic military expansion, both in terms of tactics and in number that armed yogis were finding service in the Mughal system' (Pinch 2006, 60).

While traveling through the environs of Delhi in the early sixteenth century, the Portuguese traveller, Duarte Barbosa, encountered large bands of yogis wandering about 'like the gipsies' but 'naked, barefooted, and bareheaded', their only covering tight brass belts and heavy chains draped about their necks and waists and legs (cited by Pinch 2006, 62). According to Barbosa, 'In their own speech they are called Zoame [swami], which means servant of God.'

> [Barbosa asked them] many times why they went in this fashion. And they answered me, that they wore those chains upon their bodies as penance for the sin which they committed for allowing themselves to be captured by such bad people as the Moors, and that they went naked as a sign of dishonour, because they had allowed their lands and houses to be lost, in which God brought them up; and that they did want more property since they had lost their own, for which they ought to have died; and that they smeared themselves with ashes in order to remind themselves perpetually that they were born of earth and had to return again to earth, and that all the rest was falsehood. (Pinch 2006, 62)

The shift from the armed yogi bands of the sixteenth century to the soldiering naga akharas of the eighteenth century was both demographic and tactical. By the late eighteenth century, the sheer size of the naga armies was of an entirely different order compared to the numbers given in sixteenth-century accounts. Anupgiri and

Umraogiri commanded upwards of 20,000 men in the late 1700s (Pinch 2006, 70).

They fought primarily with swords and daggers, bows and arrows, and metal discs and stones. These weapons were the tools of a specific trade, namely, engaging an enemy at fairly close quarters and rapidly closing in for the kill. This was not the material that made an Indian empire in the sixteenth century. For that task, cannons were required, primarily to breach the walls of forts built prior to the days of field artillery and secondarily to overawe the opponent. Of equal importance, when opposing armies were amassed on an open field, was a well-trained archery, with some men specializing in long-distance accuracy with massive bows and others trained in dispatching arrows in rapid succession and with an astonishingly high degree of accuracy while mounted and at full gallop. When properly deployed in tandem, such a force could quickly harass the enemy into submission. Sword, arrow, discus, and stone had utility—not for making an empire but for keeping it. Akbar recognized this and retained experts in the art of stone combat (Pinch 2006, 70–71).

By the late eighteenth century, not only had the numbers of armed ascetics increased dramatically, there was much greater tactical variety. Sanyasis, Gosains, Bairagis, fakirs, and (especially) nagas, as these soldiering ascetics were increasingly known, generally carried muskets and served widely in infantry as well as cavalry units. There is abundant evidence of this, not least of which are the celebrated careers of Rajendragiri, Anupgiri, and Umraogiri Gosain and their naga armies of Bundelkhand, Awadh, and the Delhi-Agra hinterland. There is a variety of anecdotal evidence as well of the increasingly routine participation of armed ascetics in the military economy of northern India. Lieutenant-Colonel Valentine Blacker included Gosains in his reflection on the rise of infantry forces in India in the 1700s. He described them as 'a Hindoo cast of peculiar habits, scattered over different parts of India', who 'have been always considered as good troops' on a par with Rohillah Afghans, Jatas, and Khalsa (military) Sikhs (quoting Blacker, Pinch 2006, 73). Thomas Broughton remarked in 1809 that 'as soldiers, they [Gosains] are accounted brave and faithful' (quoted in Pinch 2006, 73).

Skinner included an illustration of a naga soldier in his early nineteenth-century caste compendium. In this illustration, the warrior wears what appears to be a leather belt from which is suspended a sabre and pouches for gunpowder, ammunition, and flint. He is otherwise naked and barefoot, and his long, matted hair is wrapped around his head like a helmet; he holds a long double-ended spear or lance over his right shoulder and a long-barrelled musket over his left (cited in Pinch 2006, 75).

The shift into a more conventional infantry and cavalry role does not mean that the nagas had altogether abandoned the close-quarter combat and small-scale guerrilla action of their yogi predecessors. Quite to the contrary, they remained conspicuous for the hand-to-hand skills they could bring to bear (Pinch 2006, 76).

The new demands of military conflict help to explain how bands of armed sadhus could expand so rapidly into widespread military entrepreneurship in the eighteenth century. Yogis were accustomed to physical disciplines; their bodies were hardened by ascetic austerities and itinerancy as well as and habitual exposure to the elements. Organizationally, the non-biological bonds of loyalty that tied disciples to their gurus would have enabled smaller bands of armed ascetics to expand over time into larger and more institutionally complex—Dashanami or Ramanandi—regiments and armies (Pinch 2006, 80).

From the late sixteenth century until the early decades of the nineteenth century, many prominent regional regents recruited bands of nagas to fight in interregional struggles for power. The Mughal emperor Aurangzeb authorized in 1693/4 five Ramanandi commanders and their armies to move without hindrance. They were particularly renowned for their nocturnal guerrilla operations: naked, sometimes slippery with oil, and dangerous with the dagger. The disposition of regents to employ naga armies may have also been partly due to their reputation for supernatural yogic abilities (Sarkar 2018, 16).

In 1764, Prithvi Narayan Shah, a Gorkha king and the founder of modern Nepal, was engaged in a campaign to extend his empire into Kathmandu Valley. His chief advisor and strategist was a Nath siddha named Bhavantnath, who used his influence to negotiate various matrimonial and military alliances between Gorkha and some of the other forty-five kingdoms of western Nepal.

Sarkar notes that even as the Dashanami nagas participated in fighting as mercenaries, they still continued their ascetic way of life by attending the religious fairs and festivals like Kumbha Mela. (Sarkar 2018, 17).

Prowess and Power of the Warrior Sadhus

Padmakar recited the praises of Anupgiri Gosain, *c*.1795:

> He scorches his humbled enemies in their jungle hideaways. He touches the poor with long-armed compassion and ritual sacrifice. He gives endowments to support dharma and is the clothing that covers Hindu shame. He is the embodiment of radiant splendour, but an insatiable demon when his anger is provoked. (Pinch 2006, 104)

Bhattacharya notes that there is at least one exceptional case on record in which even the British employed a sannyasi, Puran Giri, in diplomatic negotiations. In 1774, Hastings sent Puran Giri to accompany George Bogle on his mission to Tibet. Bogle was greatly helped by Puran Giri who was highly competent to act both as interpreter and guide to the English mission on account of his knowledge of Tibetan and other languages and his experience of travelling in the Himalayan region. When Bogle was held up in Bhutan by message from the Panchen Lama asking him to go back, it was Puran Giri who first entered Tibet and persuaded the Lama to allow Bogle to visit his country. In fact, the sadhu enjoyed the full confidence of the Tibetan authorities and the respect of the Tibetan people. In this way, he became a close associate of the Panchen Lama in China and was introduced by him to the emperor (Sarkar 2018, 64).

The nagas became so powerful that they started becoming influential in the politics of the Mughal courts. Prithviraj Chauhan favourably treated them by renovating their akharas in different parts of India (Sarkar 2018, 66). The status and prestige enjoyed by the sannyasis demonstrate how greatly the regional powers valued their services. This favouritism was also marked in them having the freedom to undertake religious activities, including their long-distance pilgrimages with armed groups of followers in Bengal and outside. Their free movement was likely a root cause of conflict with the East India Company (Sarkar 2018, 68). Bhattacharya notes that from the evidence gathered to date, it is clear that the nagas were a much sought-after military and commercial force (Sarkar 2018, 77).

Tod describes the Gosains of Rajputana as follows:

> The Gosains who profess arms, partake of the character of the Knights of St John of Jerusalem. They live in monasteries scattered over the country, possess lands, and beg, or serve for pay when called upon. As defensive soldiers they are good [...] In Mewar they can always muster many hundreds of the Kanfora Jogi or split-ear ascetics. (Sarkar 2018, 236)

A naga force rendered valuable service to Maha Rao Bhar Mal II of Cutch-Bhoj (r. 1813–19), and their descendants were retained permanently in the state army. Their place of honour is the fifth in the line of procession of the Maha Rao on the Naga Panchami day. They were regarded as very brave soldiers (Sarkar 2018, 240–241).

Warrior Sadhus and the Defence of Hinduism

The Sannyasi Rebellion, which was the inspiration for *Anandamath*, the great Bengali novel written in the early 1880s by Bankim Chandra Chatterjee, originated from the united efforts of these bands of fighting sadhus and yogis, as well as fakirs, to take on the East India Company. Pinch's characterization here is fair:

> Though armed sanyasis and fakirs were not Indian nationalists, they did possess a consciously articulated tie to the land and country through which they travelled and, more importantly, to sacred geographic points on their routes. The homage that some people paid them suggests, moreover, that they themselves were regarded as an integral part of a sacred landscape—rendering them less proto-nationalists perhaps than a physical feature of the proto-nation (and, hence, the object of proto-nationalist 'territorial' devotion). In any case, sanyasi and fakir clashes with Company arms were, at least in part, predicated on the desire to retain periodic access to that sacred landscape and to the moneyed people in it. (Pinch 2006, 96)

It is clear that the warrior sadhus were motivated in large part by their consciousness of a sacred geography and the landscape tied together by various holy sites that they still assiduously travelled to in pilgrimage.

The naga sannyasis were called by the Greeks 'gymnosophists', which literally means 'naked philosophers'. Alexander's dealings with the naked sages are described by Plutarch:

> In the course of this expedition [against the Malloi tribe], he took ten of the Gymno-sophists, who had been principally concerned in instigating Sambos [*Shambhu*] to revolt and had brought numberless other troubles upon the Macedonians. As these ten men were reckoned the most acute and concise in their answers, he put the most difficult questions to them that could be thought of. [At the end,] the king loaded them with presents, and dismissed them. (Sarkar 2018, 159)

Mahant Lakshman Giri, the head of the Maha Nirvani Akhara, Allahabad, wrote a Hindi account of the akharas on 5 January 1929, part of which notes the motivation of the naga sadhus to fight in defence of Hinduism:

> The Atal Akhara is the oldest of the seven akharas. In the time of the Delhi Badshahs, there used to be three hundred thousand men in it. ... The Atal Akhara has produced many heroes and fighters for the defence of the Hindu religion. It used to reside mostly in the Jodphur State. When Muslims from Kabul and Baluchistan invaded Jodhpur and levied tribute from the Rajah, the force of the Atal Sannyasis arrived there, defeated the Muslims, took away their arms and made them swear on the Quran that they would never again invade Marwar. The Rajah in gratitude granted Nagor *taluqa* to the Gosains, whose Nagor *berhe* still holds it. (Sarkar 2018, 144)

Sarkar makes a profound point about the Hindu caste system. The entire discussion of this point is worth recording here:

> It is a general belief in Europe and India alike that the Hindu caste system has rigidly divided men according to their functions in life and that each caste follows one profession exclusively, with the result that Brahmans cannot do any other work than serving as priests and teachers of sacred books, or that Kshatriyas must not do anything except fighting battles and governing kingdoms, and a violation of this rule would be a sinful encroachment of one caste upon the divinely ordained functions of another caste. But true oriental scholars know this popular theory to be false, and even the modern history of our country furnished many instances to the contrary of it. Thus, the priestly caste has produced warriors from the earliest age of the *Rg Veda* down to the nineteenth century when the East India Company's Bengal Army was mostly recruited from Oudh Brahmans.
>
> Similarly, the warrior caste of Kshatriyas is known to have produced not only soldiers and governors, but also sages and teachers of God-knowledge [*Brahma vidya*] like Janak and Gautam Buddha, besides numberless sadhus or wandering monks and

even a world honoured female saint, Mirabai. Hence, there is nothing incongruous to reason or opposed to the root principles of Hinduism, if a member of the priestly caste takes up arms in defence of faith and country or a member of the warrior caste by birth turns hermit and teaches religion. The Dasnami akharas are only one more illustration of this elasticity in Hinduism. (Sarkar 2018, 157–158)

That is the key point here. The warrior sadhus epitomize the highest standard of Hindu dharma in their dynamic spirit of adaptation, fearlessness, personal valour, commitment to Dharma and the bonds of sacred geography and sadhana. Surely, some of their actions may have been motivated by personal desire or even greed, but on the whole, it is indisputable—even based on the works of Western scholars who do not have rose-tinted views of Hinduism—that they were animated to a large extent by loyalty to their sampradaya, their fellow monks, to Hindu dharma, and the bonds of sacred geography.

It is also lamentable that today sadhus and sannyasins are stereotyped and ridiculed as quasi-eunuchs, mocked as being superstitious, cowardly, and corrupt. This history lesson is an important reminder to us all of the strength of will and incredible character that our sadhus have always cultivated through sadhana and shraddha.

Many bands of naga sannyasis and their mahants rendered important military service to the rajas of Rajputana, Gujrat and other states, and they were rewarded with grants of land and yearly money allowance as the records of these states prove. Sarkar notes,

> Though they did not rise to the rank of barons like Himmat Bahadur, their loyalty and heroism in defence of the right cause may be totally forgotten if their deeds are not included in this general history of the ten Orders. Our only disadvantage is that these acts of heroism and loyalty were done in many scattered States and at different times, and detailed descriptions of these fights are not available, because the records of the feudal States of India have

not been searched and indexed for the use of historical research scholars.

Many other orders of Hindu religious warriors took part in these wars of Rajputana and Malwa along with the Dasnamis. But the exact proportion of naga and non-naga fighters in those old half-forgotten battles and the names of their captains cannot be clearly distinguished now for want of detailed records. The only information that we get from the Persian, Marathi and Hindi manuscripts in that Gosain and Vairagis [and some called Ramanandis and Vishnu-swamis], under the general name of Maha-purushas or Gosains fought in defence of our Rajahs, and only the general result of their actions is given in our old history. I have included all such Hindu religious warriors in this volume. However, the readers must remember that some of these heroes were outside the Ten Orders. But that does not matter: the Hindu religious and martial spirit is the same, whatever the monk's title and the colour of his dress. (Sarkar 2018, 236–236)

A few of these examples documented by Sarkar are worth recounting here:

1. In Jodhpur, Bijay Singh became initiated as a follower of the Vaishnava mahant of the Nathadwara Temple. He used to make long visits to this holy place, where the Mahapurusha soldiers were the hereditary defenders of the god. He greatly liked these Gosain troops for their valour and fidelity and took delight in improving their equipment. In approximately 1780, he enlisted a large body of these Gosains in the regular army of his kingdom. The Marwar state history declares, 'The Mahapurushas formed the cheapest, hardiest yet most trustworthy fighters. They used to get rupees three to three and a half per month as pay for each soldier, and fodder and corn for their horses as well as ammunition free from the government' (Sarkar 2018, 237). In fact, the nagas helped to remove two grave defects of the Rajput clan army, because they supplied the

steadiness that the impetuous Rathor horsemen lacked and the use of firearms that the Rajputs neglected and despised as unworthy of heroes (Sarkar 2018, 238).

2. The holy city of Pushkar had been occupied by the wandering robber tribe of Gujars. But on the Diwali night of AD 1157, naga sannyasi troops defeated and expelled the Gujars and restored the city to the Brahmans. They planted the Bharatis in the Varaha Temple, the Jnan-Naths in the Vaidyanath Temple, and the Puris in the temples of Brahma and Savitri where they are still in possession (Sarkar 2018, 241).

3. Jhansi was the chief centre of the nagas in the early eighteenth century. The Gosain militia continued to live there and to serve the new masters of that state up to the time of the Sepoy Mutiny. They formed the bodyguard of the heroic Rani Lakshmi Bai, when she fled away from the fort of Jhansi during its siege by Sir Hugh Rose in 1858 (Sarkar 2018, 241–242).

Physical Culture in Kashi

This fighting spirit was not the province of the warrior sadhus alone. Rather, Kashi has always been famous for its attention to physical culture since ancient times. Life was vigorous and physical fitness essential for survival. The Kshatriyas, Vaishyas, and Shudras all had to cultivate bodily strength (Sukul 1974, 119).

With respect to Kashi specifically, the 'Brahma Khanda' of the *Skanda Purana* mentions an athlete from Varanasi named Ashoka Datta Vaishya who served in the court of a particular king. An athlete from southern India once came to the court of this king and challenged the athlete from Varanasi. He was promptly defeated by the Varanasi athlete. So, even in the most ancient of times, Varanasi had a reputation for physical prowess.

Sukul notes that there are no records available that document the development of physical prowess in Varanasi, but still he describes the rich tradition of bodybuilding in Varanasi:

Up to the end of the last century the number of athletic bodied individuals in Varanasi was legion. Out of every hundred young men one met with about ninety were equipped with well-built muscular bodies, and on questioning would mention the particular akhara [gymnasium] where they took their exercise. Rich and poor, one and all, insisted on their sons going to some akhara or other regularly, and most of the Raises of the times themselves had been pupils at one of these gymnasia, which they continued to patronise; and the incidents connected with the athletes—masters of those akharas were on every one's lips. The beautiful bodies of the Varanasi youth were always a matter of pride to their elders and of wonder to the outsiders.

In fact a weakling was treated with such derision that he felt ashamed of himself and if his age permitted straightaway took to exercise. In Varanasi still exist akharas that have been running for three hundred years and have produced a steady tale of athletic giants. Some of these akharas have come to grief and are no longer in existence but the physical abilities of their alumni are still remembered with pride. (Sukul 1974, 120-121).

CHAPTER 21

Revival and Renaissance: The Contributions of All Bharatiyas

One of the remarkable aspects of Kashi's history is not just the ubiquitous reverence with which it is regarded across Bharat but also how it has been a magnet drawing the sacrifice, service, and contributions of Hindus from all across Bharat.

The horror through which Hindus lived during the centuries of invasion and Mughal rule can poignantly be understood through verses in the *Kashi Rahasya* that prescribe the following of acts of *prayaschitta* (penance or purification), which are encouraged to be undertaken: (i) repairing a ruined Shiva temple (ii) constructing a roof over a Shivalinga that has no temple to house it (iii) sponsoring the building of a house for a Brahmana and (iv) sponsoring the construction of a new temple (*Kashi Rahasya* verses 7, 12 in Eck 1982, 468). One can only imagine the dire straits of the shrines and temples of the city of Kashi that such acts had to be encouraged to shelter the sacred deities of Kashi.

Indeed, the five hundred years between AD 1194 and 1708 were very difficult years for Hindus everywhere and particularly in Varanasi. Vedic learning had gone into decline, and in earlier centuries of this period, scholars had fled Varanasi to southern India or in remote villages. In the sixteenth century, however, some learned pandits of Maharashtra and Karnataka came to Varanasi to pass their last days in this holy city, and they revived the study of the Vedas here once again. After AD 1735, Varanasi had once completely revived its old glory of Vedic learning (Sukul 1974, 158–159).

After the disintegration of the Mughal Empire in the late seventeenth century, Kashi passed into the hands of a ruling family that has retained the throne and the title of Kashiraj ever since. For the first time in over five hundred years, the city was under the jurisdiction of Hindu kings. There was Mansaram and his successor Balwant Singh in the early eighteenth century. Then there was the famous Chet Singh, who resisted the tax demands of the British, even when the Governor-General of India, Warren Hastings, came personally to Kashi to confront him. Chet Singh, imprisoned in his own palace at Shivala Ghat, escaped on a makeshift rope of turbans and rallied a local rebellion strong enough to make Hastings flee for his life. That was in 1781. By 1794, however, Kashi came under the British administration. The maharajas continued to play a significant leadership role, though, especially in culture and religion (Eck 1982, 139).

After the death of Aurangzeb, Muslim rule started tottering and the rise of the Maratha power, too, had its restraining influence on the Delhi and Oudh rulers. Varanasi thus had no further religious tyrannies to face after AD 1708 when Aurangzeb died. The restoration and reconstruction of temples started with great enthusiasm. Most of the important temples were built on a moderately grand scale and Maharani Ahilyabai Holkar of Indore and Rani Bhavani of Natore in Bengal spent lavishly in such efforts. Then the other Maratha princes and the Peshwas had their own share of temple restoration, and most of the important temples of Varanasi today owe their grandeur to them. It was also the Marathas who established the world-famous Varanasi ghats (Sukul 1974, 158).

Contributions of Ahilyabai Holkar and Rani Bhavani

Though the Grand Trunk Road from Bengal to Lahore via Varanasi had been in existence from the time of Sher Shah, it was practically unusable because of the lack of regular maintenance. Rani Bhavani, a lady zamindar of Bengal renowned for her munificence, constructed a road from Bengal to Varanasi around the third quarter of the eighteenth century. This road from Kolkata to Varanasi was also repaired by Rani Ahilyabai Holkar possibly towards the last part of the eighteenth century (Medhasananda 2002, 96). Dharmashalas, too, had been constructed by Rani Bhavani and Rani Ahilyabai Holkar; later other Indian princes, zamindaris, and other people of wealth followed suit (Medhasananda 2002, 173).

The Omkareshvara Temple was constructed by Rani Bhavani of Bengal around the middle of the eighteenth century; the original temple had been destroyed by Muslims. The ancient Omkareshvara Temple must have been an impressive structure, occupying the entire hilltop. The temple that sits there today is quite small, however. It is said to have been built upon that site with the patronage of the Marathi queen Bhavani in the eighteenth century and then given in patronage to a Banaras priestly family (Eck 1982, 173–174). During Rani Bhavani's visit to Kashi around 1753, she spent liberally on the construction and renovation of temples and installation of deities, the building of houses for Brahmanas, the digging of big kundas, or tanks, and in undertaking numerous other religious and charitable works. She was so renowned for her charity and piety and was so much loved and respected by the locals of Varanasi that she was popularly called the Annapurna of Kashi.

A building complex was constructed by her in 1770 in Bengali Tola for the installation of deities and also as a residence for her own family. The deities installed there were Durga, Vishalakshi, and Bhavani, located in the northern side of the complex; Gopal and Radha-Govinda, installed in the centre of the complex beyond a gate; and Kali and also a deity of Tara kept in full seclusion. Oral tradition holds that the daughter of Rani Bhavani, the princess Tara, was remarkably beautiful and desired by a Muslim ruler or warlord. Rather than be taken by him, it is said that Tara entombed herself in the complex, over which the deity of Tara was installed.

Rani Bhavani also renovated the entire tract of the Panchakroshi Yatra, built dharmashalas, renovated temples and kundas at every five miles of this long tract, consecrated the Bhavanishwara Temple in 1753, and also constructed the famous Durgavati Temple at Durga Kunda. She also paved the Kapal Mochana Kunda, Omkareshvara Kunda, and Kurukshetra Kunda.

There is hearsay—believed to be true by many in Varanasi—that Rani Bhavani constructed 365 houses in Kashi, installed a deity of Shiva in each of those houses and wished to make a gift of them to the local Brahmanas. But the Brahmanas from Bengal and northern India refused to accept the gift. Consequently, south Indian and Maratha Brahmanas accepted these houses and thus gained an important foothold in the intellectual circles of the city.

From an inscription, it appears that the renovation of the Kardameshwara temple and kunda, undertaken in 1802, was perhaps Rani Bhavani's last public work in the city as she died that same year at the age of seventy-nine (Medhasananda 2002, 746–747).

Rani Ahilyabai Holkar (1725–1795) similarly made great contributions to Kashi. As Swami Medhasananda notes, 'The two ladies to whom present day Varanasi remains immensely grateful for various works of beautification and munificence were Rani Ahilyabai Holkar of Indore and Rani Bhavani of Bengal' (Medhasananda 2002, 830).

It is Queen Ahilyabai Holkar who constructed the present temple of Vishvanatha. We do not know exactly when she visited the city or where she stayed, but that she kept close contact with the city through Beniram Pathak, her appointed official, is quite evident, according to Swami Medhasananda. Beniram continued to manage her property and supervise the construction work already undertaken, even after the passing away of the queen. He also purchased a plot of land in the Rag Ghat Fort ground for constructing a dharamshala. In a letter to the government, the queen requested the former to ensure that her men should not be interrupted in any way in their construction of the dharamshalas and ghats in Kashi and at other places for charitable and sacred purposes. Other munificent works of Rani Ahilyabai include the construction of Dashashvamedha and Manikarnika Ghats and a ghat for the exclusive use of the female bathers in Manikarnika, the building of the Tarakeshvara Temple and the Ganga Temple and three other temples on the ghats of the Ganga, and six more temples in the city, and one Brahmapuri for the settlement of Brahmanas (Medhasananda 2002, 830).

Reconstruction and Revival

In 1738, when Balwant Singh became the ruler of Varanasi, in spite of wars and political unrest, religious activity in Varanasi continued at a brisk pace. Most of the temples that were in ruins were reconstructed. The Maratha chiefs and chieftains lent their hand in this religious reconstruction and Varanasi ghats and prominent temples were re-consecrated in a grand way. Rani Bhavani of Bengal and Maharani Ahilyabai of Indore were prominent in this respect, but there were other citizens and leaders from all across Bharat who contributed to this revival (Sukul 1974, 278–279).

During the Mughal period, the rajas of Jaipur became highly influential and powerful in consequence of their close connections to the Mughal emperors. It was during and after this period that they undertook various construction projects in different places, including pilgrim centres like Varanasi. In one of these buildings, situated in Varanasi and later called Shantikutir, there was a pathashala—traditional Hindu schools imparting Vedic education from childhood onward—where Jaipur princes were sent for education (Medhasananda 2002, 835).

The reputation of Queen Ahilyabai Holkar's Vishvanatha Temple, built in 1777, attracted later rulers from other places in India to contribute to its splendour; even the British contributed.

In 1781, Warren Hastings instructed the magistrate of Varanasi to build a gatehouse for the temple. Following this trend, the twenty-four-bayed pavilion with Mughal-styled fluted columns and lobed arched brackets sheltering the sacred Gyaanavapi, immediately north of the temple, was contributed by Rai Bijabai, widow of Daulat Rao Scindia of Gwalior in 1828. A decade later in 1838, the embossed gold sheets cloaking the spires and dome were added by the Sikh Maharaja, Ranjit Singh of Lahore (Singh 2008, 112–113).

Cultural Renaissance

In the difficult days of Muslim rule, the emergence of the Bhakti school was highly influential in keeping up the morale of Hindus across Bharat. Even as their temples and holy sites were taken away from them, the writings of the acharyas and poets of the Bhakti school brought their deities to them through the practice of Bhakti and storytelling. Quite a large portion of this literature was produced at Varanasi (Sukul 1974, 157). Tulsidas Maharaj had completed his famous *Ramcharitmanas* and written several of his other books at Varanasi, and he had installed a Shivalinga and twenty-four icons of Hanuman while living there, the famous Sankatmochan being one of them.

From the seventeenth century onward, large colonies of Maharashtrian Brahmanas began to settle in Kashi, and with them came Vedic learning as well. After 1680, the Marathas replaced the Rajputs as major donors to the three holy places, the *tristhali*: Banaras, Prayaga, and Gaya. A fresh wave of cultural renaissance overtook Kashi during the eighteenth century under the influence of the Marathas (1734–1785), who substantially rebuilt the city.

The city, which had sheltered the rebel Maratha hero, Shivaji, in his challenge to Mughal power, now became the recipient of the gratitude, wealth, skill, and energy of the Marathas. Bajirao Peshawa I (reign, 1720–40) patronized the construction of Manikarnika and Dashashvamedha Ghats and the nearby residential quarters. A number of ghats, water pools along with the noted temples of

Vishvanatha, Trilochana, Annapurna, Sakshi Vinayaka and Kaala Bhairava were rebuilt under Maratha patronage (Singh 2008, 110).

It is evident that at least during the first half of the eighteenth century, Rajputs and Maharashtrians formed the largest groups among all Indians migrating to Kashi from provinces other than Uttar Pradesh (Medhasananda 2002, 111).

Coda of Christian Rule

With the advent of British rule, Christian missions started their work of proselytization. The Baptist Society started work at Varanasi in 1816, the Church Missionary Society in 1817, and the London Missionary Society in 1820. In 1867, the Zenana Bible and Medical Mission and in 1878 the Wesleyan Missionary Society took up work here. In ninety-three years, though, despite all their efforts, only eight hundred Hindus were converted (Sukul 1974, 159–160).

After suppressing the revolt of 1857, and for some time even afterwards, such terrorizing measures were taken by the British authorities in Varanasi—and especially at Allahabad, where even innocent people were hanged from neem trees in the heart of the city; trees that still stand there today—that a mortal dread of Europeans seized the hearts of the citizens, and Varanasi was no exception to this (Sukul 1974, 285). Thus, Sukul remarks, for several years thereafter, the word of an Englishman was law, and no one dared to oppose his wishes in any matter and in any manner whatsoever. It was for this reason that Reverend Sherring was able to enter every Hindu temple in Varanasi without shedding his shoes, as he boastfully records in his book on Varanasi. A time was soon to come, though, when no Englishman could enter a Hindu temple, with or without shedding his shoes, not even the elites (Sukul 1974, 285).

Conclusion

This chapter of Kashi's history, ending on a note of hope, can best be summarized by Sukul:

Varanasi has had the resilience of rising even from its ashes time and again, and who knows its culture may also have a similar renaissance, and arise once again with a fresher vigour and a greater glory! (Sukul 1974, 326)

IV
The Gyanvapi Dispute

CHAPTER 22

The History of Past and Current Litigation in the Courts of India

The following is a timeline of past and current litigation in the courts of India centred around the Gyanvapi site:[10]

The Gyanvapi Mosque stands adjacent to the Kashi Vishwanath Temple in Varanasi. According to the available historical record, it was built in the seventeenth century on the orders of the Mughal Emperor Aurangzeb after destroying the original Kashi Vishwanath Temple.

1991

- The first petition of the case was filed by Swayambhu Jyotirlinga Bhagwan Vishweshwar in a Varanasi court in 1991. Three demands were expressed by the petitioner: (i) declaring the entire Gyanvapi complex as a part of the Kashi temple (ii) removal of Muslims from the complex area and (iii) demolition of the mosque.

1998

- Another case was filed by Anjuman Intezamia Masjid Committee, which approached the Allahabad high court, asserting that the dispute between the temple and mosque

---

10 https://www.financialexpress.com/india-news/gyanvapi-case-a-complete-timeline-of-eventsnbsp/3200200/

could not be decided by a civil court as it was not permissible by the law. As a result, the high court stayed the proceedings for twenty-two years.

2019
- The case was revived when the 'next friend' of Swayambhu Jyotirlinga Bhagwan Vishweshwar, Vijay Shankar Rastogi, filed a plea in Varanasi court demanding an archaeological survey of the disputed area.

2020
- This plea further encouraged the Anjuman Intezamia Masjid committee to oppose the petition seeking an ASI survey of the entire Gyanvapi complex.
- In the same year, the petitioner approached the lower court for the resumption of the hearing of 1991 petition.

March 2021
- The Places of Worship Act 1991 was taken up by a bench in the Supreme Court led by the former Chief Justice S.A. Bobde to examine its substantiality. The bench demanded a response from the Central Government of India on a PIL filed by advocate Ashwini Kumar Upadhyay that questioned the validity of the act.

August 2021
- The case again gained momentum when five female devotees filed a petition in the Varanasi court seeking permission to worship deities—Hanuman, Nandi, and Shringar Gauri—inside the premises of Gyanvapi.

September 2021
- In the judgment given by a single judge bench of the Allahabad high court, it was announced that the court should wait for further judgement in the already proceeding cases of the matter.

April 2022

- On the basis of the petition filed in August 2021, the Varanasi court appointed an advocate commissioner and ordered a videography survey of the complex. The order was again challenged by the Anjuman Intezamia Masjid committee in the Allahabad high court, which upheld the order of the lower court. This time, the party also filed a Special Leave Petition in the Supreme Court.

May 2022

- 6 May: The videographic survey of the Gyanvapi complex began.
- 12 May: The court appointed senior advocate, Vishal Singh, to supervise the survey and he was also appointed as special advocate commissioner. The team was directed to report all the recorded details of the survey by 17 May.
- 14–19 May: The survey resumed again and was conducted for two days. All the survey findings were submitted in a report to the court.
- 20 May: The case proceedings were transferred to a district judge by the apex court, saying that case required involvement of a more 'seasoned hand' to deal with the case. The Supreme Court subsequently said it would intervene only after the district judge had decided on the preliminary aspects of the case.
- 26 May: The district court began hearing the maintainability petition of the case. However, the argument given by the petitioner's side, that of the Anjuman Intezamia Masjid committee, remained incomplete till that date. This led to further extension of the date of the hearing.

August 2022

- Varanasi district judge Ajai Krishna Vishvesha reserved his order till 12 September. The time was given to both parties to complete their arguments.

October 2022

- The Varanasi district court rejected the plea for carbon dating of the Shivalinga claimed to have been found in the Gyanvapi Mosque.

November 2022

- The Supreme Court agreed to set up a bench to hear the case.

May 2023

- 12 May: The Allahabad high court ordered the determination of the age of the Shivalinga by using modern technology.
- 19 May: The Supreme Court deferred the scientific survey to determine the age of the Shivalinga.

July 2023

- 21 July: The Varanasi district court directed the Archaeological Survey of India (ASI) to conduct the survey, including excavations, wherever necessary, to determine if the mosque was built at a place where a temple existed earlier.
- 24 July: The Supreme Court halted ASI's survey and asked the High Court to hear the masjid committee's plea.
- 27 July: The Allahabad high court extended the stay on the ASI's survey until 3 August.

August 2023

- 3 August: The Allahabad high court allowed the scientific survey of the Gyanvapi premises 'in the interest of justice'. The Anjuman Intezamia Masjid committee submitted to the Supreme Court a challenge to the Allahabad high court order that refused to stay the Varanasi court's direction for a scientific survey.
- 4 August: The Supreme Court refused to stay the ASI survey of the Gyanvapi Mosque at Varanasi, except for the 'wazukhana' area where a Shivalinga was claimed to have been found in 2022.

January 2024

- A local court in Varanasi granted permission to Hindus to conduct puja inside one of the sealed cellars located inside the Gyanvapi Mosque complex. It directed the district magistrate of Varanasi to make necessary arrangements within seven days so that the plaintiff, Shailendra Kumar Pathak Vyas, and the Kashi Vishwanath Temple trust board could appoint a purohit to carry out the rites. Worship has since commenced. The order is the result of a plea filed by the plaintiff, who had submitted that rites had been performed in that cellar for hundreds of years and had been arbitrarily stopped by orders of the Mulayam Singh government in 1993 (*Economic Times,* Varanasi court allows pujas, 2024).
- The court also made public the ASI (Archaeological Survey of India) report on its survey of the Gyanvapi complex. The ASI survey report has confirmed the existence of a pre-existing Hindu temple at the Gyanvapi Mosque. The lawyers for the Hindu plaintiffs have separately filed a plea in the Supreme Court of India to unseal the 'wazukhana' area within the Gyanvapi complex based on the results of this report (*Economic Times,* Gyanvapi Case, 2024).

CHAPTER 23

Reframing the Dispute: The Sacred Geography of Gyaanavapi

What becomes immediately obvious from even a cursory glance at the history of litigation in the courts is that the legal framework being applied to this and similar cases is woefully inadequate.

First, the very idea of the Places of Worship Act of 1991 is convoluted—the idea that a law can arbitrarily freeze the religious classification of a site based on a date picked out of thin air. This will never satisfy the needs for justice and equity of different communities. Second, the idea of the legal question at the heart of this case being whether or not the mosque was built atop a temple is ludicrous; it is obvious to anyone and everyone that this is exactly what happened.

See the following passage by Diana L. Eck, for example:

Today's 'Golden Temple' of Kashi Vishvanatha replaced a much grander sixteenth-century Vishvanatha temple built by Narayana Bhatta at the time of the Mughal Emperor Akbar. That temple was partially destroyed in the seventeenth century, under the rule of the deeply conservative Aurangzeb. It was turned into a mosque, and another Vishvanatha Temple was built a short distance away. *The mosque today bears the popular name Jnana Vapi Mosque, so called because of the sacred Well of Wisdom, the Jnana Vapi, located in a pillared arcade between today's mosque and temple. For more than three hundred years, they have sat side by side, temple and mosque. Whether or not the mosque is built of a ruined temple is hardly contested, as it is in Ayodhya. One side of the old temple still stands, ornamented and broken, the rest having been incorporated into the mosque* (emphasis added). (Eck 2012, 324–325)

However, it is easier to tie ourselves up in complex legalese and jargon than face the uncomfortable but simple truth that great violence was done to the sacred geography of Kashi, one of the holiest if not the holiest of Hindu cities, and that there is a legitimate desire and even a need felt by the Hindu community to restore that sacred geography.

This does not mean that there should be disenfranchisement of the Muslim residents of Kashi. On the contrary, all such arrangements should be made to ensure freedom of worship for all communities including the establishment of access to places of worship. But one cannot hide behind the banner of secularism to waive away and dismiss the fact that in Hinduism there is a concept of the sacred kshetra, which cannot be reduced to title deeds and property maps, which cannot be distorted and conformed into Abrahamic worldviews that are fixated on historical dates and human-centred history.

In a worldview that at least acknowledges the concept of sacred geography, it is very obvious that the entire Gyanvapi site, which obviously bears its name from the Gyaanavapi well, and the Kashi Vishwanath compound has been one of the most sacred sites of Hinduism, not just in Kashi, not just in Bharat, but in the entire world, for that matter. Whatever the archaeological evidence may or may not uncover, the sacred geography as captured in the lore and oral tradition of Hindus, as sanctified by the footsteps of pilgrimage taken generation after generation, as documented meticulously by the work of numberless pandits and acharyas who tirelessly worked for the preservation and restoration of sacred sites and pilgrimage circuits, cannot be denied.

And this is the problem with the discourse and debates today: there is no acknowledgement of the concept of sacred geography. Gyaanavapi and Vishvanatha are just reduced to the status of a singular temple or building with no independent significance that ties it back to the Kashi kshetra. This is a Eurocentric worldview that does not accommodate the lived spiritual reality and cosmology of non-European religious traditions, like Hinduism.

With this background and context, let us, once more, for the last time, delve into the sacred geography of Vishvanatha and Gyaanavapi.

Avimukteshvara and Vishveshvara

The story of Vishvanatha and Gyaanavapi cannot begin without mentioning Avimukteshvara. After all, it is Avimukteshvara who is said to be the guru of Vishveshvara. In the Kashi Khanda, Vishveshvara and Avimukteshvara are described as the two right hands of Kashi.

Avimukteshvara is mentioned as the reigning deity of Kashi in the sixth-century *Dashakumaracharita*, which mentions the pilgrimage of a young man to Kashi, where he bathes at Manikarnika and worships Avimukteshvara. The name Avimukteshvara also occurs on as many as eight separate seals from the Rajghat excavations in Kashi, dating from Gupta times to the tenth or eleventh centuries (Phatak in Eck 1982, 195-198).

Puranic sources claim that Avimukteshvara is the primordial linga without beginning, so no one knows just how it came into being. The Kashi Khanda states that this linga was established here by Shiva himself when he left Kashi for exile to Mount Mandara during the reign of King Divodasa.

The relationship between Avimukteshvara and Vishveshvara is clarified in both the *Linga Purana* and the Kashi Khanda of the *Skanda Purana*. While everybody worships Vishveshvara, Vishveshvara worships Avimukteshvara, which bestows both *bhukti* (enjoyment) and *mukti* (liberation). Avimukteshvara is thus often referred to as the guru of Vishveshvara. Alas, today, there is only a trace left of that hallowed Avimukteshvara Linga: an ancient fragment of stone hidden amidst three Muslim graves on the north side of the Gyaanavapi Mosque, sprinkled with flowers once a year on the day of Shivaratri (Eck 1982, 198–199).

Sukul explains the transition of prominence from Avimukteshvara to Vishveshvara. He starts with the fact that all the temples of Varanasi were demolished in AD 1194 and lay in ruins for several decades. During this time, Razia's mosque was built on the original site of the Vishveshvara Mandir between AD 1236 and 1240. When the strictures of Islamic rule loosened a bit, most temples were rebuilt at their original sites, but Vishveshvara's original site was inaccessible because the mosque was built under imperial orders.

In order to accommodate it, a space was made for the Vishveshvara Linga in the Avimukteshvara compound, situated at the foot of the mound on which the temple had first stood. Naturally, the other deities whose temples had stood there and were now being rebuilt at their original sites had to be installed in smaller temples and in this process Avimukteshvara was shifted a little northward. Space was thus found for Vishveshvara between Avimukteshvara and Gyaanavapi. This latter well thus became situated immediately to the south of Vishveshvara, which had been rebuilt on a grand and extensive scale in tune with its popular importance. Consequently, it was the most imposing structure in the locality.

Soon after, another iconoclastic storm burst over Varanasi and all these temples were once again razed to the ground. Some decades later, there was another reconstruction. This time, Avimukteshvara was given a corner in Vishveshvara's temple itself (Sukul 1974, 179). His independent existence was now lost, but his importance was still recognized. Even the Kashi Khanda says that in the Kashi kshetra presided over by Vishveshvara, those who do not visit the noble Avimukteshvara Linga are fools and again that in this world everyone worships Vishveshvara but Vishveshvara worships Avimukteshvara.

Later came another wave of Muslim fanaticism and the temples lay in ruins again, and in the next reconstruction Avimukteshvara lost his identity entirely. His was now only another name for Vishveshvara. Even some Hindu religious authorities, in the second half of the fifteenth century and after, incorrectly believed that Vishveshvara and Avimukteshvara were the same—two names of the same lingam (Sukul 1974, 180). This is why the precise cataloguing of sacred sites in the Sthala Purana is so important and necessary, so that the uniqueness and importance of different sacred sites does not become obscured by the mists of time and the fog of history.

Between AD 1494 and 1496, Sikandar Lodi again pulled down all the temples of Varanasi and these remained in ruins for about ninety years, and the common belief that Avimukteshvara and Vishveshvara were the same persisted. Even such a great authority on Varanasi as Bhatta Narayana, by whose efforts Vishveshvara's temple was rebuilt, said in his *Tristhali Setu* that Avimukteshvara was Vishveshvara. It was only in AD 1620 that Mittra Misra in his book *Viramittdrodaya: Tirtha Prakash Khand* questioned this view as erroneous. He proved on the strength of the Kashi Khanda itself that these two great lingas were not the same, as Vishveshvara is said to worship Avimukteshvara, and in the tirtha yatra prescribed of the fourteen Shivalinga in Kashi both the lingas are separately mentioned. Thus, their separate existence was recognized once again, and a small temple was built near the northeastern corner of the great edifice of the Vishveshvara Temple. This eventually became the place where Muslim tombs are situated as one enters the Gyanvapi enclosure from its northern gate.

In 1669, there was the final iconoclastic storm under the order of Aurangzeb in which the Gyanvapi temples—there were at least eleven there—were demolished and this time a mosque was built in place of the partially demolished Vishveshvara Temple, the western portion of which was broken but not demolished. As Sukul notes, it was left in that condition to spite the Hindus for all time to come (Sukul 1974, 181).

As Eck notes, 'Ironically, the mosque is popularly known in Varanasi as the Jnana Vapi Mosque, taking on the very name of the Hindu sacred precinct on which it stands' (Eck 1982, 192).

The Geography of the Vishvanatha/Gyaanavapi Compound

The Gyaanavapi Kupa is at the back of Vishvanatha Mandir. It is said that Vishvanatha Linga was dropped into this well when the main temple was destroyed by the Mughals. To the north of this well is the mosque built by Aurangzeb after the destruction of Vishvanatha Mandir (Chandramouli 2018, 35).

In the *Linga Purana* quoted by Lakshmidhara, Avimukteshvara is said to be located just to the north of the sacred well, Gyaanavapi, precisely where the mosque sits today and where Vishveshvara was previously located. According to that Purana, around Avimukteshvara stood the shrines of Dandapani, Taraka, and Mahakala—all of which still have their places today near the Gyanvapi Mosque and the Vishwanath Mandir. Clearly, Avimukteshvara occupied the spot that Vishveshvara later came to dominate.

It is said that a picture is worth a thousand words. The following map tells the whole story. Note that the Vishveshvara Antargrha Yatra encompasses the site of the mosque and Gyanvapi. It is clear here that the three are part of one indivisible whole; the site of the mosque was the site of the earlier Vishveshvara Temple and before that the site of Avimukteshvara. The sanctity of this site to Hindus and the sacred geography of the entire Kashi kshetra, which is centred around this very site, cannot be overstated.

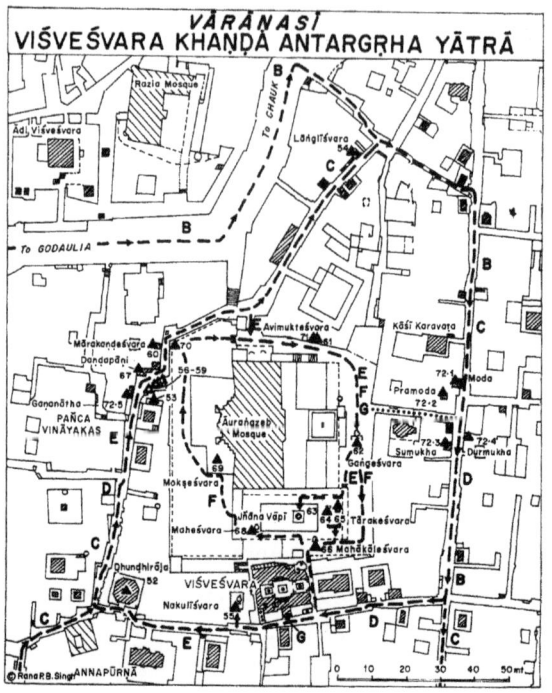

Source: Singh 1993b, 53

Importance of Vishveshvara

We know that by the twelfth century Vishveshvara attracted the worship of King Govindachandra, for he left an inscription proclaiming so (Sukul 1974, 178). In the same century, an inscription from south India records that a certain king of Karnataka set up a fund to help the pilgrims of his area pay the Muslim-imposed tax so they could visit Vishveshvara in Varanasi (Eck 1982, 200).

Perhaps the strongest, if ironic, indication of Vishveshvara's importance in the twelfth century is that it was singled out for destruction by Muhammad Ghori's captain Qutb-ud-din Aibak in AD 1194. Rebuilding on that site was pre-empted by the construction of a mosque there by the famous ruling princess of the Delhi sultanate, Raziyyat-ud-din (Razia) during her short reign (1236–1240). Known as Razia's Mosque, it still stands today.

In the years that followed the building of Razia's Mosque on Vishvanatha's hilltop, the Vishvanatha Temple was rebuilt in another location, probably a short distance down the hill in the vicinity of Avimukteshvara Temple, an area it soon came to dominate. A 1353 inscription records the establishment of a large temple called Padmeshvara near Vishveshvara, which indicates that by that time the Vishveshvara Temple had been re-established.

In the late fourteenth and fifteenth centuries, however, the temples of Kashi were destroyed several times under the reigns of Tughluq of Delhi, Mahmud Shah Sharqi of Jaunpur, and Sikandar Lodi of Delhi. When the great scholar and religious leader Narayana Bhatta began his career in the sixteenth century, Vishveshvara again lay in ruins.

Narayana Bhatta, who compiled a digest of Puranic verses on Kashi, Gaya, and Prayaga in his *Tristhali Setu*, comments on some of the passages that concern Vishveshvara in a manner that tells a great deal about the times:

> Even if the linga of Vishveshvara here is taken off somewhere and another is brought in and established by human hands, on account of the difficulty of the times, whatever is established in that place should be worshipped. [...] And if, owing to the power of foreign rulers, there is no linga at all in that place, even so, the dharma of the place itself should be observed, with rites of circumambulation, salutation, etc., and in this way the daily pilgrimage [*nityayatra*] shall be performed. (Bhatta in Eck 1982, 202–204)

This again underscores the importance of sacred geography. Narayana Bhatta, the greatest exponent of the tirthas in Kashi, tells us that even if there is no longer a Shivalinga in the place where Vishveshvara once stood, we should still worship the site. This has ongoing relevance to the litigation today, because from the standpoint of sacred geography, whether or not the object discovered in the mosque is a Shivalinga, the site itself is of ongoing sacred import and relevance to Hindus.

According to legend, the linga of Vishveshvara was saved from the temple before it was desecrated by the armies of Aurangzeb. It was thrown by a provident priest into the deep waters of the Gyaanavapi. In 1777, Ahilyabai Holkar, the Queen of Indore, sponsored the construction of the present temple. Her royal inscription makes no mention of her having established another linga (Eck 1982, 202–204).

Up until the time of Ahilyabai Holkar's installation of the new temple, devotees would pour water into the well as offerings to Vishveshvara until Ahilyabai reportedly installed a new idol of Shiva, brought from the Narmada river, in the present temple she built for it in 1777. Contrary to the story of this installation by Ahilyabai Holkar, it has been claimed that the *pandas*, the traditional priests of Vishvanatha, recovered the old idol of Vishvanatha from the Gyanvapi shortly after the iconoclastic storm of 1669. A cut mark found at the top of the linga, which could have been caused when the idol was tossed into Gyanvapi, also suggests this possibility.

After the recovery, the linga was finally installed in an inconspicuous corner to the south of the Gyanvapi and was worshipped without ostentation till the date of the construction of the present temple. In support of this claim, information about some royal personages visiting the city and worshipping Vishvanatha between AD 1672 and 1765 has been documented in various pilgrimage record books preserved by the pandas (Medhasananda 2002, 176).

According to Swami Medhasananda, '[T]he above data leads us to believe that the continuity of the worship of Vishvanatha did not break during the intervening period. It is also likely that Ahilyabai Holkar did not install a new idol of Shiva, but only reconsecrated the old one' (Medhasananda 2002, 176).

Eck notes that, in one corner of the Gyanvapi Mosque, Hindus were allowed to honour the ancient site of Avimukteshvara, which had since become a Muslim grave site, with flowers (Eck 1982, 405–406).

The ongoing importance of Vishveshvara can be understood through the actions of Daulat Rao Sindhia, who had given shelter to Varanasi's deposed king, Chet Singh. Once, Sindhia requested the British to grant necessary permission so that the Vishvanatha Temple could be restored to its original site at Gyanvapi. The government, unwilling to incur the displeasure of the Muslims did not comply with his request (Medhasananda 2002, 832). This shows that Hindus never forgot or ceased desiring the restoration of the old sacred geography of Kashi.

Sukul notes that even today all the Hindu dancing girls of Varanasi go to the Adi Vishveshvara Temple once a year on a fixed day and dance there the whole night free of charge on the pain of excommunication from their own society. The Adi Vishveshvara Temple is situated within a few yards of the original site of Vishveshvara's temple, and only a wall divides it from Razia's Mosque. This temple was built by Maharaja Sawa Jai Singh of Amber, who was a persona non grata with the Mughal emperors, as a memorial to the original site of Vishveshvara's temple and was therefore called Adi-Vishveshvara, the prefix 'Adi' denoting that this was the site of the original Vishveshvara Temple. Since there was another duly consecrated Vishveshvara Temple already in existence, this name was quite appropriate. Tradition says that the *argha*—the ovoid seat on which the Shivalinga rests—of this temple is the one that belonged to the Vishveshvara of the Gyaanavapi Temple, which the Maharaja obtained by the Mughal king's favour (Sukul 1974, 177).

Sukul underlines the ongoing importance of the Vishvanatha Temple by pointing to the following facts:

- When Razia Sultana wanted to build a mosque on the site of a demolished temple in Varanasi, it was this temple that was chosen for the purpose. It is a well-known fact that on such occasions of display of power and religious animosity, sites of the most important temples alone have been utilized. (Babar built his mosque on the site of the Janmasthan Temple at Ayodhya, and Aurangzeb on the site of the Janmasthan Temple

at Mathura and also on the sites of three most important temples at Varanasi).
- When Jaziya tax was imposed on the pilgrims visiting Varanasi, a Hoysala king of Karnataka, Nrisimha III, donated a village with a revenue of 645 Niskhkas in AD 1279 to provide money for the payment of this tax by the residents of Karnataka, Telengana, Talvi, Tirthut, and Gauda countries, and for the worship of Vishveshvara. Similarly, about the same time, Seth Vastupal of Gujrat sent one lakh rupees for the worship of Vishvesvhara (Sukul 1974, 178).

There is an interesting reference about the Gyanvapi Mosque preserved in Persian literature. There was a Hindu poet in the court of Shah Jahan, who had proclaimed before the king that he was a Brahmana and would always remain a Brahmana even if he were to be taken to Kaaba a hundred times. He had then said, 'My heart is so enamoured of Kafra [all Hindus were called kafirs and the Hindu religion was Kafra according to Muslims] that even if I go to Kaaba a hundred times I will still return a Brahmana.' His name was Chandrabhan, and his penname was Barahman. He had then escaped death by the courtiers quoting Saadi's words, which said that if Christ's donkey went to Kaaba, it would still be a donkey on return. He continued to be in the court of Aurangzeb, and when the Gyanvapi Mosque had been built Aurangzeb asked him if he could or would say something on the occasion. It was a cruel cut to the old poet, and he instantly re-joined with a couplet: 'Oh Sheikh see the wondrous greatness of my temple in that it became the house of [your] god only after its downfall!' implying how much higher it was when in its full glory. The king was very angry but kept quiet (Sukul 1974, 183).

Conclusion

It is said that a book is only successful if it has surprised the author along the way. If an author has not learned anything in the journey of writing the book, then why should anyone read their book?

When I first set about the project of writing this book, I had a very clear thesis in my mind. My mind was full of sharp legal arguments and logical points all about what I deemed to be the appropriate solution for the controversy of the Gyanvapi site.

What transformed me, what surprised me, what taught me so much in the process of writing this book was the experience of reading in full the Kashi Khanda of the *Skanda Purana*. I had meant to summarize it in a few paragraphs, but I became so entranced by the story, by the experience of discovering the sacred geography of Kashi simply through reading the Puranic text, that I felt compelled to take up nearly half the book with a summary of its contents.

For, sacred geography is not abstract or intellectual. It is experiential, and this book would have been an exercise in hypocrisy if it had merely talked about the concept of sacred geography without actually delving into the meticulous details of Kashi's sacred geography. I now wish to go to Kashi again and again to undertake all the various yatras and have darshana of all the various shrines about which I have written here.

Perhaps when I first set out to write this book, I fancied that I had some intricate, complex, sophisticated arguments to make. Now I no longer harbour such delusions. The meaning and the purpose I take away from writing this book is simple. Sacred geography matters. The modern world may have divorced itself from the notions of entire territories, kshetras, being holy and needing to be kept intact to preserve and channel spiritual energies and invite the presence of the Devatas into those spaces, but that does not mean it is not real. The moment one steps back from archaeological digs and exercises in dating and surveying, the moment one just reads a few lines from the Puranas and looks at the circuit of prescribed pilgrimages over the ages, it becomes obvious that the Gyanvapi site is an integral part of the current Kashi Vishwanath compound as it was of the earlier Vishveshvara Mandir and the original Avimukteshvara site. There are few sites of greater import to Hindus and Hinduism than this one.

The fact that there is no agency or space to even acknowledge this claim of sacred geography is deeply problematic. A court or a society can always overrule one valid claim for another; it does not have to be dispositive if there are great enough countervailing weights on the other side to push back against the claims of sacred geography. That is the workings of democracy and a society of law and order. What is unacceptable, though, is to use the pretext of pseudo-secularism to claim that such notions of sacred geography do not exist or are unimportant. That is silencing a civilization and a religion. To delegitimize a viscerally felt claim, based on the civilizational and metaphysical DNA of a people over the course of thousands of years, is the worst kind of violence and disenfranchisement, and it is nothing but the continuity of foreign rule Hindus and Bharatiyas have fought so hard to shake off.

In the end, I go back to the *Skanda Purana*, to the Kashi Khanda, to the story of Shiva, who in his compassion and kindness allowed himself to become exiled from his favourite abode. Yet, the beauty of Kashi was such that he longed to come back home. The time had come, the time has come, for his exile to end.

References

Aiyangar, K.V. Rangaswami (ed.). 1942. *Tirthavievecana Kanda*, by Lakshmidhara, Vol. III of *Krityakalpataru*. Gaekwad's Oriental Series, Vol. XCVIII. Baroda: Oriental Institute.

Barbosa, Duarte. 1866. *A Description of the Coasts of East Africa and Malabar in the Beginning of the Sixteenth Century*, trans., notes, and preface Henry E.J. Stanley. London.

Bhardwaj, Surinder M. 1973. *Hindu Places of Pilgrimage in India: A Study in Cultural Geography*. Berkeley: University of California Press.

Bisschop, Peter C. 2021. *The Varanasimahatmya of the Bharavapradurbhava*. Pondicherry: Institut Francais de Pondichery.

Black, John. 2012. 'The Meaning of the Word Myth.' *Ancient Origins: Reconstructing the Story of Humanity's Past*. August 30. Accessed November 18, 2023. https://www.ancient-origins.net/human-origins/meaning-word-myth-0061

Blacker, Valentine. 1821. *Memoir of the Operations of the British Army in India, during the Mahratta Ware of 1817, 1818, and 1819*. London.

Chandramouli, K. 2018. *Holy Kashi to Vibrant Varanasi*. Varanasi: Indica Books.

CNN 2017. 'Face to face with a cannibalistic sect: Believer with Reza Aslan.' CNN. January 20. Accessed November 18, 2023 . https://www.cnn.com/videos/tv/2017/01/20/believer-reza-aslan-india-clip-1.cnn

Eck, Diana L. 1982. *Banaras: City of Light*. New York: Alfred A. Knopf.

———. 1993. 'A Survey of Sanskrit Sources for the Study of Varanasi.' In *Banaras (Varanasi): Cosmic Order, Sacred City and Hindu Traditions*, by Rana P.B. Singh. Varanasi: Tara Book Agency.

———. 2012. *India: A Sacred Geography*. New York: Harmony Books.

Elliot, Henry Miers. 2013. *The History of India, as Told by Its Own Historians: The Muhammadan Period*. United Kingdom: Cambridge University Press.

Farquhar, J.N. 1925a. 'The Fighting Ascetics of India.' *Bulletin of the John Rylands Library* 431–452.

———. 1925b. 'The Organization of the Sannyasis of the Vedanta.' *Journal of the Royal Asiatic Society* 479–486.

Forbes-Boyte, Kari. 2011. 'Sacred Geography.' *Encyclopedia of the Great Plains*. Edited by David J. Wishart. University of Nebraska Lincoln. Accessed November 21, 2023. http://plainshumanities.unl.edu/encyclopedia/doc/egp.na.102

Goswami, C.L. (trans.). 1971. *Srimad Bhagavata Mahapurana*, with Sanskrit text and English translation. Gorakhpur: Gita Press.

Havell, Ernest Binfield. 1905. *Benares the Sacred City: Sketches of Hindu Life and Religion*. London: W. Thacker & Co.

Jain, Meenakshi. 2019. *Flight of Deities and Rebirth of Temples: Episodes from Indian History*. New Delhi: Aryan Books International.

Jayaswal, Vidula. 2019. *Kashi and Varanasi: Emergence of State, City and Religious Landscapes*. New Delhi: Aryan Books International.

Kamakoti.org. n.d. 'Importance of Sthala Puranas from the Chapter "Puranas".' *Hindu Dharma*. Accessed October 1, 2022. https://www.kamakoti.org/hindudharma/part14/chap18.htm

Lawrence-Zuniga, Denise. n.d. 'Space and Place.' *Oxford Bibliographies*. Accessed October 7, 2023. https://www.oxfordbibliographies.com/view/document/obo-9780199766567/obo-9780199766567-0170.xml

Lochtefeld, James G. 2002. *The Illustrated Encyclopedia of Hinduism*, Vol. 1 (A–M). Rosen.

Lorenzen, David. 1978. 'Warrior Ascetics in Indian History.' *Journal of the American Oriental Society*.

Macleod, Norman. *Days in North India*. Philadelphia: J.B. Lippincott & Co.

Medhasananda, Swami. 2002. *Varanasi at the Crossroads: A Panoramic View of Early Modern Varanasi and the Story of its Transition*, Vol. 1. Kolkata: The Ramakrishna Mission Institute of Culture.

Meyer, Jeffrey F. 1991. *The Dragons of Tiananmen: Being as a Sacred City*. Columbia: University of South Carolina Press.

Mittal, Sushil and Thursby, G. (eds). 2004. *The Hindu World*. New York: Routledge.

Muhanna, Elias. 2017. 'The Contradictions of Reza Aslan's "Believer".' *The New Yorker*. April 9. Accessed November 18, 2023. https://www.newyorker.com/culture/culture-desk/the-contradictions-of-reza-aslans-believer

Wiktionary. 2023. 'Mythos.' *Wiktionary*. August 31. Accessed November 18, 2023. https://en.wiktionary.org/wiki/mythos.

Phatak, V.S. 1957. 'Religious Sealings from Rajghat.' *Journal of the Numismatic Society of India*, Vol. XIX, part II, pp.171–175.

Pinch, William R. 2006. *Warrior Ascetics and Indian Empires*. Cambridge: Cambridge University Press.

Rana, Pravin S. 2003. 'Pilgrimage and Ecotourism in Varanasi Region: Resources, Perspectives and Prospects.' Unpublished PhD thesis in Public

Administration and Tourism Studies, Lucknow University, Lucknow UP, India.

Richer, Jean. 1994. *Sacred Geography of the Greeks: Astrological Symbolism in Art, Architecture, and Landscape.* State University of New York Press.

Safi, Michael. 2017. 'Reza Aslan Outrages Hindus by Eating Human Brains in CNN Documentary.' *The Guardian.* March 10. Accessed November 18, 2023. https://www.theguardian.com/world/2017/mar/10/reza-aslan-criticised-for-documentary-on-cannibalistic-hindus.

Sarkar, Jadunath. 2018. *A History of the Dasnami Naga Sannyasis.* Edited by Ananda Bhattacharyya. New Delhi: Manohar Publishers and Distributors.

———. 2019. *A Short History of Aurangzib 1618–1707: Abridged From the Larger Work in Five Volumes, with a Map, Chronology and Index.* Delhi: B.R. Publishing Corporation.

Sax, William S. 1991. *Mountain Goddesses. Gender and Politics in a Himalayan Pilgrimage.* Oxford University Press, New York.

Seamon, D., and J. Sowers. 2008. 'Place and Placelessness, Edward Relph.' In *Key Texts in Geography.* London: Sage Publications Ltd.

Sherring, M.A. 1868. *The Sacred City of the Hindus: An Account of Benares in Ancient and Modern Times.* London: Trubner and Co.

Singh, Rana P.B. 1993a. 'Varanasi: Chronology of Historical Events.' In *Banaras (Varanasi): Cosmic Order, Sacred City and Hindu Traditions,* by Rana P.B. Singh. Varanasi: Tara Book Agency.

———. 1993b. 'Varanasi: The Pilgrimage Mandala, Geomantic Map and Cosmic Numbers.' In *Banaras (Varnasi): Cosmic Order, Sacred City, and Hindu Traditions,* by Rana P.B. Singh. Varanasi: Tara Book Agency.

———. 2002. *Towards the Pilgrimage Archetype: The Panchakroshi Yatra of Banaras.* Varanasi: Indica Books.

———. 2004. *Cultural Landscapes and the Lifeworld. Literary Images of Banaras.* Varanasi: Indica Books.

———. 2008. *Banaras, the Heritage City of India: Geography, History, and Bibliography.* Varanasi: Indica Books.

———. 2013. *Hindu Tradition of Pilgrimage: Sacred Space and System.* New Delhi: Dev Publishers and Distributors.

Sukul, Kuber Nath. 1974. *Varanasi Down the Ages.* Varanasi: Bhargava Bhushan Press.

Tagare, G.V. 1950. 'Chapter 6 of Kashi Khanda: Tirthadhyaya (Sacred Places).' *Wisdom Library.* Accessed October 09, 2023. https://www.wisdomlib.org/hinduism/book/the-skanda-purana/d/doc423743.html#note-e-145992

———. 1950a. 'Chapter 25 of Kashi Khanda: Agastya Visits Skanda.' *Skanda Purana.* Wisdom Library. Accessed October 8, 2023. https://www.wisdomlib.org/hinduism/book/the-skanda-purana/d/doc423763.html

———. 1950b. 'Chapter 26 of Kashi Khanda: Description of Manikarnika.' Wisdom Library. Accessed October 8, 2023. https://wisdomlib.org/hinduism/book/the-skanda-purana/d/doc423764.html

———. 1950c. 'Chapter 32 of Kashi Khanda: The Manifestation of Dandapani.' Wisdom Library. Accessed October 12, 2023. https://www.wisdomlib.org/hinduism/book/the-skanda-purana/d/doc423770.html

———. 1950d. 'Chapter 39 of Kashi Khanda: Manifestation of the Lord of Avimukta.' Wisdom Library. Accessed October 08, 2023. https://www.wisdomlib.org/hinduism/book/the-skanda-purana/d/doc423777.html

———. 1950e. 'Chapter 45 of Kashi Khanda: The Arrival of Sixty-Four Yoginis.' Wisdom Library. Accessed October 12, 2023. https://www.wisdomlib.org/hinduism/book/the-skanda-purana/d/doc423783.html#note-t-146076

———. 1950f. 'Chapter 47 of Kashi Khanda: Description of Uttararka.' Wisdom Library. Accessed October 13, 2023. https://www.wisdomlib.org/hinduism/book/the-skanda-purana/d/doc423785.html

———. 1950g. 'Chapter 48 of Kashi Khanda: The Greatness of Shambaditya.' Wisdom Library. Accessed October 13 2023. https://www.wisdomlib.org/hinduism/book/the-skanda-purana/d/doc423786.html

———. 2020. 'Chapter 6 of Kashi Khanda: Tirthadhyaya (Sacred Places).' *Skanda Purana*. September 6. Accessed November 23, 2023. https://www.wisdomlib.org/hinduism/book/the-skanda-purana/d/doc423743.html#note-e-145992

———. n.d.[a]. 'Chapter 33 of Kashi Khanda.' *Skanda Purana: Description of Jnanavapi*. Accessed November 21, 2023. https://www.wisdomlib.org/hinduism/book/the-skanda-purana/d/doc423771.html#note-t-146047

———. n.d.[b]. 'Chapter 58 of Kashi Khanda: Attainment of Salvation by Divodasa.' *Skanda Purana*. Accessed November 23, 2023. https://www.wisdomlib.org/hinduism/book/the-skanda-purana/d/doc423797.html

———. n.d.[c]. 'Chapter 59 of Kashi Khanda: Panchanada Comes Into Being.' *Skanda Purana*. Accessed November 23, 2023. https://www.wisdomlib.org/hinduism/book/the-skanda-purana/d/doc423798.html

———. n.d.[d]. 'Chapter 68: The Origin of Krttivasas.' *Skanda Purana*. Accessed November 23, 2023. https://www.wisdomlib.org/hinduism/book/the-skanda-purana/d/doc423807.html

———. n.d.[e]. 'Chapter 73: The Greatness of Omkara.' *Skanda Purana*. Accessed November 23, 2023. https://www.wisdomlib.org/hinduism/book/the-skanda-purana/d/doc423812.html

Twain, Mark. 1898. *Following the Equator, A Journey Around the World*. Hartford: The American Publishing Company.

Varanasi-temples.com. n.d. *Avi Mukti Vinayak*. Accessed September 1, 2023. https://varanasitemples.in/vinayak-temples/avi-mukta-vinayak-3/

———. n.d. *Avimukteshwar Temple*. Accessed September 1, 2023. https://varanasitemples.in/category/shiva-temples/other-shiva-temples-a-d/avimukteshwar/

Visuvalingam, Elizabeth-Chalier. 1993. 'Bhairava: Kotwal of Varanasi.' In *Banaras (Varanasi): Cosmic Order, Sacred City and Hindu Traditions*, by Rana P.B. Singh. Varanasi: Tara Book Agency.

The Take. n.d. 'What Was the Indian Response to "Indiana Jones and the Temple of Doom" Upon Release?' the-take.com. Accessed November 20, 2023. https://the-take.com/read/what-was-the-indian-response-to-aindiana-jones-and-the-temple-of-dooma-upon-release.

World Pilgrimage Guide. n.d. 'Sacred Geography: The Location of Sacred Sites According to Regional Configurations of Sacred Geography.' *Sacred Sites*. Accessed November 5, 2022. https://sacredsites.com/sacred_places/sacred_geography.html

About the Author

Aditi Banerjee is a bestselling author based in the US. Her debut novel, *The Curse of Gandhari*, was published by Bloomsbury India in 2019 and her second, *The Vow of Parvati*, came out in 2022. Her third book, *Hindu Love Stories: Dharmically Ever After*, is a collection of stories from Hindu literature and history. She co-edited *Invading the Sacred: An Analysis of Hinduism Studies in America* in collaboration with Rajiv Malhotra and has authored several essays in publications such as *The Columbia Documentary History of Religion in America Since 1945* and *Buddhists, Hindus, and Sikhs in America: A Short History*. Her articles have appeared in *Outlook* magazine and other publications. She is a devout Hindu and frequently writes about Hinduism and the Hindu-American experience.

Aditi is a practicing attorney at a Fortune 500 financial services company in the US and a member of the Indic Academy. She completed her executive MBA programme from Columbia University, New York, and earned a juris doctor from Yale Law School. She is a magna cum laude graduate in international relations from Tufts University, Massachusetts.

www.ingramcontent.com/pod-product-compliance
Ingram Content Group UK Ltd.
Pitfield, Milton Keynes, MK11 3LW, UK
UKHW042003230426
12048UKWH00009B/514